Legislating in the Dark

Chicago Studies in American Politics

A SERIES EDITED BY BENJAMIN I. PAGE, SUSAN HERBST,
LAWRENCE R. JACOBS, AND ADAM J. BERINSKY

Also in the series:

Additional series titles follow index

Legislating in the Dark

Information and Power in the House of Representatives

JAMES M. CURRY

THE UNIVERSITY OF CHICAGO PRESS   CHICAGO AND LONDON

JAMES M. CURRY is assistant professor of political science at the University of Utah. In 2011 and 2012, he was an APSA Congressional Fellow in the office of Illinois congressman Daniel Lipinski.

The University of Chicago Press, Chicago 60637
The University of Chicago Press, Ltd., London
© 2015 by The University of Chicago
All rights reserved. Published 2015.
Printed in the United States of America
24 23 22 21 20 19 18 17 16 15   1 2 3 4 5

ISBN-13: 978-0-226-28168-1 (cloth)
ISBN-13: 978-0-226-28171-1 (paper)
ISBN-13: 978-0-226-28185-8 (e-book)
DOI: 10.7208/chicago/9780226281858.001.0001

Library of Congress Cataloging-in-Publication Data

Curry, James M., author.
    Legislating in the dark : information and power in the House of Representatives /
James M. Curry.
        pages cm — (Chicago studies in American politics)
    Includes bibliographical references and index.
    ISBN 978-0-226-28168-1 (cloth : alk. paper) — ISBN 978-0-226-28171-1 (pbk. : alk.
paper) — ISBN 978-0-226-28185-8 (ebook)   1. United States. Congress. House.
2. Legislative bodies—United States.   I. Title.   II. Series: Chicago studies in American
politics.
    JK1319.C89 2015
    328.73′072—dc23

                                                                            2015008521

♾ This paper meets the requirements of ANSI/NISO Z39.48-1992 (Permanence of Paper).

FOR JILL, LOUISE, AND HENRY

Contents

Acknowledgments

This book was born in the summer of 2007 within the close quarters of a House Appropriations subcommittee office in the Longworth House Office Building in Washington, DC. There I experienced the efforts of committee leaders and their staff to craft and manage a bill, and then navigate it through subcommittee, committee, and the House floor. It matured in 2012 during my time as an American Political Science Association congressional fellow. In the only slightly less cramped quarters of a member's office, I lived the battle to help my boss legislate. This book would not have been possible without these experiences and the generosity of the people I worked for and alongside. To Deborah Bilek, Bob Bonner, Frank Carrillo, Karyn Kendall, and Dale Oak—the majority staff of the House Appropriations Subcommittee on Financial Services and General Government—and to Congressman Dan Lipinski and his impressive staff, Jason Day, Eric Lausten, Sofya Leonova, Brian Oszakiewski, Frank Pigulski, Jennifer Sypolt, John Veysey, and Nathaniel Zimmer, I am forever indebted.

I am no less in debt to the thirty-two anonymous members of Congress and congressional staffers who took time out of their busy schedules to talk with an inquisitive political scientist. For all the ways this book may appear critical of the United States Congress, it is not a criticism of the individuals who serve and work there. Members of Congress and their staffs are among the hardest-working people I know. Their jobs are stressful, grueling, and often demoralizing, and as a reward they earn the public's ire. Yet I have no doubt that if more people had the opportunity to experience their world as I have, their public approval would be much higher.

My debts extend well beyond Capitol Hill. The University of Maryland and the University of Utah were stimulating intellectual homes as I conducted this research. At both, numerous supportive colleagues and faculty offered feedback and advice. At Maryland an early attempt at this research benefited greatly from presentation at the American Politics Workshop, where I received a tremendous amount of helpful feedback. At Utah I have continued to profit from generous institutional support, including Matt Haydon's invaluable research assistance.

Along the way, a number of people from these institutions and elsewhere provided important commentary and advice, including Michael Bailey, Jeff Biggs, Janet Box-Steffensmeier, Chris Foreman, Matt Green, Thad Hall, Laurel Harbridge, Paul Herrnson, Irwin Morris, Tracy Sulkin, and Jeffrey Taylor. I am especially indebted to Peri Schwartz-Shea, who read and commented on multiple drafts. Her advice focused my attention on things I had not even perceived as important and shaped how I view and understand my own research and the way it is presented in this book. Sarah Binder too gave instrumental feedback and posed several challenging questions at a crucial stage in this project. She also suggested the book's title, which is undoubtedly superior to anything I could have given it.

Frances Lee deserves particular recognition. Frances has been a part of this project from the beginning, as an adviser, a mentor, and a friend. It is through her that I was introduced to scholarship on Congress, and she has made an indelible impression on how I think about congressional politics. She provided vital feedback, support, and advice as this book progressed over the years. I cannot even begin to express my gratitude.

It has been a pleasure working with the University of Chicago Press. John Tryneski has been an enthusiastic and supportive editor from the start, and he guided the book through a fruitful review process. The anonymous readers he selected provided comments and critiques that helped me greatly improve the manuscript. Others at the Press deserve mention as well, including Rodney Powell for his assistance and for answering my many questions and freelancer Alice Bennett for her thorough copy editing. Larry Jacobs, the series editor, was also supportive from the start and provided timely advice on framing the book.

Of course, nothing is possible without supportive family and friends, and I have both. My parents, Mark and Jill Curry, have been supportive of my quest to complete this book for far too many years. Now they can finally see a tangible result. My sister, Liz, has also been encouraging and as a bonus has promised to buy a copy of the book for her library (so I know at least one copy will be sold). Since I began this project my family has expanded numerous times, adding mother-, father-, brothers-, and sisters-in-law, nieces and nephews, cousins, and more. Each has provided welcome diversions. My friends have likewise helped me focus on things besides research. Working on a book can be all-consuming. It is good to have people who keep you from being completely devoured.

Most important, I am grateful to my wife, Jill, who has been with me since this project's conception. Jill's love and support throughout have been matched only by her intellectual contributions. She has read numerous drafts (more than I can count), commenting, fixing typos, and offering encouragement. She has also done more than her share in allowing me time to work on "the book" as well as letting me vent my frustrations too often. Without her I am not sure I would have ever finished this thing. Over the past few years our family has grown to include our daughter Louise and our son Henry, who keep me focused on what is really important. It is to the three of them that this book is dedicated.

CHAPTER ONE

Introduction

No man can be a competent legislator who does not add to an upright intention and a sound judgment a certain degree of knowledge of the subjects on which he is to legislate. —James Madison, *Federalist Papers* 53

I love these members; they get up and say, "Read the bill." What good is reading the bill if it's a thousand pages and you don't have two days and two lawyers to find out what it means after you read the bill?—Representative John Conyers (D-MI)[1]

John Boehner (R-OH) was livid. On the afternoon of Friday the thirteenth in February 2009, the House of Representatives was finishing debate on the 340,000-word conference report on the American Recovery and Reinvestment Act of 2009 (ARRA). As the visibly tired minority leader took to the floor to denounce the stimulus package, he did not focus on his disagreement with the policies included in the bill. Instead, he underlined his displeasure with the expedited means of considering the bill. Filed by the conference committee late the night before, the final text, split into two documents, had been available to view only since early morning. Slamming his copy onto the chamber floor, Boehner raged, "Here we are with 1,100 pages—1,100 pages not one member of this body has read. Not one. There may be some staffer over in the Appropriations Committee that read all of this last night—I don't know how you could read 1,100 pages between midnight and now. Not one member has read this."[2]

Boehner was right. No member of the House of Representatives could possibly have read the entire conference report in the thirteen hours between the time it was filed and the time debate began on the floor, even without breaking for food, sleep, the call of nature, or to think through its implications. A person reading at two hundred words a minute would need more than twenty-eight hours to read the bill from start to finish.[3] But despite the bill's having changed considerably since its initial consideration in the House, and having grown substantially in size, it cleared the chamber by a nearly perfect party-line vote, with just seven Democrats voting with the opposition and one voting present. The overwhelming majority of the 246 Democrats who voted for passage could not have fully considered the details of the legislation, nor could the 176 Republicans who voted against it.

The process by which ARRA was considered is not an aberration. It is representative of the considerable influence that legislative leaders in the House of Representatives exercise over policymaking. The central theme of this book derives from a simple notion: information provides power in Congress. More specifically, the argument is that meaningful and pervasive inequalities exist among members of Congress regarding the information they possess during the legislative process, and these inequalities affect the balance of power and influence in the House. Namely, those holding formal leadership positions—party leaders and committee chairs—have extensive information about the legislation being considered and the political dynamics surrounding that legislation. Rank-and-file members of Congress, in contrast, have limited resources and find it very difficult to become informed about most of the legislation being considered at any time. Because of these limitations, they concentrate their legislative efforts on developing expertise in one or two issue topics, yet they must still obtain enough information about all bills considered in their committees or on the floor so they can cast votes. Consequently, they often must rely on those who have the information, their leaders, for the knowledge and cues they need to make decisions.

Information thus is a key source of power for legislative leaders, shaping the tactics and strategies by which they exercise leadership. Because their rank and file rely on them for information and cues, leaders can shape how their followers view policy proposals and the preferences they develop. Party leaders and committee chairs can provide their rank and file with information and frame legislation to focus their attention on reasons to support the leadership's position on a bill and away from reasons to oppose it. Leaders expend considerable resources developing the talking points and messaging points that will be most effective in this regard, relying on their large staffs to gather intelligence about what is likely to persuade their rank-and-file members to stand with them on final votes while undercutting the messages and tactics of the opposition.

Furthermore, both party leaders and committee chairs have tactics to aggravate the informational inequalities in the chamber, making their rank and file even more dependent on them for information. These tactics include drafting bills behind closed doors and keeping legislative language secret throughout most of the process, changing the contents of legislation immediately before consideration in committee or on the floor, and exploiting or exacerbating the complexity of the legislation and legislative language. In taking these steps on some bills, leaders keep their rank and file and the opposition in the dark about the details of policy proposals until the last second, giving them little time to independently understand and evaluate items they are supposed to vote on. As these bills are rushed through committee or floor consideration, rank-and-file lawmakers often have nowhere to turn for information except to their leaders.

These leadership tactics—gathering, disseminating, and restricting access to information—will be explored extensively in this book, but ARRA is instructive as an introduction. Drafted and negotiated behind closed doors by a few key lawmakers in each chamber, the final text of the bill was not available for members to view until the midnight before floor consideration. Posted on the Rules Committee website, the final text was split between two documents. The first, intended to be an integrated copy, erroneously omitted several sections of the bill. Consequently the second document, a photo image of part of the original copy of the bill including these omitted sections, was posted a few hours later. Thus lawmakers and their staffs had two documents totaling over 1,100 pages to peruse if they were to understand the bill. Convening the House at 9:00 a.m., the leadership moved to immediately begin consideration of the bill, with the final vote that afternoon. In all, members had just a few hours to assess the bill and decide how to vote. Given its size and the confusion surrounding the actual text, anyone would have been hard-pressed to make an independent judgment. The Democratic leadership and the key committee chairs involved in drafting the final language, however, were standing by with meticulously crafted talking points meant to assure their rank and file that the bill met Democratic priorities, that it was a good stimulus package, that it would go over well with their constituents, and that they could feel safe in supporting it on the floor. The Republican rank and file likewise had to turn to their leaders, including Boehner, whose histrionics were clearly aimed at fostering opposition.

This information-based power has numerous implications for how we understand Congress and congressional lawmaking. As discussed in more detail in the next section, most congressional scholarship pays little attention to the institutionalized inequalities among members of Congress, including informational inequalities, and the effects these inequalities have on policymaking. Additionally, while most scholars see congressional leaders as important, they usually understand their independent influence as limited. Here, by contrast, I place legislative leaders front and center in the policymaking process and present their influence as significant and pervasive.

Additionally, the findings in this book further our understanding of the underpinnings of party power in Congress. Congressional leaders oversee parties that, although more unified than in the past, are still fairly decentralized and heterogeneous. Unlike their contemporaries in most parliamentary systems, leaders cannot control membership in the party or who wins the party's nomination to run for a seat in the chamber. Furthermore, each representative is elected from a distinct geographic district, represents a distinct constituency, and thus faces electoral pressures that can conflict with the party's goals. In shaping the information these lawmakers have about the legislation being considered, leaders can mobilize their diverse followers to act like programmatic parties and enact partisan agendas. But as effective as it is, this method of leadership comes at a cost. In shutting most lawmakers out of the legislative process, stifling their voices, and keeping them in the dark, leaders undermine the quality of legislative deliberations and dyadic representation in the House of Representatives.

The principles of this theory likely extend beyond the House of Representatives. In any legislature where informational inequalities benefit leaders, these dynamics are likely to be found to some degree. Although there is more parity among US senators in terms of the information and resources they possess, leaders routinely have information their rank and file lack. In many state legislatures, the dynamics uncovered here are likely to be even more dramatic, especially in part-time or citizen legislatures whose rank-and-file representatives have little or no staff and spend most of the year away from the capitol. Under these conditions, leaders are likely to have remarkable ability to leverage information to mobilize their ranks.

The evidence in this book draws on a number of methods of investigation, including participant observation in congressional offices, elite interviews with members of Congress and their staffs, and quantitative analyses of a dataset of important bills considered in the House from 1999 to 2010. However, before discussing these details, it is important to make clear how this book contributes to our understanding of congressional leadership and of Congress in general.

Scholarly Perspectives on Congressional Leadership

Within congressional studies, leaders are poorly understood. Despite decades of interest, we lack a complete understanding of the factors that constitute congressional leadership, the sources of power that leaders rely on, and how greatly they can exercise these powers. As David Truman (1959, 94) put it decades ago, "Everyone knows something of leaders and leadership of various sorts, but no one knows very much. Leadership, especially in the political realm, unavoidably or by design often is suffused by an atmosphere of the mystic and the magical, and these mysteries have been little penetrated by systematic observation."

Despite some excellent studies of congressional leaders and leadership, these words continue to ring true.[4] The study of legislative leaders in Congress not only is underdeveloped, it has been misdirected. Specifically, there are three broad tendencies that have led to a scholarly misreading of congressional leadership. This book addresses and challenges each of them.

Inattention to Inequalities

The first tendency has been a lack of attention to the deep inequalities among members of Congress, particularly in the information they possess during the legislative process. While congressional scholars generally do not view lawmakers as perfect equals, how institutionally unequal they are is underappreciated, and the consequences of these inequalities are not well understood.[5] This trend has been accentuated by an empirical focus on roll-call voting (on this point see Clinton 2012; Clinton and Lapinski 2008). It is at the voting stage that members appear most equal, with each possessing one vote regardless of institutional position. But a focus on roll calls obscures the significance of activities before the vote, during which members of Congress are less likely to engage as equals. What is more, these earlier, often unseen stages are perhaps even more important than voting. As Richard Hall (1996, 2) put it after years qualitatively investigating congressional committees, "floor voting is only one and probably not the most important form of participation in the legislative process."

Underscoring this trend has been a scholarly focus on lawmaker preferences. As Lee (2009, 24–46) extensively covers, in recent decades the preeminent paradigm in the study of Congress has centered on how legislative decisions are driven by the policy preferences, or ideologies, of individual lawmakers. This focus has paired well with using roll-call voting as the primary means of studying Congress. Scholars have used this approach to analyze how well legislator preferences explain numerous congressional phenomena, including policy outcomes, gridlock, committee composition, and more. However, as Lee (2009, 46) puts it, this focus has "led to diminishing scholarly interest in patterns of communication among members, cue-taking, caucus deliberation, and party consensus-building." Especially relevant to this study, it effectively buries concerns about informational inequalities, about how informed members of Congress are on the details of the policy proposals they vote on, and about the way lawmakers become informed. The most abstract studies in this tradition, those employing a spatial modeling approach, often assume away concerns about information in the interest of parsimony, assuming ab initio that lawmakers have complete information about legislative proposals and how they relate to their own ideological preferences (e.g., Krehbiel 1998). While few of these scholars would likely argue that this assumption is perfectly true, that informational concerns are often assumed away suggests that many scholars do not view them as important or influential enough to take into consideration when studying Congress.

Some studies do recognize information disparities in Congress, but they ultimately conclude that these inequities do not strongly influence policymaking. For Krehbiel (1991) informational problems are central to legislative organization, but committees and other legislative institutions effectively minimize any negative effects of informational disparities and instead leverage informational differences to benefit the chamber majority. Yet Krehbiel's evidence cannot determine whether members of Congress react positively or negatively to the actions taken by those with superior information because they approve or disapprove of these actions or because they simply do not have enough information to judge them. Kiewiet and McCubbins (1991) also recognize that "hidden information" is a problem in congressional delegation to leaders and other entities, and like Krehbiel they find that this problem can be mitigated. However, their analyses focus primarily on the delegation of authority to standing committees and executive branch agencies rather than to committee chairs or party leaders.[6]

This book argues instead that information asymmetries are central to understanding the influence of party leaders and committee chairs, and that the limited attention congressional scholars have paid to informational inequalities has undermined our understanding of lawmaking in the House of Representatives. This lack of attention is curious given the prevalence of such attention in other areas of study, including bureaucratic power (see Weber 1991; Niskanen 1971; Banks and Weingast 1992), presidential power (see Schlesinger 2004; Rudalevige 2005), organizational leadership (see Mulder 1971), and economics (see Akerlof 1970; Spence 1973).[7] As will be shown, information asymmetries systematically benefit those holding formal leadership positions in Congress, as they leverage their advantages to influence how legislation is drafted, how lawmakers perceive that legislation, and ultimately what is passed in committee and on the floor.

Underestimating Leadership Influence and Power

A second tendency in the study of Congress has been to underestimate the power and influence of legislative leaders. While congressional scholars generally view leaders as important, the dominant framework for understanding their influence—a principal-agent framework—has led them to systematically understate how much leeway leaders have to act and how much influence those actions have on the behavior of rank-and-file members of Congress and on the policymaking process.

Some scholarship sees legislative leaders virtually as clerks. For example, Krehbiel (1991) presents delegation to legislative leaders as a division of labor meant to create specialization, reduce informational barriers for the chamber as a whole, and reduce the inefficiencies inherent in collective action. Party leaders exist to grease the skids for successful policymaking, but their actions are aimed at pleasing the parent chamber. Similarly, committees exist to accrue the specialized knowledge needed to draft informed legislation, but they must produce policies satisfactory to the chamber's majority or risk rebuke on the floor. While legislative leaders are expected to play an important role in policymaking, because all their decisions must be ratified by majority votes, the real power lies with the rank and file.

In recent decades, theories emphasizing the importance of contextual and environmental factors for legislative leadership have gained prominence. While most of these studies present leaders as an integral part of the legislative process, they see their influence as constrained by the preferences of their rank and file. In other words, leaders can and do exercise significant authority in the House of Representatives, but only when there is broad agreement within the party to act aggressively to achieve generally agreed-on goals. Cooper and Brady (1981), for example, find that differences in the leadership styles of speakers Joseph Cannon (R-IL) and Sam Rayburn (D-TX) are explained by party strength during their times in office. Cannon was able to act more aggressively than Rayburn because a unified Republican caucus granted him the authority and the procedural powers to do so. Aldrich and Rohde's (2000) theory of conditional party government extends this perspective, arguing that under conditions of intraparty unity and interparty polarization, lawmakers will give their leaders more authority to aggressively push the party's agreed-on policies. Kiewiet and McCubbins (1991, 54–55) likewise find that the checks on the actions of party leaders decrease as preference homogeneity increases. Sinclair (2012, 140–42) highlights the extensive influence legislative leaders have in the contemporary legislative process but similarly argues that their unorthodox tactics stem, to a large degree, from a rise in party polarization and conflict. Accordingly, if legislative leaders can act aggressively only when their followers want them to, it calls into question whether these actions constitute leadership or if instead their followers are acting as the leaders.[8]

Cox and McCubbins (2005) likewise present legislative leaders as important actors in the legislative process. They find that to control the agenda of the House, the majority party delegates substantial agenda-setting powers to party leaders and committee chairs. This gives them some leeway to decide what legislation should be on the chamber's agenda, largely based on what would be good or bad for the party's image or brand. However, while Cox and McCubbins find that negative agenda control, or leaders' abilities to block legislation, is absolute, positive agenda control is conditional. As the authors put it elsewhere, "positive agenda control is ever present, but the frequency with which the party uses this power varies with the degree to which the party membership agrees on what the party's collective reputation should be, hence on what should be done" (Cox and McCubbins 2002, 109). For making anything happen, leaders are still constrained by the preferences of their followers.

None of this is meant to dispute that principal-agent perspectives on congressional leadership tell us a great deal. Congressional leaders are undoubtedly limited by their followers, and many of the lessons in this book are broadly consistent with a principal-agent take on delegation of leadership. However, most principal-agent studies of congressional leadership underestimate the leeway leaders have to act, in part because they do not adequately take into account the way their informational advantages empower them. As discussed in more detail in subsequent chapters, rank-and-file lawmakers cannot easily check or constrain leadership actions when they lack information about those actions. Furthermore, leaders can use their informational advantages to influence the very preferences that contextual theories claim limit their authority. In sum, understanding the nature of informational inequalities in the House of Representatives helps us understand how much influence legislative leaders can exercise, and it suggests they are more influential than typically recognized.

Limited Understanding of Leadership Activities

A third tendency in the study of Congress is an underdeveloped understanding of the daily actions legislative leaders take to influence policymaking. While various studies assert ways congressional leaders can exercise influence, or identify certain foundations of leadership power, the search for these pillars of power has been constrained both by an acceptance of the limitations on leadership power discussed above and by a discipline-wide trend toward quantitative analysis.[9] In other words, scholars have focused the hunt for influential leadership actions not only on those that fit within the limitations established by principal-agent theories of congressional leadership, but also on those actions that can be observed and assessed using quantifiable data, usually in terms of the ability to influence or change roll-call votes.

As a consequence, perhaps the most commonly asserted pillar of power has been leaders' abilities to control and distribute select resources and incentives. In other words, leaders can force, cajole, convince, or threaten their members to act a certain way by offering or withholding tangible benefits. Both party leaders and committee chairs, for example, can use their fund-raising advantages to distribute millions of dollars in campaign cash to fellow partisans to ensure their loyalty and support in future legislative battles (Cann 2008). Similarly, both sets of leaders can use their positions of power to direct federal expenditures toward the districts of those who are loyal (Cann and Sidman 2011). Party leaders can also reward loyal partisans with favorable committee assignments and other institutional perquisites (Smith and Ray 1983; Rohde 1991, 77–78). Conversely, disloyalty can be discouraged with threats of punishment, including withholding these same benefits. Additionally, there is evidence that leaders extract promises to support the party in future battles in return for these select benefits, then call in these promises at key moments (King and Zeckhauser 2003).

The ability to control the chamber's agenda is another recognized source of power. With some leeway over which legislation is considered on the floor of the House, party leaders influence what is considered and passed (Cox and McCubbins 2005). Additionally, leaders can use their agenda powers to reward loyalists by allowing their bills and amendments to be considered and punish disloyalists by keeping their legislative items off the agenda. For committee chairs, agenda control has long been seen as a major source of power. At least since Woodrow Wilson (1885), conceptions of committee power have focused on gatekeeping abilities (see also Bryce 1893; Snyder 1992; Shepsle and Weingast 1987; Weingast 1989; Deering and Smith 1997). With substantial control over their agendas, committee chairs hold the lion's share of committee gatekeeping powers.

These sources of power are real, and their importance to leaders should not be discounted. Control over chamber resources has been important to legislative leaders since early in Congress's history (see Jenkins and Stewart 2013). Nevertheless, if these are their pillars of power, leadership influence in Congress rests on a weak foundation, since there are good reasons to believe there are inherent limitations on their ability to pressure their rank and file to act a certain way by distributing money, committee seats, and the like. Although committee assignments are often viewed as among the most important resources at a leader's disposal, the contemporary committee assignment process is driven by a host of factors including lawmakers' seniority, electoral vulnerability, constituent interests, and changes in the majority's share of seats from Congress to Congress (see Frisch and Kelly 2006; Grimmer and

Powell 2013). Loyalty to the party and the leadership is only one factor in making committee assignments. Furthermore, the hypothetical punishment for disloyalty—being stripped of one's committee seats—is rare (Schickler and Rich 1997). Part of the reason Speaker Boehner's decision to strip four recalcitrant Republicans of their committee assignments at the start of the 113th Congress was so newsworthy is that similar episodes are difficult to recall. Just as often, it seems, leaders are unable to remove uncooperative lawmakers from committees. For example, when Speaker Newt Gingrich (R-GA) and Chairman David Livingston (R-LA) attempted to remove freshman representative Mark Neumann (R-WI) from an Appropriations subcommittee for opposing a leadership-supported bill in 1995, the large class of Republican freshmen revolted, forcing his reinstatement and securing him a seat on the Budget Committee as well. The attempt at muting Neumann actually gave him a bigger voice.[10]

Leaders' abilities to leverage various other resources—such as campaign funds, chamber seniority, and caucus membership—may be limited as well. There is mixed evidence, for example, that parties allocate campaign funds to reward loyalty or that distributing these funds induces loyalty. While Cann (2008) finds compelling evidence that the interchange of party funds relates to loyalty and unity in the House, other studies do not (e.g., Cantor and Herrnson 1997; Damore and Hansford 1999). Most studies find that party funds are distributed primarily based on electoral need (see Herrnson 2011, 91–135). Regarding seniority and caucus membership, there is even less evidence. Systematic study of the use of these perquisites as sticks is nonexistent, largely because their use is rare. While this does not mean leaders cannot effectively threaten to use these powers, if examples of members' losing their accrued seniority, being exiled from the party, or being punished in other ways are rare, then at the very least the *centrality* of these carrots and sticks to leadership power should be questioned.

How greatly legislative leaders can leverage their agenda powers should also be questioned. As noted above, while party leaders' abilities to exercise negative agenda control may be absolute, their positive agenda control is conditional. Even the gatekeeping power of committee chairs is questionable as a primary source of influence in the contemporary House. Although single committee referral for nearly all legislation and party leaders' unwillingness to bypass committee consideration before the 1970s made this power substantial, the rise since then in multiple referral and committee bypass has considerably muted committees' ability to keep legislation bottled up. Among the bills analyzed for this study, roughly 30 percent were referred to more than one committee, and almost 34 percent bypassed at least one committee's jurisdiction. While none of this implies that negative agenda powers are not beneficial to leaders, it suggests agenda control may not be a sufficient explanation of leadership power. Ultimately, if we are to understand legislative leaders as influential in the legislative process, we need to look elsewhere for the sources of their power.

Again, part of the reason contemporary scholars' understanding of leadership power is underdeveloped is a focus on quantitative data analysis. The forms of influence identified above can be seen and evaluated using statistical data that are publicly available, such as data on committee assignments, the movement of campaign funds among lawmakers, or the content of the floor agenda. But studies employing other methodological approaches suggest that leadership power goes beyond these highly visible exercises of influence, and that their influence may rest primarily on actions behind the scenes.

For example, Caro's (2002) study of Lyndon Johnson as "master of the Senate" draws on extensive interviews, archival research, and the historical method to understand Johnson's power as Senate majority leader. His means of influence are found to rest on actions and factors that are behind the scenes and nonquantifiable, including the relationships he forged with key lawmakers, direct pressure he applied during private conversations, his creativity in structuring procedure and action on and off the Senate floor, and to some degree his good fortune. Early studies of the House Speakership focused on the personal and biographical aspects of powerful leadership, emphasizing how "men of strong character" such as Henry Clay and Thomas Reed were able to exercise significant power (Follett 1896, 64; see also Fuller 1909; Brown 1922; Hasbrouck 1927; Chui 1928; and recently, Davidson, Hammond, and Smock 1998). Peters's (1997) historical analysis investigates how the power and influence of the Speaker evolved throughout the course of congressional history. Strahan's (2007) historical case studies document how leaders actively shape the preferences of their rank and file and subsequently alter legislative outcomes in a variety of contexts. Richard Hall's extensive interviewing and direct observation of committee politics (e.g., 1987, 1996) reveals that committee chairs' enhanced abilities to participate in the legislative process heightens their influence, placing them at "the epicenter of the communications network in which most important legislative interactions take place" (Hall 1996, 94). Green's (2010) study of the House Speaker draws on interviews with former Speaker Jim Wright (D-TX, 1987–89) and other Capitol Hill actors as well as quantitative data to understand the Speaker's influence in the House.

Each of these studies finds leaders to be powerful actors in congressional policymaking, more powerful than most other scholarship indicates, suggesting that the search for their influence needs to go beyond publicly visible actions to look at action that takes place behind the scenes or that may not be so obviously identifiable. This book is devoted to this task. The rest of this chapter describes the data and methodologies employed and gives a brief outline of the book. First, however, comes an important matter of definition.

Defining "Legislative Leaders"

Distinctly important is the meaning of "legislative leader." As noted above, legislative leaders include both those in the majority party leadership and committee chairs. But whom do those definitions include? The latter is relatively straightforward. Committee chairs are those lawmakers who chair each of the full standing, special, and select committees of the House of Representatives. This definition does not include subcommittee chairs: while they undoubtedly have more influence than most rank-and-file members of Congress, their control over committee affairs is far less than, and sometimes subservient to, that of the chair of the full committee. In particular, subcommittee chairs lack access to the resources and information held by full committee chairs. Specifically, although they are assigned staff to help run their subcommittees, these staffers serve at the pleasure of the full committee chair. As such, these staffers bear no loyalty to the subcommittee chairs and do not necessarily work in their interests. Although subcommittee chairs sometimes exert substantial influence, they are not considered leaders for the purposes of this study.[11]

Defining majority party leaders is a bit more complicated. Some studies of congressional leadership focus only on the Speaker of the House (Peters 1997; Davidson, Hammond, and Smock 1998; Green 2010; Peters and Rosenthal 2010). Others studies define the majority party leadership more broadly to include other members of the leadership team (e.g.,

Ripley 1967; Sinclair 2012). In this book the majority leadership is understood as the latter, but also as a fluid entity. In any Congress, the set of representatives who constitute the majority party leadership can evolve. The Speaker of the House and the majority leader are always a part of the leadership, but the influence of the majority whip, the caucus chairperson, the chair of the party's campaign committee, some deputy whips, and other actors can vary. Sometimes the leadership table is larger, other times it is smaller; and sometimes lawmakers selected to traditional leadership positions do not have as much influence as those who previously held the post. Roy Blunt's (R-MO) testy relationship with then majority leader Tom DeLay (R-TX) is often cited as evidence that Blunt was less influential as a majority whip than were previous and subsequent holders of the position.[12] Generally, however, the core of the majority leadership is understood as the Speaker, the majority leader, and the majority whip. As one staffer interviewed for this study put it, "The party leadership is Boehner, Cantor, and McCarthy. Practically, when people around here say 'leadership' they mean the Speaker, the majority leader, and the whip."[13]

It is also important to briefly discuss the nature of the relationship between the party leadership and committee chairs. Studies have often portrayed these two sets of leaders as power centers at odds with each other in the legislative process. Undoubtedly this has sometimes been true. But leaders and chairs are not necessarily opposed. In fact, in times of unified parties, at least, they should find plenty of common ground. Cox and McCubbins (2005) portray the members of the party leadership and the committee chairs as senior partners in a firm, sharing in the profits and damages to the caucus as a whole. As such they have incentives to work together for common interests. They may often find more reasons to work together harmoniously than to compete.

Design of the Study

A lot of what accounts for leadership influence in Congress takes place behind the scenes. Leaders' efforts to manage information flows in the House, restrict lawmakers' access to legislative language, or otherwise exploit their informational advantages cannot be understood through public records of congressional action alone. Furthermore, lawmakers' motivations cannot be understood solely by looking at their actions but require deeper investigation. For these reasons I used a combination of methods for this study.

Methods of qualitative investigation—specifically, participant observation on Capitol Hill and elite interviews with members of Congress and staff—lay the foundation for the study. These methods allow for insight into the importance of information in the legislative process, how leaders work to use their informational advantages, and how rank-and-file lawmakers are affected. Quantitative analyses build on the lessons learned through the qualitative research. I leverage insights obtained through interviews and observations to develop unique quantitative indicators of leaders' efforts to use their informational advantages for influence. Using these measures, the behaviors, activities, and expectations theorized about, and studied qualitatively, are further investigated via statistical analyses. Specifically, I employ an original dataset of more than five hundred important bills considered from 1999 to 2010. Finally, case studies of action on specific bills build on the quantitative and qualitative research and provide additional insight. Combining these methods gives a more complete picture of leadership actions and influence and also allows this book to provide a rich and detailed account of how party leaders and committee chairs manage day-to-day policymaking.

Participant Observation

This study draws on two extended periods of participant observation in the House of Representatives. Specifically, in 2007, during the 110th Congress, I spent four months as a fellow with the majority staff of the House Appropriations Committee's Subcommittee on Financial Services and General Government. In 2012, during the 112th Congress, I spent eight months as an American Political Science Association (APSA) congressional fellow with the Office of Representative Daniel Lipinski (D-IL). These experiences allowed me to observe and participate in congressional action in ways not otherwise possible. Working as a staffer in a committee office, I took part in coordinated efforts to restrict access to information. Later, working in a member's office, I lived the struggle to obtain the information needed to help my boss legislate.

More than just observing or "interacting with these politicians in their natural habitats" (Fenno 1978, 56), my experiences as a participant observer are characterized by engagement in the role of legislative staffer and immersion in the world of congressional politics. Schwartz-

Shea and Yanow (2012, 63–66) describe participant observation research as varying along a continuum from nearly pure observation to heavily participatory. My experience tended toward the latter. While the observation of political actors and action was undoubtedly important, the focus was on participating as a member of a legislative staff on Capitol Hill and developing what Schatz (2009) calls "ethnographic sensibility." In other words, my approach was not just to watch what lawmakers and congressional staffers do, but to tap into the inner logic behind their actions myself and make sense of their world. In this way my approach was decidedly interpretive.[14]

The benefits of "close, person-to-person contact that is attuned to the worldviews of people we study" are hard to overstate (Schatz 2009, 4). Perhaps the greatest benefit of this method of study is that it allows for discovery of facts, trends, and insights that were not anticipated or that conflict with tacit assumptions in the scholarly literature. Additionally, in taking part in the Capitol Hill world I was studying, I could better observe and understand the behind-the-scenes activities so crucial to comprehending leadership, as well as discern the motivations of the actors involved. I draw on these participant observation experiences throughout this book. At times I tap my experiences explicitly, and these instances are clearly noted. However, the broader theoretical and organization framework of the book was fundamentally shaped by these experiences. More detail on my participant observation is found in appendix A.

Elite Interviews

This study also draws heavily on elite interviews with members of Congress and key legislative staff, past and present. Specifically, I conducted thirty-two interviews, which build on the participant observation research, studying the role information asymmetries play in House policymaking among a broader set of actors and letting these actors describe their experiences, motivations, and behaviors in their own words. In general, the two methods complement each other, allowing me to understand how a variety of congressional actors see the role information plays in power relations in the House.

Interviews within Congress are notoriously hard to obtain (see Goldstein 2002; Baker 2011; Beckmann and Hall 2013). Consequently, I used a snowball selection technique (Biernacki and Waldorf 1981; Esterberg 2002, 93–94). Beginning with an initial set of interviews with people I was already acquainted with, I asked each of them to refer me to others who might be willing to talk. Each subsequent interview provided opportunities for more referrals, and my access to potential interviewees "snowballed." During this period I also cold-contacted the offices of current and former members of Congress to request more interviews. This recruitment method provided access to individuals I would not have reached had I simply sought interviews from a random selection of offices. In the end, the set of interviewees was quite diverse (see appendix A).

The interviews themselves lasted twenty to forty minutes and were semistructured, consisting primarily of open-ended questions. Every interview was conducted with the understanding that all communications would be used anonymously. In conducting the interviews, I wanted to avoid letting my expectations limit the interviewees' responses or the insights I could attain. The first several interviews were the most exploratory. I used them to refine the interview procedure and structure subsequent interviews. To a degree, each interview was unique. The questions were tailored to interviewees' roles in the House (leader or rank and file, member or staffer) and whether they were currently in or out of office. Still, each interview aimed at answering the same broad questions (e.g., how members of Congress obtain information about legislation; how, and to what degree, leaders influence this process, etc.).

Evidence from these interviews is presented throughout the book. Each interviewee was assigned a number, and all quotations are designated by those numbers. In addition, all interviewees are identified by their role in Congress. Specifically, interviewees are noted as either members of Congress or staffers and are further identified as party leaders, committee leaders, or rank-and-file members. Beyond this, however, their identities are protected. Appendix A provides a more detailed overview of the set of interviewees, how they were contacted, the structure of the interviews, the questions asked, and my method of transcription and analysis. These interviews provided valuable insights. In addition, along with the participant observation, they allowed me to develop quantitative indicators of leadership actions and use statistical analyses for further investigation.

Dataset of Important Bills

All the quantitative analyses in this book, unless otherwise noted, draw on a dataset of important legislation considered in the House of Representatives from 1999 to 2010 (the 106th through 111th Congresses). The selection of bills is intended to capture all legislation deemed meaningful, consequential, or important at the time it was considered. Congress deliberates on many minor or trivial bills each year. Understanding how bills like these are considered is not particularly enlightening about consequential leadership influence. Understanding how leaders influence the consideration of important legislation tells us something more substantive.

Scholars have used a number of methods to categorize legislation as important or major. Mayhew (1991) analyzed *New York Times* and *Washington Post* wrap-ups of congressional activity to determine which legislation could be considered "major" contemporaneously and retrospectively. Roughly twelve bills a year were designated as major legislation. Sinclair (2012), looking to develop a more inclusive collection of important legislation, uses the bills listed in *CQ Weekly*'s weekly list of important bills (see also Taylor 1998). This section has most recently been titled "Bills to Watch," but at times it has also been known as "This Week in Congress" and "What's Ahead." Forty to fifty bills are listed each year.

This book draws on Sinclair's approach, for two reasons. First, it is relatively inclusive, so the data analysis can pertain to more legislation. Second, it is primarily current in that it captures legislation that was deemed important by actors in the legislative process *at the time of consideration*. It is this level of importance that drives how lawmakers act. In addition to the legislation captured by this method, all regular appropriations bills are included in the dataset. This is done, first, because these bills are purposely left out of *CQ Weekly*'s listing of bills and, second, because appropriations compose a significant amount of the activity in the House each year. Furthermore, battles over spending bills are often long and contentious. All together, 518 legislative items—including regular bills, resolutions, joint resolutions, and concurrent resolutions—are included.

Each legislative item in this dataset is coded for its issue content, using the typology established by the Policy Agendas Project.[15] This typology categorizes issues into nineteen major issue areas and a total of 225 specific topics. The Congressional Bills Project, maintained by E. Scott Adler and John Wilkerson, codes each bill as primarily addressing one of the 225 topics. I use their coding here.[16] Additionally, each legislative item is coded for *all* the major issue areas addressed. While some bills address just one topic, other bills address topics across a variety of issue areas and dimensions. This coding is not provided by the Congressional Bills Project, so, using the Policy Agenda Project's codebook, I coded every legislative item for each of the nineteen major issue areas addressed by any part of the bill. Bills range from addressing one major issue area to addressing all nineteen.[17] These issue codings are instrumental in the development of various measures introduced and employed throughout the book. More detail on the dataset of legislative items can be found in appendix B.

These data are advantageous for several additional reasons. The time span studied (1999–2010) covers congressional action that took place during at least part of three presidential administrations (Clinton, Bush, and Obama), representing control of the White House by both parties. These years also cover both Democratic and Republican control of the House (eight years of Republican and four years of Democratic control) and every iteration of unified and divided government. The dataset also includes legislation that had varying success in the House, including bills that were never reported out of committee, bills that both passed and failed on the floor (though they overwhelmingly passed), bills that were stalled in the Senate or in bicameral negotiations or were vetoed, and bills that ultimately became law.

These data allow for a variety of analyses. Primarily, I use them to build on the insights garnered from the qualitative study and to develop and test indicators of leadership influence in the House of Representatives. The combination of these methods allows this book to provide both breadth and depth of evidence of leadership influence and the way leaders use their informational advantages to gain power.

Organization of the Book

Chapter 2 presents a theory of information and power in the House of Representatives. This theory rests on a threefold foundation: that information is a valuable commodity in Congress; that possession of information is not evenly distributed, but is heavily concentrated among lawmakers holding formal leadership positions; and that because leaders and rank-and-file lawmakers have distinct goals in legislating, leaders will employ their information power to push policies and drive congressional action in a different direction than would happen in a more deliberative, equal legislature.

Chapter 3 draws on participant observation and interview evidence to illustrate how the goals and resources of leaders and rank-and-file lawmakers affect the flow of information in the House and the degree of influence leaders have throughout the process. Rank-and-file lawmakers have to rely on shortcuts and cues to obtain the information they need, directing them toward sources of information, such as their party and committee leaders, that are likely to reinforce their partisan predispositions. Leaders take advantage of this dynamic, working to gather intelligence about their members' preferences and using this information to sell the bills they have created.

Chapter 4 analyzes the actions leaders can take to restrict the information available to members of Congress about the legislation being considered. A combination of qualitative and quantitative research uncovers the specific tactics party leaders and committee chairs employ, and it finds that while leaders cannot use these aggressive tactics on all bills, they are able to apply them strategically on bills of the highest importance to the leadership or when their informational hegemony is imperiled by strong interest from outside groups.

Chapter 5 quantitatively analyzes how greatly leaders can use the powers identified in chapters 3 and 4 to increase partisan support for legislation on the floor. Various analyses of the important bills dataset indicate that using restrictive informational tactics increases the partisan nature of final passage votes. These results, in concert with the qualitative evidence presented throughout the book, suggest that the ability of leaders to influence what information their rank-and-file members consider when making voting decisions is an important underpinning of party power in Congress.

Chapter 6 presents two case studies of the use of informational tactics by legislative leaders in committee and on the floor. Specifically, the chapter looks at the consideration of the American Clean Energy and Security Act of 2009 by the Committee on Energy and Commerce and the consideration of the REAL ID Act of 2005 on the floor of the House. Each case details how party leaders and committee chairs can exercise their informational powers to lead the legislative process, influence how legislation is considered, and affect what passes through committees and through the chamber.

Chapter 7 explores the limits of informational leadership. Drawing primarily on the interview research, I find that legislative leaders' use of informational tactics has the potential to frustrate rank-and-file members and engender distrust among them, especially among moderates and other lawmakers out of step with their party's orthodoxy. Examining the struggles of the new Republican leadership during the 112th Congress (2011–12), I conclude that while a lack of trust can hamper legislative leaders, the source of power persists.

Chapter 8 discusses the insights that can be gained from this book. First, in recognizing important inequalities in the House of Representatives, legislative leaders are shown to be far more consequential and influential than they are typically portrayed in political scholarship. Second, the book contributes to our understanding of the underpinnings of party power and discipline in Congress. Party leaders and committee chairs can encourage partisan behavior in the House by influencing the information lawmakers consider when making decisions, and by directing them toward reasons to support the party rather than oppose it. Finally, my findings underscore the tensions and trade-offs between legislative deliberation and responsible party governance in Congress. While using informational tactics helps legislative leaders get their parties to overcome collective action problems and act like programmatic, responsible parties, it reduces, degrades, and sometimes eliminates individual lawmakers' ability to participate and to represent their constituents on questions before the chamber.

CHAPTER TWO

Information and Power in the House

Scientia potentia est [Knowledge is power].—Attributed to Sir Francis Bacon

Information is a commodity here, perhaps the most valuable one.—Party leadership staffer[1]

The influence wielded by political leaders has evoked respect and concern ever since the country's founding. James Madison and Alexander Hamilton both dedicated important passages in the *Federalist Papers* to discussing political leadership's ramifications for the burgeoning republic. Both believed that strong leadership could be either a boon or a bane (Strahan 2003). For example, in *Federalist Papers* 62 Madison argues that legislatures are prone to "[seduction] by factious leaders, into intemperate and pernicious resolutions" (Hamilton, Madison, and Jay 1999, 377). However, in other essays he repeatedly mentions the importance of finding "fit characters" and politicians of "generous principles" who could be kept working in American government (Strahan 2003, 64). Despite the attention the founders paid to this topic, scholarly understanding of leaders and leadership in Congress remains underdeveloped.

This chapter lays out a theory of information and power in the House of Representatives. The principles underlying this theory are simple. The first is an understanding that information is a valuable commodity in Congress. Before lawmakers can act on legislation—propose an amendment, make a statement on the floor, or cast a vote—they have to understand what they are amending, debating, or voting on, and the implications of those actions. Furthermore, information is empowering. The more members of Congress know about a bill, the more involved they can be in its development. And other members of Congress often rely on informed members for knowledge and insight.

The second founding principle is that information is not evenly distributed. The typical member of Congress has limited time, resources, and information and simply cannot become informed about most legislation or deeply analyze it. Legislative leaders—both majority party leaders and committee chairs—by contrast, leverage their considerable staff resources both to accrue information about most legislation and to become deeply involved in its development and consideration. Consequently, rank-and-file lawmakers often must rely on their leaders for enough information so they can make decisions. In providing information, leaders can exploit lawmakers' predispositions toward partisanship, ambiguous policy preferences, and limited ability to control or check the decisions and actions of their leaders.

The third principle is that leaders' goals and motivations are distinct from those of their fellow lawmakers. If leaders and rank-and-file lawmakers shared identical goals in the legislative process, the information disparity would be meaningless. Leaders would simply be providing a shortcut to help party or committee members achieve an agreed-on outcome. However, leaders are far more concerned than other lawmakers with achieving big-picture, partisan priorities and goals. Consequently, they work to influence the information rank-and-file lawmakers are exposed to and direct their attention to reasons to support their leaders rather than defect.

This chapter discusses each of these principles in detail, presenting information as a source of power that legislative leaders routinely and persistently rely on to influence the legislative process. Ultimately, in understanding how leaders leverage their informational advantage in Congress, we can understand the pervasiveness of their influence and see how that influence shapes congressional policymaking.

The Value of Information in Congress

Gathering and processing information about legislative items is a principal concern for all members of Congress. To cast a responsible vote, offer an amendment, or take any other action, lawmakers first need to understand what they are voting on, amending, or acting on. But the demands on members' time and resources make it unrealistic for them to

closely consider most items (see Kingdon 1989). Legislators' schedules
are loaded, often with overlapping meetings with constituents, caucuses,
and other legislators or executive branch officials, with committee hearings and markups, and with floor deliberation and votes, fund-raising
events, and trips to and from the district, as well as meetings and briefings with staff. Congressional staffers' schedules are similarly booked
with meetings, briefings, hearings, markups, and events in and around
the Capitol complex. As one representative told Richard Hall, "I feel
like I'm spread thin all the time. There's never any time to read or think
an issue through or anything like that" (Hall 1996, 23).

Lawmakers today may be busier than ever before, since the congressional workload has increased dramatically over the past several decades. As figure 2.1 shows, despite popular complaints that Congress
takes too much time off, the data suggest that legislators are working
more than ever. Between the 80th and 109th Congresses (1947–2006) the
total hours the House was in session rose from 1,224 to 1,918, a 57 percent increase. Similarly, the number of hours a day that the House is
in session has grown. During the 80th Congress the House was in session, on average, 4.8 hours a day. By the 109th Congress that average had
reached roughly 8 hours, a 67 percent increase.

Similarly, the House is taking more votes than in the past. Figure 2.2

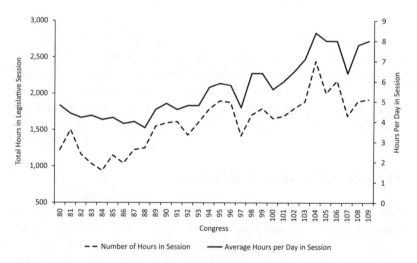

FIGURE 2.1. Time in legislative session for the House of Representatives, 80th to 109th
Congresses. Source: Ornstein, Mann, and Malbin 2008, 124.

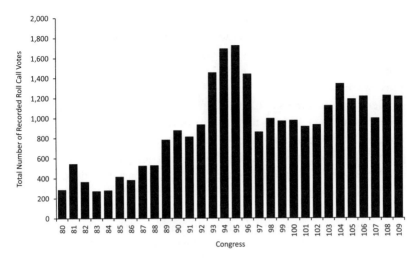

FIGURE 2.2. Number of roll-call votes taken by the House of Representatives, 80th to 109th Congresses. Source: Ornstein, Mann, and Malbin 2008, 124.

presents the number of recorded roll-call votes taken in the House of Representatives between the 80th and 109th Congresses. While the use of electronic voting beginning in the 93rd Congress clearly led to an initial rise and subsequent fall in the number of recorded votes, it is also clear that a general increase in recorded roll-calls preceded this date and continued thereafter, increasing by 325 percent over the time series. Arguably, these votes are taken on more complex legislative items as well. In the 80th Congress the average public bill was just 2.5 pages. By the 109th Congress it was more than 15 pages. Similarly, over the same period the *Federal Register* grew by more than 500 percent, from 14,736 pages to 78,724 (Ornstein, Mann, and Malbin 2008, 127).

Lawmakers today must spend significant time away from the Capitol as well. The need for members of Congress to campaign constantly during their time in office is now well documented (see Ornstein and Mann 2000). Lawmakers lead permanent campaign apparatuses, always looking toward the next primary or general election. Most representatives and senators fly home on weekends to take part in events around their district or state, conduct meet and greets with constituents, give speeches to local groups, and take part in ceremonial events. When they are in Washington, the campaign is not suspended. Members of Congress spend hours making fund-raising calls by phone and attending lunches, dinners, and receptions to meet potential donors and solicit cash. At a new-member orientation event for incoming freshmen of the 113th Congress, House Democrats told their new colleagues they should expect to spend four hours a day calling and soliciting donors and another hour on "strategic outreach," which includes attending events and press work.[2]

Generally, members of Congress are overwhelmed by the tremendous demands on their limited time and resources. Historically, the need to cope with logistical and informational demands has driven the way lawmakers have organized and structured their jobs. At the institutional level, party leadership posts were established, in part, to reduce the inefficiency of having every lawmaker participate in scheduling and agenda setting (Bach and Smith 1988; Baron 2000). Increasing workloads and demands on Congress similarly heralded the formation of standing committees to more efficiently process information and develop policy responses (Cooper 1970). As Gamm and Shepsle (1989, 60) put it, "Increased workloads, increased responsibilities, and an increased longing for independence from the executive branch demanded a more efficient and orderly system of processing legislation and reaching decisions."

Members of Congress have also structured their individual behavior to deal with their limited resources and to process information more effectively. Typically, lawmakers specialize in a small subset of issues that are important to their constituents and seek committee assignments related to these specialties (Adler and Lapinski 1997). Within committees they further specialize, becoming involved in proceedings especially relevant to their districts' concerns and their own policy interests (Hall 1996). In focusing on just a handful of issues, lawmakers can become knowledgeable on the substance of relevant policies, informed on the political dynamics surrounding them, and acquainted with the key players. In short, with time lawmakers can become experts on a couple of issues.

However, this system of specialization tends to leave lawmakers relatively uninformed about other issues. But to be responsible representatives, they need to know enough about the policy and political implications of each bill scheduled for floor or committee consideration to cast an informed vote. Lawmakers generally want to avoid casting votes that may come back to haunt them (Arnold 1990). For legislation that reaches beyond their specializations, this goal can be hard to attain. Their limited resources and hectic schedules make it difficult to analyze bills independently. Even if they have plenty of time, they may lack the knowledge to understand the intent and implications of legislation addressing complex or technical issues such as the tax code, science and technology policy, or regulation of high finance. Ultimately, lawmakers have to find other ways to obtain enough information to make responsible and intelligent decisions.

To become informed efficiently, most lawmakers rely on cues and information provided by other political actors. Kingdon (1989) finds that two of the primary sources they turn to are interest groups and other lawmakers. The positions interest groups take on a bill can provide useful information. In assessing the list of supporters and opponents across the universe of interests, members of Congress can get an idea of how their constituents may react to a yea or nay vote. Additionally, most members have strong ties to groups who share their policy priorities and goals (Hall and Deardorff 2006). The information and cues these groups provide can help a lawmaker feel more confident about a voting decision.

Lawmakers also turn to their fellow representatives for cues on how to react to particular legislation. Specifically, they ask members of Congress whom they believe they can trust and who have "some expertise on the legislation in question" (Kingdon 1989, 85). Trust follows from partisanship and policy preferences, since lawmakers are more likely to trust their fellow partisans, and within their party they are most likely to trust lawmakers who are ideologically similar to them (Kingdon 1989, 81). Expertise is often understood as lawmakers' sitting on the committee(s) of jurisdiction for a particular bill. As noted above, these lawmakers are likely to be specialized in the issues the bill addresses and potentially involved in hearings or committee markups on the bill early in the legislative process. By turning to trusted, knowledgeable colleagues, lawmakers can obtain information and cues on legislation they know little about or lack the expertise to fully understand so they can cast an informed vote.

This system of specialization and information sharing is efficient, but it alters the power dynamics in the chamber. On any particular bill, those in the know are empowered. Without the time, resources, or ability to become independently informed, most lawmakers rely on those who do know, putting themselves at their mercy. Knowledgeable lawmakers can use their platform to influence their colleagues, providing information and cues to bolster support for bills they like and foster opposition to bills they dislike. Scholars have previously recognized that specialization and the nonrandom distribution of information to members of congressional committees can bias policy outcomes toward preference outliers (see, for example, Fenno 1973). As the next section suggests, however, on a lot of important legislation, information is heavily concentrated among the small cadre of lawmakers holding formal leadership positions, empowering them to influence their rank and file on most bills considered in the House of Representatives.

Information and Leaders in Congress

Lawmakers' level of involvement on any issue or bill can be understood as a function of their *interest* in the bill and the *resources* they have to commit to it (see Hall 1987, 1996). Interest can arise from a variety of sources, including constituents' concerns and the member's personal policy preferences, and across the range of issues it is likely to be fairly evenly distributed throughout the chamber. Resources, however, are largely a function of a lawmaker's position in the chamber. Specifically, lawmakers holding party and committee leadership posts benefit from larger staff resources than rank-and-file lawmakers. While most lawmakers can commit their limited resources only to the legislative items of greatest interest, legislative leaders have enough resources to be involved on nearly every important issue or bill.

As shown in figure 2.3, majority party leaders and committees have far more resources than the typical rank-and-file lawmaker. In 2010, for example, rank-and-file members were limited to hiring a maximum of eighteen staffers and were allotted an average of $1.5 million for salaries and offices expenses. By contrast, majority party leadership and committee offices have routinely been appropriated millions of additional dollars for salaries and other expenses. In 2010 majority leadership offices were given $14 million for their expenses, and the average committee benefited from $7.4 million to be used at the chair's disposal.[3] Furthermore, the disparity is growing over time. As shown, funding to all offices grew from 1998 to 2010. Funding to personal and committee offices grew at relatively the same pace. Specifically, funds appropriated to personal offices grew 27 percent and funds to committee offices grew 22 percent. Funds to majority leadership offices, by contrast, grew by 50 percent from 1998 to 2010.

With more funds on hand, party and committee leaders can hire far more staff. In 2009, for example, the majority and minority leadership

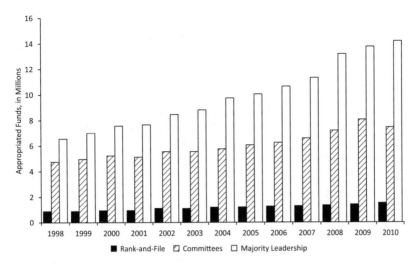

FIGURE 2.3. Funds appropriated to rank-and-file, committee, and majority party leadership offices, fiscal years 1998 to 2010. Sources: Legislative Branch Appropriations, fiscal years 1998–2010. Figures are in 2010 constant dollars.

offices employed 219 staffers, and the average House committee employed 59 (Petersen, Reynolds, and Wilhelm 2010). In each instance, most of these staffers worked for the majority party. In 2010, Nancy Pelosi (D-CA) employed 59 people in the Speaker's office alone (Glassman 2012, 26).[4] By comparison, while the average rank-and-file lawmaker hired 16 staffers in 2009, on average just 8 of them worked in the Capitol Hill office, with the others employed back in the district and likely working on casework and other constituent services rather than on legislating. The staffers leaders can hire also are typically more experienced and knowledgeable and can focus more assiduously on fewer tasks and policy issues than the staff of rank-and-file lawmakers. Committee staffers, for example, can concentrate solely on a subset of issues within the committee's jurisdiction. Leadership staffers can focus on narrow areas of policy and procedure as well. By comparison, the staffers of typical lawmakers have to work on numerous policy areas and typically have less experience and expertise.

Using these staffers, leaders can become intimately involved in and knowledgeable about every important bill and issue before their committees or before the House. They can lead the crafting, negotiating, and drafting of legislative language and keep a keen eye on the political dynamics surrounding the bill or issue as it moves through the legislative process. Committee chairs, for instance, can use their impressive staff resources in combination with their procedural powers to gather information about the moods of rank-and-file committee members, draft or redraft legislation entirely within their offices, then sell the bill to committee members ahead of the markup, emphasizing information that may encourage support. Party leaders can rely on their vast whip organizations to assess how rank-and-file lawmakers might react to specific policy ideas or provisions, then delegate other staffers to either draft the bill behind closed doors, coordinate the drafting among a few key players, or alter the contents of the bill before it is considered on the floor. With control over the floor agenda, the majority party leadership can schedule consideration of the bill when the timing is right and aggressively sell it to rank-and-file lawmakers looking for cues about what the bill does, how it might be perceived, and how it will affect their districts and their political fortunes.

Consequently, when rank-and-file lawmakers are looking for trusted and knowledgeable sources late in the legislative process, their party and committee leaders will often be the most informed actors they can find, and those leaders will be eager to explain why they should support (or oppose) the bill in question. While lawmakers are not fools and do not blindly follow their leaders, there are several reasons to believe that rank-and-file lawmakers are persuadable and that legislative leaders can use their informational advantages in influential ways. (1) Lawmakers are predisposed to be partisan and have various incentives to go along with their leaders in the absence of compelling reasons to the contrary; (2) rather than clearly defined policy preferences, lawmakers often have only general or vague preferences that can be shaped; and (3) it is not feasible for the rank and file to adequately check or control many of their leaders' actions.

Partisan Incentives and Dispositions

Congressional lawmakers are predisposed to act as partisans and work together for reasons that go well beyond ideology and policy agreement. Lee (2009) exhaustively covers the subject and finds that lawmakers are inclined to exhibit partisan behavior because of collective political interests. As she adroitly puts it, "Members' electoral and institutional interests are bound up with the fate of their parties" (Lee 2009, 3). Electorally, lawmakers are tied together by public perception of their party (see also Cox and McCubbins 2005). They do not win or lose elections entirely independent of each other, but are affected by the general standings of the parties with the public and by voters' partisan leanings (Jacobson 2009, 135–44). As such, lawmakers have an interest not only in improving public opinion of their own party, but in tarnishing the opposing party's reputation. Doing so requires coordinated action by party members to deliver a popular policy agenda as well as exploit opportunities to make the other side look bad.

Institutionally, lawmakers are tied together by collective power interests (see also Schattschneider 1942). Control over Congress confers collective benefits that include control over the legislature's agenda, the ability to use the floor for political messaging, and control over which policy proposals become law. These collective benefits in turn confer individual benefits for members of the majority party, including more money for district projects (Balla et al. 2002; Levitt and Snyder 1995), more campaign cash (Cox and Magar 1999; Rudolph 1999), opportunities to obtain chairmanships and other powerful positions, and improved capacities to influence public policy and exercise power within the government. By working together, partisans can improve not only their individual odds of reelection, but the odds that their party does well as a whole and takes and retains control over Congress.

Because of these collective incentives, lawmakers would much rather go along with their party in committee and on the floor than go against it. Early scholarship on roll-call voting strongly suggests that most lawmakers approach the legislative process assuming they will support their party's position. Deviation occurs when information comes to light that makes a bill unpalatable (Ripley 1967, 139–59; Matthews and Stimson 1975; Kingdon 1989). When no compelling reason to oppose the party arises, the default is to be a good partisan, knowing the collective benefits it entails. In other words, lawmakers generally do not want to anger party leaders and their fellow partisans or risk embarrassing or damaging the party without a very good reason.

The implications of this general partisan posture toward the legislative process are dual. First, lawmakers have reasons to *want* strong leaders and leadership. Strong leaders can grease the skids and help legislative majorities overcome collective action problems, pass legislation, and take positions that help them win elections and obtain future majorities (see Rohde 1991). Second, leaders' influence over what information lawmakers are exposed to should make members even more likely to support their parties in committee and on the floor. When leaders act as gatekeepers to policy and political information, it makes it less likely that lawmakers will be exposed to information that may encourage them to defect. Leaders are going to obscure or downplay this potentially damaging information in favor of information that encourages the rank and file to go along with the party. This provides a way for legislative leaders to reinforce partisanship in committee and on the floor, even among diverse and heterogeneous caucuses.

The Ambiguity of Preferences

In addition to an inclination to support their leaders, there is evidence that, rather than clearly defined policy preferences, members of Congress have what would more accurately be defined as "broad orientations" or "zones of acceptable outcomes" that can be molded and influenced by leaders' actions (Cooper and Hering 2003; Weaver 1986, 2000). Congressional scholars often portray lawmakers' behavior as deterministic, guided by the preferences of their districts and constituents and largely fixed until the next election (see, for example, Krehbiel 1998; Brady and Volden 1998). From this viewpoint, there seems little reason to believe their leaders' information would be influential. However, there is a great deal of evidence, anecdotal and otherwise, that lawmakers have significant leeway to act independently of their constituents. The representatives Fenno (1978) interviewed, for one, indicated that they had leeway as long as they could convincingly explain their votes to their constituents. Arnold (1990) furthered this argument, suggesting that lawmakers could take nearly any reasonable position on a bill if they could do so obscurely. If the meaning or consequences of a vote are unclear, a member of Congress can act with relative latitude. Furthermore, not every individual in a district needs to approve of the policy positions a representative takes. Members need to please only a large enough subpopulation to secure reelection. Lawmakers are not pure delegates in the Burkean sense but can often act as trustees.

As well as having flexibility in their decisions, lawmakers hold preferences that vary in intensity from issue to issue and bill to bill. Just as no rank-and-file lawmaker could be fully informed on every issue, no lawmaker could possibly be intensely concerned about every issue (see Hall 1987, 1996). This variation in intensity affects which issues members of

Congress try get involved in, as well as how clearly defined their preferences are. On some issues members may simply be uninterested. A legislator from an eastern urban district, for example, may not care whether dairy subsidies favor midwestern or California farmers. Other times, members may be apathetic simply because they did not have time to consider the legislation closely. Regardless of the reason, on issues where members have less interest and less at stake, they are likely to have less well-defined policy preferences.

Even on issues and bills where members of Congress do have solid preferences, there is evidence that majority party leaders can have influence. Evans and Oleszek (1999) find, for example, that party leaders not only respond to their rank and file's preferences on legislation, but actively work to shape those preferences. Specifically, leaders routinely use their whip organization to mobilize support for policy proposals. Forgette (2004) finds that exposure to leadership messages at caucus meetings increases lawmakers' likelihood of voting with the party, and Burden and Frisby (2004) find that targeted whip efforts change the positions of rank-and-file partisans ahead of floor votes. Furthermore, Evans and Grandy (2009, 197) demonstrate that whips may be most effective when "significant pockets of disagreement" exist within a party caucus.

Underlying lawmakers' susceptibility to persuasion is that they may simply have a tough time making decisions. According to research done by Behringer, Evans, and Materese (2006), lawmakers sometimes remain unsure how they will vote even as they are headed to the floor for the roll call; and this occurs not just on minor legislation, but on items of great importance. The implications of preference ambiguity for information-based leadership are clear. By influencing what information rank-and-file lawmakers are exposed to, leaders can influence their positions on bills and issues. They can provide them with justifications for voting with their party so that they can explain their votes when they go back to their districts. Furthermore, by shaping information they can influence lawmakers' preferences on new issues, policies, and bills as they emerge and evolve. In short, leaders can use their informational advantages to persuade lawmakers, in part because lawmakers are persuadable.

The Difficulty of Checking Leaders

Finally, legislative leaders can use their informational advantages to influence lawmakers because it is often difficult for rank-and-file members

to control or check their leaders' actions. The process of leadership selection is often understood to ensure the rank and file's control over the
type of leaders they have and ultimately the actions those leaders take.
Because those holding leadership positions are subject to reelection every two years, their party caucus will select people whose policy preferences are similar to the party median and will replace unfaithful leaders.
However, there is substantial evidence that leaders are selected primarily based on other concerns. For example, there is a strong relationship
between candidate-to-candidate campaign donations and leadership selection. Lawmakers can improve their odds of obtaining a party leadership post by aggressively distributing campaign funds to fellow partisans (Deering and Wahlbeck 2006; Heberlig, Hetherington, and Larson
2006; Green and Harris 2007; Cann 2008).

Historically, and still to a large degree, the selection of committee
chairs has reflected chamber seniority. The importance of seniority to
legislative organization in Congress has been well documented (Goodwin 1959; Polsby, Gallaher, and Rundquist 1969; Hinckley 1971). Although the final selection may reflect contribution totals, the list of
candidates is largely determined by seniority. Without extensive experience in Congress and on the committee in question, a member has little chance of becoming the chair. This remains true even though under
Speaker Newt Gingrich (R-GA), seniority was often bypassed in select-
ing committee chairs (Owens 1997).

Beyond the selection procedure, there are various reasons it is difficult for lawmakers to check their leaders' actions. Particularly relating to
information, rank-and-file lawmakers are largely unable to be discern-
ing about the information their leaders provide. If members are turning to the leadership for information, it is because they cannot get it elsewhere or acquire it independently. If they do not have time to collect
the information on their own or from any other sources, they probably
do not have time to question what their leaders provide. Even if a few
skeptical lawmakers do allocate the time necessary to scrutinize the information legislative leaders give them on a particular bill and find it
is misleading, insufficient, or incomplete, these efforts will have consequences only if these skeptical lawmakers have the resources, contacts,
and clout to convince a significant number of their colleagues that their
leaders are misleading them. This task is unlikely to be achieved, even
if there are some dissatisfied rank and filers. As noted above, rank-and-
file lawmakers have numerous incentives to go along with their leaders,

and most of them, most of the time will not be interested in proving their leaders wrong.

Even if rank-and-file lawmakers are unhappy with a committee chair or a party leader, removing a leader from power can be quite difficult. Removal has been rare in the House of Representatives.[5] For various reasons, once lawmakers are selected for a leadership or committee post, it is difficult for the rank and file to remove even the most troublesome agents. The longer members spend on a committee or in a leadership position, the more experience and expertise they acquire regarding legislative procedure and policy. Removing such experienced leaders may be detrimental for the committee, the chamber, or the party. Furthermore, legislative leaders work to protect their power, building alliances by striking deals with other members over legislation, distributing campaign contributions, and otherwise shoring up support.

Even if lawmakers have the will and the votes to remove a leader, there may be no agreement on a successor. Consider the deliberations over Representative Les Aspin's (D-WI) chairmanship of the House Armed Services Committee in 1987. After he became chair in 1985, Apsin's conservative stances on military and foreign policy, and his support for the Reagan administration's policy proposals, clashed with the more liberal Democratic rank and file. At the start of the next Congress in 1987, House Democrats voted to remove Aspin from his post and select a successor. However, nothing in the Democratic caucus by-laws restricted Aspin from running to regain the gavel. Along with Aspin, three other committee members were nominated for the post: Charles E. Bennett (D-FL), an ethics reformer and political moderate; Nicholas Mavroules (D-MA), a leading liberal on the committee; and Marvin Leath (D-TX), one of the few committee Democrats even more conservative than Aspin. Early rounds of voting eliminated Bennett and Mavroules from consideration, leaving the conservative Aspin to face off against the even more conservative Leath. Realizing Leath would be even more troublesome, liberal Democrats swung strongly for Aspin in the final vote. Despite continuing to clash with his fellow partisans, Aspin would hold on to his chairmanship until 1993, when President Clinton appointed him secretary of defense.[6]

In short, holding leaders in check is not easy. Historically, only extreme abuses of power have led to rebuke or removal. Serious challenges to party leaders have been relatively uncommon. From 1863 to 1977, there were only six serious challenges to Democratic Party leadership posts in the House of Representatives and nine to Republican posts (Nelson 1977, 935). Since the 1970s, leadership challenges have been neither more common nor more successful. Successful challenges to committee chairs have also been relatively few. Except for a handful of disposals by the Democratic caucus in the 1970s (see Rohde 1991, 22–23), few chairs in either party have been forcibly removed. Most of the time it is simply more rational for rank-and-file lawmakers to trust their leaders and keep their own time free for other activities like campaigning, tending to constituents, and working on the legislation that is important to their particular interests. This arrangement gives leaders significant leeway to influence policymaking in Congress. Members of Congress do not always want to constrain their leaders, but even when they do it may be prohibitively difficult.

Combined, these three dynamics—lawmakers' incentives and predispositions to be partisan, the ambiguity of lawmakers' policy preferences, and the difficulty of restraining leaders' actions—amplify the ability of majority party leaders and committee chairs to leverage their informational advantages into influence. However, information power would not be very meaningful if leaders and followers were in complete agreement about what policies should take priority and how to address them. Under these conditions, leaders' controlling and providing information would simply make legislating more efficient, with leaders using their resources to inform their time-pressed rank and file about legislation they all agree on. However, as the next section suggests, leaders hold unique goals, directing their efforts to different policies and priorities than the typical lawmaker.

Leadership Goals and Leadership Action

Members of Congress are understood to act purposively to achieve their goals. In his seminal research, Fenno (1973) stresses that not only do lawmakers act in response to their goals, but they *adapt their goals* to match the positions they hold in the chamber. Relevant to this study, obtaining a chairmanship or a leadership post is likely to alter lawmakers' priorities.

Recent studies by Strahan (2007) and Green (2010) have emphasized that leadership action is driven by several leadership-specific goals. Conceptually, leaders' goals are neither completely distinct from nor completely compatible with goals held by typical members of Congress. In some ways, pursuing leadership goals benefits both leaders and their rank and file, but in other ways it acts to the detriment of the rank and file's interests, influence, and objectives. Understanding how this is so requires understanding legislative leaders' three primary, interrelated goals: remaining a leader, winning and holding chamber majorities, and passing a partisan agenda.[7]

Among existing studies of Congress, the first goal—remaining a leader—is by far the most prominently discussed. Much like all lawmakers seeking reelection, congressional leaders cannot pursue any other goals unless they first obtain and hold their positions. The overwhelming attention to this goal contributes to the scholarly focus on the limitations to leaders' influence. Since party leaders and committee chairs stand for reelection to their posts every two years, they have to satisfy members of their party or risk being cast off. Congressional history is not replete with cases of leaders being overthrown, but even a few cases—such as Joseph Cannon's (R-IL) removal from power in 1911, Gerald Ford's (R-MI) defeat of Charles Halleck (R-IN) for Republican leader in 1965, and the removal of conservative Democratic chairs in the 1970s—along with the presence of ambitious up-and-comers, may be enough to keep leaders on their toes. With the sword of Damocles perpetually over their heads, leaders will feel some need to be responsive to their rank and file. Yet assuming this is the only consequence of this leadership goal is off the mark. Leaders must indeed be responsive to their followers, but they are held responsible for far more than responsiveness, and the other leadership goals motivate action that often conflicts with those efforts.

In addition to demanding responsiveness, leaders' rank and file judge the efforts they put toward achieving the second leadership goal—helping the party win and hold chamber majorities. Put bluntly, leaders risk losing power if their party does poorly at the polls. As noted above, there are numerous collective benefits to majority status. Arguably, majority status is even more beneficial for legislative leaders than for the rank and file. For one thing, leaders' powers are greatly diminished when they are in the minority. The majority leadership sets the agenda, determines committee seat allocations, influences bill referral, and determines the rules by which legislation will be considered on the floor. Committee chairs, similarly, control the agendas of their committees and determine how bills will be written and considered in committee meetings. The minority leadership and minority ranking members on committees, by con-

trast, can only respond to these actions. Second, a party's good show-
ing at the polls enhances a leader's job security. Few leaders are thrown
out after their party wins an election; they run a much higher risk of attracting opposition if the party is struggling (Peabody 1976). This means
leaders' efforts to keep their posts may entail more than just responsiveness, and at times their actions to bolster the party's electoral fortunes
may conflict with responsiveness to the desires of their rank and file.

The third leadership goal—passing a partisan agenda—informs some
leadership actions that may conflict with responsiveness. To some degree, all members of a party caucus hold this goal. Lawmakers have incentives to help their party pass a successful policy platform and bolster
the party's collective image with voters. However, rank-and-file lawmakers have numerous competing incentives, interests, and goals that
may conflict with broad party priorities. For one thing, the preferences
of lawmakers' constituents, and the priorities of their party do not always
align (Kingdon 1989; Sullivan and Uslaner 1978). In these instances lawmakers need to balance their individual goals of reelection with the collective goals of the party. Legislative leaders, by contrast, have unique
incentives to advance partisan priorities rather than focus on their own
particular interests.[8] One of these incentives is the previous leadership
goal. Needing to build a positive party image for the next election, leaders typically focus on achieving big-picture partisan items, establishing
a record of success and a contrast with the other party. These efforts, in
turn, can help them maintain their power by placating most members of
the caucus with improved electoral odds.

Leaders focus on major partisan items for other reasons as well. Their
institutional positions require them to take the lead in the president's efforts to set the policy agenda. The president's influence on congressional
politics is foremost (Bond and Fleisher 1990; Edwards and Wood 1999).
Although they cannot dictate policy outcomes, presidents have substantial influence over the congressional agenda and, because of their veto
power, over the final substance of bills signed into law. To a large degree,
legislative leaders have to respond to the presidential agenda. If there is
unified government, this means majority party leaders and committee
chairs often become the chief supporters of the president's legislation.
If there is divided government, it means becoming a leader of the opposition. This is especially true for party leaders. Modern Speakers of the
House feel it is their duty to support a president who is a member of their
party (Peters 1997; Green 2010). Peters (1997) also suggests that Speak-

ers feel responsible for leading the opposition when the president is of the other party. While typical lawmakers have an interest in bolstering presidents from their own party and damaging presidents of the other party, they do not have the same obligation to take the lead on presidential initiatives. Instead, they can largely act according to how presidential actions will be received by their constituents.

Another incentive for leaders to pass a partisan agenda is their historical reputations. Strahan demonstrates that Speakers act, in part, to build reputations for themselves based on the policies passed during their tenure. This concern naturally leads them to focus on the big picture. As he puts it, "Parochial concerns of rank-and-file legislators may cause them to pay insufficient attention to broader, long-term interests, while advancing these broader interests is precisely what confers lasting 'fame' on a leader" (2007, 31). In other words, prominent statesmen and stateswomen do not gain national fame by accruing pork or focusing narrowly on their constituents' preferences. They do so by influencing the enactment of nationally significant legislation. Undoubtedly this should concern not only Speakers, but well-known committee chairs and other representatives as well. Much like presidents, these actors are likely to be concerned with building positive, and national, records.[9]

Generally, the responsibility that comes with party and committee leadership redirects lawmakers' priorities toward broader items and concerns. Consider the evolution of Representative Maxine Waters (D-CA).[10] During her first twenty years representing southern Los Angeles, "Kerosene" Maxine was a firebrand of populist opposition to banks, big business, and financial institutions. For her reliably liberal, Democratic, and blue-collar district, Waters's public tirades—including calling bank executives "gangsters" and threatening to tax their companies "out of business"—won her local popularity and acclaim.[11] However, when Representative Barney Frank (D-MA) retired in 2012 at the end of the 112th Congress, Waters became the top Democrat on the House Financial Services Committee. Since then, her famously caustic stances have softened. Since taking the leadership post, she has met publicly with banking executives, expressed her concern for their interests, and told them her door is open. Her new position, incentives, and responsibilities have altered her goals as a newly minted ranking member. As Kenneth Bentsen, former Democratic member of Congress and member of the Financial Services Committee, told the *New York Times*, "[Waters] clearly understands that her role has changed."[12]

With great power comes great responsibility, and for legislative leaders in the House these new obligations beget a new set of goals and ultimately a set of priorities different from those of their rank and file. While rank-and-file lawmakers want their party to succeed, they also see legislative questions through the lens of their individual reelection goals. Partisan leaders endeavor to get rank-and-file lawmakers to consider the big picture rather than the details. In other words, they want them to weigh the collective benefits of supporting the bill (or opposing it if in the minority) against any reasons to do otherwise.[13]

Their informational advantages help leaders achieve these ends. As discussed in the subsequent chapters, party leaders and committee chairs take aggressive actions to influence what information lawmakers have about the intent of legislation, the specific language and provisions included, and the political dynamics related to the bill. They hope to get lawmakers to see the legislation their leaders have crafted, or the position their leaders have taken on a bill, amendment, or provision, as in their interest as well as the party's. Because of the incongruence of goals, these efforts may encourage rank-and-file lawmakers to support something they might have opposed had they had different information. They may also dissuade them from actions they otherwise might have taken or undermine the minority's ability to put up an effective opposition. While aggressive, information-based leadership may result in legislation that benefits the entire majority party, that legislation might have looked different under a more open, informed, and deliberative legislative process.

Conclusion

Information plays a central role in congressional lawmaking. Lawmakers need information to make decisions, and the information they have influences the decisions they make. Because they often do not have the time, resources, or expertise to accrue this information independently, lawmakers rely heavily on their well-informed legislative leaders. This combination of informational asymmetry and reliance places leaders in a position of power. Playing off lawmakers' partisan predispositions, shapable policy preferences, and limited ability to check their actions, leaders strategically exploit this reliance to lead the chamber and drive action. This power is pervasive, and they use it regularly to achieve their goals in committee and on the floor.

What expectations can we have for when and how legislative leaders will leverage their informational advantages into influence? What effects should these efforts have on lawmakers' behavior and on congressional action? The implications are inherent throughout this chapter, but they warrant elucidation here. Regarding the first question, we should find that leaders use their informational power strategically in pursuit of their leadership goals. Leaders should try to manage what information their rank and file have and use information to reinforce partisan positions. They will expend much time, energy, and resources accruing, dispensing, and generally shaping the flow of information throughout the chamber, their committees, and the legislative process. Leaders will at times strategically keep lawmakers on both sides of the aisle in the dark about the contents and implications of legislation, increasing their partisans' reliance and undercutting the minority's ability to craft an effective opposition strategy that siphons off majority support. Consistent with their goals, leaders will be most aggressive in their actions on high-priority partisan bills and issues. They will also be most aggressive when the influence of outside groups and other political actors threatens their control over what information is out there.

We should find that these efforts reinforce legislators' partisanship. When directed toward partisan reasons to support a bill or provision, rank-and-file members of the majority should find fewer reasons to defect and more reasons to stand with their leaders and cast roll-call votes consistent with their partisanship. Minority lawmakers should do the opposite. Having been shut out, the minority will find more cause to oppose the majority's position and will more consistently cast votes against it. Consequently, bills subject to heavy information tactics will present more partisanship on roll-call votes. This may give legislative leaders in the majority more leeway to shape legislation to their liking, but it has serious implications for relations between the parties and between leaders and their rank-and-file members.

The next chapter begins to flesh out these implications of information-based leadership power by delving into the mechanisms of information flows in the House of Representatives, looking at how rank-and-file lawmakers seek information and how leaders provide it. We thus can see specifically how leadership control over information flows creates the space for significant influence.

CHAPTER THREE

Flows of Information in the House

One of the most difficult parts of being a member of Congress is not being able to get enough information on how to cast a vote.—Rank-and-file member of Congress[1]

The individual member could probably obtain this information himself if he took the trouble, but he rarely has time to request or digest it. The material supplied by leaders helps him overcome these limitations.—Randall B. Ripley 1967

Members of Congress are always looking for information, but the nature of the search and their ultimate use of the information they obtain differ for rank-and-file lawmakers and legislative leaders. The differences reflect the distinct priorities and resources they bring to the legislative process. On one hand, rank-and-file lawmakers first act to please their constituents, or at the very least to avoid hurting themselves in the next election. Even though only one or two votes or decisions may ultimately matter during their next reelection fight, lawmakers will consider each decision important because, as Fenno (1978, 143) quotes one representative, "you don't know which one it will be." But before they can decide how to vote, whether to amend, what to support or oppose, or make any other decision, lawmakers need to know enough about the legislation to decide how it relates to their constituents' preferences. Because they have limited time and resources, they need to get information as efficiently as possible.

Legislative leaders, by contrast, give priority to the big picture for their party: passing major legislation, getting wins, making their party look good and the other party look bad, and doing what it takes to help the party win and hold chamber majorities. With substantial resources at their disposal, information becomes a means to achieving these things, and ultimately a means to power and influence in the chamber. Party and committee leaders operate information-gathering enterprises that let them constantly take stock of legislation being developed and considered, the reactions of other lawmakers, outside groups, and the public to legislative provisions, and the potential moves of political opponents. Armed with this information, they can strategically craft policy positions and legislation and sell them to their rank and file, gaining support both inside and outside Congress.

Drawing on evidence from interviews with members of Congress and staffers, as well as my experiences as a participant observer, this chapter illustrates how the different goals and resources of rank-and-file lawmakers and their legislative leaders affect the flow of information in the House and the influence of leaders. Ultimately, because of their limited resources, the rank and file have to rely on shortcuts and cues to obtain the information they need. They typically must limit their search to finding material that confirms their predispositions or else turn to informed and trustworthy sources like their legislative leaders. Leaders can use the information they have accrued to take advantage of this dynamic, selling their position to their rank and file. When successful, these efforts help leaders shape the way lawmakers view legislation and the actions they take, though some may be more easily influenced than others.

This chapter begins by demonstrating the different orientations leaders and rank and file lawmakers bring to legislating. I then detail how rank-and-file lawmakers gather information, stressing how they are constrained and susceptible to leaders' influence. Subsequently, the information enterprises of legislative leaders are detailed, including their efforts to gather intelligence and then use the information to sell their positions to their rank and file. Ultimately, these efforts help leaders overcome the collective action problems inherent in trying to pass legislation in a relatively decentralized legislature like the House of Representatives.

The Different Orientations of Rank-and-File Lawmakers and Legislative Leaders

As explained in chapter 2, legislative leaders, because of their institutional positions, have different priorities than rank-and-file lawmakers and thus a different orientation toward policymaking. The interviews

I conducted with lawmakers and staffers stressed this point. Those in both party and committee leadership posts, and their staffs, demonstrated the priority they placed on winning by passing legislation. One leadership staffer made this clear, emphasizing that these considerations drive the way the leadership uses the tools at its disposal, such as the Rules Committee, to structure the floor consideration of legislation:

> LEADERSHIP STAFFER: One way you get things done is you just go and hammer it out in the Rules Committee. . . . And sometimes that gets you good results and sometimes that gets you bad results, but it will get you a result.[2]

This same staffer gave as an example the efforts to pass the American Clean Energy and Security Act of 2009. For the leadership, the overwhelming desire was to get *something* passed so the president had ammunition going into the UN Climate Summit in Copenhagen later in the year:

> LEADERSHIP STAFFER: [On rewriting the bill in the Rules Committee] That was backed up against the visit to the energy summit. So you had this hard deadline. Nobody wanted to embarrass themselves and go on to Copenhagen and have nothing to show.[3]

For those in the leadership, the aim of the legislative process is to advance legislation that meets broad party goals and to do it in a way that helps the party's image in the next election. Once a bill has been crafted that leaders think achieves this goal and can pass the committee or the chamber, they are reluctant to make any changes. Those in leadership posts often were unsure why a rank-and-file lawmaker in their party would want to make changes at this stage. One committee staffer reflected this general attitude when she said she didn't understand why a rank-and-file member of the committee would offer any amendment the chair opposed:

> COMMITTEE STAFFER: If the chairman or ranking member opposes it they are not going to vote for it; it's just dead. So what's the point of doing it?[4]

While rank-and-file members might have reasons for offering an amendment even if they knew it was doomed—such as signaling concern to constituents or simply because they have strong convictions on the issue—leadership and committee staff typically did not understand wasting time on something that did not help achieve the ultimate goal: advancing the bill.

For leaders, the balance struck in a bill they have crafted needs to be preserved. The final product has been carefully pieced together through negotiation with key players and interests behind the scenes in a way that will broadly benefit the party's goals. Any change could unravel the carefully crafted balance, jeopardizing the bill's prospects, its effect, or its message. Consequently they are intent on persuading their lawmakers to accept what has been produced. One committee staffer described the defensive posture his committee often took toward their bill drafts:

> COMMITTEE STAFFER: We've got our bill out there, and all of a sudden they want to make a change which, again, upsets the balance in some way—it's complicated something and we have to deal with it all at the last minute.[5]

A party leadership staffer similarly described how many committee chairs feel about the bills they work through their committees:

> LEADERSHIP STAFFER: Ninety to one hundred percent of the time the chair of the committee where a bill originated is going to say, "Hey, what came out of my committee stays." The phrase that everyone likes to use is [that it's] a "carefully crafted balance" of issues and that you can't change a thing or else it will all come crashing down.[6]

For legislative leaders the ends justify the means. While they understand that rank-and-file members have their particular interests and concerns, the goal of legislating is to pass an agenda, and whatever that might take is fair game, whether or not rank-and-file legislators are completely satisfied and have a real voice. One leadership staffer made this clear when I asked him what considerations went into the tactics the leadership chose to adopt on any particular bill:

> LEADERSHIP STAFFER: What's the best way to get the agenda passed?[7]

Or if I asked him about specific leadership actions on specific bills:

> That was the price for getting the votes. This is the place where we have to figure out what we have to do to make things happen.[8]

This staffer did not find complaints about procedure to be legitimate, including protests about how fast some legislation is considered or the amount of information rank-and-file lawmakers have about it. In fact, when I pushed back regarding these concerns, he became agitated:

> LEADERSHIP STAFFER: That's a cheesy public argument; the minority votes against it all anyway. It's not like they are trying to figure out if maybe if they knew what this was maybe they might vote for it. Never!
>
> JC: What about the majority?
>
> LEADERSHIP STAFFER: It's not like the amount of information anyone has affects the outcomes. It's just some people's best political argument— that things were done in a shoddy way. . . . It's part of a political argument. Sometimes it's true, but it's not a real argument. It's not like if we gave them another two hours, or four days, or two weeks anything would change. I think it's a political argument.[9]

This staffer best exemplified the general attitude that party and committee leaders and their staffs demonstrated toward the legislative process. Their job was to pass something broadly benefiting the party. The rank and file should act like team players, line up with their leaders on votes, and not do anything to hurt the bill's chances.[10]

While rank-and-file lawmakers share their leaders' concerns about the party's image and passing legislation and hesitate to work against their party unnecessarily, their individual priorities often conflict with those of their leaders. While leaders are intent on passing an agenda, rank-and-file lawmakers care how legislation will affect their constituents, and ultimately how their votes will affect their individual careers. A robust history of research has established that members of Congress are intensely attentive to their districts.[11] Consequently, when it comes to legislating, and to information sharing and communication, they value different things than their leaders do. Whereas their leaders are pushing to get something passed quickly, rank-and-file lawmakers want time to consider the specifics. As one put it, "When it comes down to it, it's the details that really matter."[12]

These different orientations and concerns shape the way lawmakers search for information and the way leaders try to control the knowledge their rank and file have and the decisions they make. However, in their quest for relevant information and details about the legislation before them, rank-and-file lawmakers are constrained by their limited time and resources and subject to biases that create a window for leaders to influence them.

Information and Rank-and-File Lawmakers

Despite the insistence of the lawmaker quoted in the chapter epigraph that members of Congress cannot get enough information, it would be misleading to suggest that they simply lack knowledge. Members are awash in information, data, and voices telling them this or that, pleading their case about the best course of action, recommending numerous bills and amendments as worthy or unworthy, and providing political advice on how to act, think, or vote. Contemporary lawmakers are not deprived of information; rather, the information encompassing their worlds is crushing and cacophonous. The challenge for them is not simply to accrue information but to identify the *useful* information within their time and resource constraints. A more accurate statement might be that the most difficult thing is for lawmakers to find *relevant* information that they can *trust*.[13]

For information to be useful, it must be *relevant*. Specifically, good information needs to be relevant not only to the bill being considered, but also to the lawmaker's political interests. Generally, members of Congress want two types of information: policy and political. They want information that improves their understanding of the bill's intent and shows how supporting or opposing it is likely to affect at least some people or groups in their districts. Policy information answers the questions, What's in this bill? and What does it intend to do to public policy? Political information tells who supports and opposes the bill, how vehement that support or opposition is, and how taking a position will affect lawmakers' political support, particularly within their districts.

For information to be relevant, it also has to be timely. The information must arrive close enough to the consideration of a bill for lawmakers to pay attention to it but must allow time to factor it into their decision making. Except for members intimately involved in drafting the bill or those who specialize their legislative efforts on the issue at hand, most lawmakers turn their attention to any bill only late in the process — just before or after consideration has begun in their committees or on the floor. Information must arrive within this window if lawmakers are to be attentive enough to factor it into their decision on a bill.

Lawmakers and staff alike noted the importance of timeliness. One staffer interviewed noted that sometimes he knew something was happening only because outside groups reached out at a crucial moment:

> RANK-AND-FILE STAFFER: It's definitely useful if they contact us just a little before something is coming up, because sometimes that's the only way I find out something *is* coming up! . . . But generally if they can reach out to us maybe a week before consideration then we can really get a gauge on the political climate on the bill, and that is really helpful.[14]

Another staffer noted that it was important to develop good relationships, especially with stakeholder groups, because then they would know they should reach out at the right time:

> RANK-AND-FILE STAFFER: It's always good to have the relationship previously with the groups. They're going to try to reach out to you right before something is being considered, but it's more about developing that relationship in the first place.[15]

In addition to relevance, useful information must be something a lawmaker can *trust*. In Washington, of course, everyone has an agenda, and anyone giving information to a congressional office is hoping for an outcome that may or may not mesh with the interests of the representative. Bureaucrats, for instance, owing to their specialized focus and long career histories, often have deep, intimate knowledge of their policy areas and typically keep close watch on what is happening in Congress, so they can provide relevant policy information to lawmakers. But executive departments, agencies, and bureaucrats are also biased, interested not only in defending their turf, but often in defending the status quo (see, for example, Niskanen 1971; Miller and Moe 1983). Similarly, interest groups carry clear biases, and many of the most prominent groups in Washington are strongly associated with one of the parties and work closely with it to achieve certain policy ends. As one member of Congress put it, "There aren't many independent sources out there."[16] Consequently, both lawmakers and their staff have to identify political actors, including other lawmakers, whom they can trust to help them understand legislation. A major factor in whom they trust is policy agreement (Kingdon 1989, 85; Hall and Deardorff 2006). Several lawmakers and staff stressed this trust factor:

RANK-AND-FILE MEMBER: People would say, "You mean you don't understand every vote you take?" Well certainly I don't! No way! There's not
enough time! Even my staff, as good as they were. So you find credible
members on the other committees. And staff would find other staff that
they trusted.[17]

Some of those interviewed suggested trust can stem from broader ideological agreement. This former lawmaker typically sought out individuals from his corner of the party caucus:

RANK-AND-FILE MEMBER: In my case the Tuesday Group, which is a moderate Republican clustering, would have members from the committee who
would sit there and say, "I have heard that this is coming up and it includes
X, Y, Z details that seem to have implications people haven't caught up
with."[18]

One staffer noted that state delegations can provide a good forum for
finding members with similar views. At the very least, other members of
the state delegation may have constituents with similar interests:

RANK-AND-FILE STAFFER: We would often reach out to other members of
the state delegation for their thoughts on the bill.[19]

Relevance and trust shape what information lawmakers find useful,
but the search for this information is primarily shaped by their time and
resource limitations. In an ideal world, most lawmakers would embark
on a comprehensive search for information on every bill before making decisions. This would include reaching out to all the sources who
could provide relevant information, including the leading sponsors and
opponents of a bill, the staff of the committee of jurisdiction, executive
branch agencies that might be affected, interest groups and stakeholders who have a strong interest in the issue, and their party leaders, then
weighing how trustworthy or sound they find the information so they can
make the decision they feel is best suited for their interests and those of
their constituents. But comprehensively accruing and digesting information is not possible on most bills. Consequently, legislators take shortcuts to gather enough information to make a decision that is defensible if
not ideal. If lawmakers believe they can offer a justifiable explanation to

their constituents or to important interest groups, they can feel confident enough to act. As one staffer put it:

> RANK-AND-FILE STAFFER: Ultimately you have to make something of a judgment call that isn't perfectly well grounded because the information isn't there.[20]

To make these judgment calls, rank-and-file offices rely on various shortcuts and cues. They cannot approach information gathering as a tabula rasa. Their biases, preconceptions, and experiences shape their approach. Based on who has written a bill or an amendment, who supports or opposes it, and how they have acted on similar bills in the past, lawmakers will often already be inclined toward support or opposition. For example, most will distrust proposals advanced solely by lawmakers from the other side of the aisle, or ones backed by political interests they typically disagree with. Conversely, many lawmakers will be inclined to support proposals advanced primarily by fellow partisans or other regular political allies.

Experience can sometimes be a useful shortcut. While some of the legislation each Congress considers is new, other bills are rehashed year after year, and conflict inevitably erupts around some of the same issues and policy proposals in successive Congresses. In these instances veteran lawmakers and staff, at least, can use the information they previously collected and the actions they took as a guide, seeking only to find out if anything has changed. The lawmakers and staff interviewed noted that previous consideration required them to collect less new information. This staffer described how the time he put toward a bill would vary:

> RANK-AND-FILE STAFFER: It depends on if the bill is something we've gone through before. If so, less time is needed to understand it.[21]

However, relying on experience is not as simple as it sounds. Staff turnover on Capitol Hill is frequent, so policy memory may have been lost within an office since the last time a bill was considered. A study by the Sunlight Foundation found that member offices in the House averaged 36 percent staff turnover over a two-year period between 2009 and 2011.[22] Furthermore, there is some turnover among elected members every two years. New members will not be able to rely on the same experience as veteran lawmakers. But most important, relying on experience subjects lawmakers to the same biases and predispositions that shaded their decisions in previous Congresses.

When experience is not sufficient, congressional offices take other steps to gather information. Where they look depends on whether they think support or opposition is more likely. When support is likely they search for reasons to support. This means seeking out those who support the bill, such as its lead sponsors, groups that have endorsed it, the majority staff of the committee that worked on it, or the members of the party leadership or whip office who are promoting it. When the assumption is disagreement, they look for reasons to oppose. One legislative staffer I worked with described that as trying to find out "where the body is buried." In other words, when there are reasons to believe opposition is likely, the goal is to find out what is "wrong" with the proposal so as to justify opposition. Staffers and lawmakers know they almost never agree with certain other members or with items supported by certain groups, so the aim is to figure out what is wrong with the bill "this time." This means seeking out leaders of the opposition, such as minority staff on the committee of jurisdiction, interest groups and stakeholders who have made their opposition public, or the minority party leadership.

This process narrows the search for information and makes it more efficient, but it also biases lawmakers toward a decision they might not have made were the information obtained more comprehensive. Cognitive psychologists refer to these effects, among other things, as confirmation bias and motivated reasoning. Individuals searching for information will often restrict their search in ways that confirm what they were hoping to find. Further, in uncovering evidence, they will accept confirming information at face value while being more critical of information that challenges their predispositions.[23] Calvert (1985) notes that relying on biased sources likely to reinforce their predispositions is rational behavior for political elites. Given the cost of accruing information, broadly canvassing for objective advice may not make sense even when it is possible. Nonetheless, this rational behavior can still affect the decisions lawmakers make. By limiting their search to reinforcing sources, they preclude being exposed to new information that might alter their preferences or positions on a bill or an issue or lead them to decide switching positions is safer.

Further aggravating these biases, the need for relevant information limits a lawmaker's search to sources who have adequate expertise in the policy area and are familiar with the bill at hand. As Hall (1996) finds, on any bill or issue the number of deeply engaged and informed law-makers is relatively small and typically limited to its leading proponents and opponents. On major bills that group is likely to be even smaller and is often limited to legislative leaders. In the contemporary House, signif-icant bills are often crafted by key committee chairs and members of the majority party leadership (Sinclair 2012). For rank-and-file lawmakers, this means that those they can turn to often have the greatest incentive to persuade them to either support or oppose the legislation.

Consequently, in searching for relevant and trustworthy information, lawmakers are often led toward evidence that confirms and reinforces their predispositions, both by their need to collect and process informa-tion efficiently and by the biases and agendas of their sources. Of course, how much lawmakers and staffers limit their searches varies from of-fice to office and from bill to bill. Naturally, some lawmakers will sim-ply want support for the action they are inclined to take, while others will want a more balanced picture before they act. Lawmakers who have an independent streak, or who do not fit neatly within the mainstream of their party (e.g., moderates) may be more skeptical and less sure whom to trust, since their predispositions line up with their leaders' less often than those of more orthodox partisans.[24] Nonetheless, all lawmakers must turn somewhere for information, and they may have no choice but to turn to leaders who take steps to accelerate the legislative process or keep the chamber in the dark (as described in the next chapter).

In general, rank-and-file lawmakers' susceptibility to influence as they gather information is important because, as the rest of this chap-ter and the next chapter describe, legislative leaders work to manage and control the flow of information in the House of Representatives, taking advantage of the predispositions of their rank and file and their need for trustworthy and relevant information in trying to steer the legislative process toward specific outcomes.

The Information-Gathering Enterprises of Leaders

Legislative leaders take advantage of their rank and file's need for in-formation by giving them reasons to support the leadership's positions on legislation. This begins with leaders gathering as much intelligence as possible about the preferences of rank-and-file lawmakers, the other party, and outside groups and about their potential valuations of bills, issues, and provisions. Leveraging their large staff resources, party and committee leaders allot significant time and energy to these tasks because, for them, uncertainty is failure. As one committee staffer described it, "If we're surprised, we're not doing our job."[25] Armed with the information they accrue, they can decide how to proceed and how to sell a bill to their coalition and ensure success.

Committee chairs and party leaders use similar tactics to gather information as they use their staff and resource advantages. Committees tend to gather information primarily during the early stages of the legislative process, while the majority party leadership gathers intelligence throughout.

Committee Chairs and Staff

Committee information gathering often begins even before the drafting of the chairman's mark.[26] Under the guidance of the committee chair, staffers work to find out what rank-and-file committee members may think about a proposal or an issue. Then they try to determine what leeway they have in writing the bill and which committee members will be so intensely concerned that they must be more intimately involved in the drafting and legislating. This information is gathered in several ways— through general outreach, targeted outreach, formal meetings, and discussions with the minority.

Committee staffers generally reach out to subcommittee and committee members early in the drafting process, or before, and report back to their chairs. Their aim is to take the temperature of the rank-and-file members of the committee or subcommittee about provisions that might be included in a bill. They also want to find out if there are specific policies that are of special interest to some committee members or that may provoke controversy later on. At this point, committee staffers also expect members of the committee to come to them directly if they have any special interest in a bill being drafted, or if they have distinct concerns they would like considered. A few staffers described the committee's perspective on this stage:

COMMITTEE STAFFER: We solicit. We ask at the subcommittee level; we say, "You know, if you've got any amendments you better tell us now. Let's talk about it, because we've done everything we could to accommodate you."[27]

> COMMITTEE STAFFER: The subcommittee staff is in pretty regular contact
> with the other subcommittee members. . . . They have certain programs
> they want to plus-up. They obviously have their earmarks that they want
> to fend for. So they will continue to be in touch with the subcommittee
> staff. It's not a constant thing because other members of the subcom-
> mittee may have particular parochial, or peripheral, issues they are con-
> cerned about, particular issues that their boss takes a particular interest
> in, but it's not going to cover the whole bill.[28]

Committee members don't do themselves any favors by trying to sur-
prise their chair and the staff. The committee wants to know up front
about issues members want to be involved in or items they have strong
views on. Rank-and-file members of the committee are encouraged at this
stage to send in letters requesting particular policy considerations or, with
the Appropriations Committee, to make specific requests for the funding
of projects.[29] The committee staffers I interviewed, however, also made
it clear that it is not as simple as "ask and you shall receive." Committee
staffers solicit input, requests, and ideas from their rank and file, but there
is no guarantee that these will be included in the bill as drafted or even
addressed in any way. Generally, committee members are left in the dark
about whether their requests will have any impact on the final bill:

> COMMITTEE STAFFER: All [rank-and-file] input, though, is on the front end,
> and not as we are drafting. There is no back-and-forth—you know, "we're
> thinking about doing this"—except at the discussion of the staff and the
> chairman.[30]

For committee chairs and their staff, the aim of soliciting requests is
not pleasing their rank-and-file members or including their wishes in the
final bill. It is gathering intelligence and understanding the political dynamics around the bill and issue in question. Staffers seek feedback so
they can estimate how committee members will respond to specific legislative language, which members will likely support or oppose certain
provisions, and which members may be particularly interested in the bill.

Along with general outreach, committee staffers will target specific
rank-and-file committee members if they know from experience that
these members will be intensely concerned about an issue being addressed in the bill:

COMMITTEE STAFFER: If there is something we know [a rank-and-file member] cares about and we want to make sure we get it right for them, then we may have some back-and-forth with them on it.[31]

RANK-AND-FILE STAFFER: Sometimes the committee will provide you with unsolicited information if they know it's important to your boss. Most of the time, however, you have to ask.[32]

Furthermore, rank-and-file members can signal that a particular issue is going to be very important to them, even if it hasn't been in the past, through the way they approach the committee staff:

COMMITTEE STAFFER: The offices who are really serious about things and know what they're doing will write a letter and then follow up at the staff level and the member level sometimes and say, "This is really important. Is there some way we can work this out?" and then that gets our attention and we will focus our limited time and resources on trying to deal with those issues.[33]

Unlike the interaction generated from general outreach, this type of interaction is driven by the intensity of preferences held by the rank-and-file committee members and is likely to result in a more substantive give-and-take between the staffer, or the member, and the committee. As this committee staffer indicated, it is also more likely to lead to the member's interests being reflected in the final draft of the bill. When a lawmaker shows enough interest and invests enough time and energy, staffers and the committee chair will do their best to be accommodating, and to avoid creating a problem for the bill later.

An example of this can be seen in the legislative work on the American Clean Energy and Security Act (ACES) in 2009. In their discussions while drafting the bill, Energy and Commerce Committee chairman Henry Waxman (D-CA) and subcommittee chairman Edward Markey (D-MA) made sure to involve Rick Boucher (D-VA), a senior member of the committee who was a longtime opponent of climate change legislation and an ally of the coal industry. Knowing Boucher's deep interest in the subject, and recognizing that vehement opposition from him could spell trouble for the bill, Waxman and Markey wanted to make sure Boucher felt he had been accommodated enough to stand with them on the final product, or at least not stir up opposition.[34]

Nevertheless, as one key staffer to a committee chairman noted, on any bill the members becoming this involved are few:

> COMMITTEE STAFFER: Most of the members of the subcommittee don't have daily interaction; it's very occasional interaction.[35]

Their limited time and resources do not allow typical members of Congress to be deeply involved in committee activity at all times. They have to choose their battles and concentrate on the issues most important to them and their districts (see Hall 1996). Furthermore, as another staffer said, these rank-and-file committee members still lack the ultimate authority of the committee chair. If the request runs counter to the overall direction of the bill and the broad compromises crafted, or if the request conflicts with the wishes of the chair, the request is unlikely to make its way into the bill's language. Succinctly put, "It's not a matter of [the rank-and-file] approving what we do. It's a matter of trying to accommodate them."[36]

In other words, chairs and committee staffers do not typically talk with the rank and file to determine how to write a bill that pleases them. Instead, they poll their members to find out what kind of bill they might be able to sell to them, whose interests they can or must accommodate, what policies, provisions, and items cannot be incorporated, and how the final product can be packaged and sold. Ultimately, it is about satisfying the chair rather than figuring out what the rank and file want.

In addition to the outreach described above, committee staffers also gather intelligence through formal meetings with the staff of rank-and-file members. These meetings, as described in the interviews, are general forums during which committee staffers make a few general statements and announcements about the committee's upcoming schedule, and then open the meeting to questions. More than anything, these meetings give committee leaders another opportunity to gauge their members' opinions, based on the questions asked or staffers' reactions to the announcements and schedule. As this rank-and-file staffer notes, members' offices get their voices heard, but it often feels like the committee is just creating the appearance of a deliberative process:

> RANK-AND-FILE STAFFER: In a lot of cases there would be a meeting for our particular staffer associated with the committee, or legislative staffer assigned to the committee, probably a week in advance to talk about pieces

that were being considered; things that we might want to offer. Sometimes
those were more helpful than other [times]. *Sometimes it just seemed like
a venue to say that the committee had met and gotten input from staff* and
other times it was more substantive where you could talk about possible
amendments that you might want to offer [emphasis added].[37]

In addition, at some point the committee or subcommittee chair sometimes holds a similar meeting with majority members of the committee
as another information-gathering exercise.[38]

Committee chairs and staff also keep in regular contact with the minority's ranking members and the minority committee staff throughout the drafting. They do so largely by bouncing ideas off the minority
staff to get an idea of the response if certain provisions were included in
the bill:

COMMITTEE STAFFER: The majority writes the bill, and we will seek [minor-
ity] input as we move along, and they will provide their input and we will
try to accommodate them as best we can.[39]

COMMITTEE STAFFER: It's "Let me know what your ideas are on this particular issue; What would you suggest for this account? or Is there something
that's a priority for the minority on this particular agency?"[40]

But like discussions with the rank and file, these discussions do not
mean the minority's input is incorporated into the text of the bill. Instead, these interactions are meant to give the chair and the majority
staff an idea of what the minority is concerned about, what minority
members are thinking, and what issues might cause a partisan fight in
markup or on the floor. One staffer emphasized that most of the conversations with the minority are one-way. Majority staffers may ask the minority staffers how they might react to a certain provision, but they do
not tell them what language is going to be in the final product. The majority's priorities and final plans are kept close to the vest:

COMMITTEE STAFFER: It's not extremely open. You don't want to tip [them]
off . . . [b]ecause there are negotiations to be worked out; because there
might be things you don't want out in the public domain—there's a certain
level of trust with the minority; you don't want them to work up a bunch of
opposition to something you're trying to do before the bill is moving; for
a variety of reasons you're not going to be completely forthcoming about

what you're going to do with every item in the bill. Now that's not to say input won't be solicited. Certainly, input is solicited every step of the way, but it's not an exchange of information.[41]

Minority committee staffers, under the direction of the minority's ranking member, are eager to provide input to the majority staff, hoping to obtain at least some concessions. But at the same time they realize their opinions are merely suggestions. They also know their information actually helps the majority write a stronger product by revealing what issues may raise problems later in the legislative process and helping them identify easy ways to avoid costly political fights or undercut the minority's ability to oppose the bill effectively. Giving the example of the removal of terrorist suspects from the Guantanamo Bay prison facility, this staffer also said that on items of particular sensitivity the majority staff will be even less forthcoming than usual:

> COMMITTEE STAFFER: A lot of times, in that case, they would probably be a lot less willing to include me in the conversation. A good example of that would be the policies and programs related to Guantanamo prisoners and detainees. That's been a huge issue on our bill—and I'm not sure the administration is talking to anybody—but to the extent that they are they are talking to the majority and I'm not part of that planning process because they feel that whatever they want to propose, probably rightly, that our side is going to provide opposition to.[42]

Chairs and their staffers also use committee hearings to collect information. Not only can they get feedback on proposals, policies, and bill drafts from the experts, interest groups, and other individuals invited to testify, but leaders can get a sense of where members of the committee, including the minority, stand by the questions they ask and their reactions to the witnesses. Hearings are often highly scripted affairs in which the majority staff carefully selects and approves witnesses who will provide testimony that supports what the chair wants to do on an issue. In doing so, they build a record of supportive information and testimony that they can use later to sell their position to the rank and file. The case study of committee work on ACES in chapter 6 highlights how committee leaders do this, and how they can expose minority talking points at the same time.

In short, majority committee staffers go to great lengths to gather as much information as they can on what other lawmakers are thinking about, care about, and want to see in the bill. Rank-and-file members and staff get their voices heard, and sometimes their input may even affect the details of a bill, but any real influence the input has depends on what the chair wants:

> RANK-AND-FILE STAFFER: Most of the time [committee staffers] are pretty helpful in working with you as long as it doesn't conflict in major part with the chairman or the ranking member.[43]

Ultimately, the information committee leaders gather helps them plan their legislative strategies—how to craft a bill, how to sell a bill, and how to manage the process. But committees are not the only ones gathering information. The majority party leadership is doing so as well.

The Majority Party Leadership

Majority party leaders spend just as much time gathering information, but they do it on a much larger scale. Typically, they take the temperature of the entire majority caucus, to make sure enough members will be on board for passage, or of a subset of the caucus that may have particular concerns. The party's whip apparatus does most of the information gathering, but the rest of the party leadership can get into the act as well. The whip organization is the eyes and ears of the majority party leadership, and it is heavily relied on for gathering intelligence. The whip's office has a dedicated staff and a hierarchy of command from the chief whip down to deputy whips, then down to regional and issue-specific whips who talk to members within their own jurisdictions to determine any concerns with an upcoming bill.

Whip officers and staffers take several routine steps to survey their caucus. The most frequent is called the "whip check," which these days is done as an e-mail from the whip's office to every member of the caucus. These e-mails typically list from one to several bills and amendments, sometimes with a brief summary, the party's recommendation for how caucus members should vote (if the leadership is taking a position), and a request from the whip that any members who intend to vote against the party leadership's recommendations notify them as soon as

possible. These whip checks go out to rank-and-file members of the caucus anywhere from three or four days ahead of floor action to as late as
an hour before the vote.[44]

However, whip checks are not the only way information is gathered.
The whip organization's information gathering often begins very early in
the legislative process and continues through floor action:

> LEADERSHIP STAFFER: We'll start well in advance of any bill text, and [the
> effort] gets sharper as the bill text develops.[45]
> LEADERSHIP STAFFER: [Information gathering] becomes key in the majority
> because you are trying to govern. You're trying to get 218 votes to govern
> on a daily basis on the floor. And from that perspective you need to con-
> stantly be getting intelligence from your members: on where they are; on
> where other members are; on where the minority is.[46]

Generally, the earlier the whip organization can begin collecting information the better, because it gives leaders an idea of where they are going
to have to tread lightly, use creative tactics, or gather more intelligence.

Gathering intelligence includes both formal means—like whip checks
and meetings, including those with the entire caucus and subcaucuses
like the Blue Dogs, the Republican Study Committee, or the Congressional Black Caucus—and informal means such as one-to-one conversations and e-mails to obtain firsthand and secondhand information about
what certain lawmakers might be planning to do or what the minority
may have up their sleeves.[47] Like rank-and-file lawmakers, whip officers
and staffers use information gained from experience to simplify matters. On bills addressing issues that have been similarly legislated on before, whips and whip staffers know which lawmakers and subcaucuses
they need to communicate with, who might be a problem for passing the
legislation, and what issues might cause snags if they are not addressed
properly in the bill or through the majority leadership's legislative strategy. As one staffer explained, "You can narrow it down pretty quickly
who your problem members are going to be when you're going to whip
a bill."[48]

Giving the example of energy legislation, another staffer explained
how he classified members of the party caucus into groups based on their
interests and how he could approach information gathering through
these categories:

LEADERSHIP STAFFER: Any bill that deals with energy, I automatically know I have my solar people I have to deal with and make sure they are okay. I know immediately I'm going to have to deal with my oil-patch members, particularly in the South. So immediately I have to go to them to find out what exactly they do or don't like about this energy bill. . . . Then you have your coal members, who have their own batch of issues, and then, of course, you have what I like to call your rate-payer coalition.[49]

Based on experience with energy legislation, the whip office knew whom to talk to and what to talk about, and even had an idea of what bill features these groups might be concerned about.

The whip organizations will also adjust their strategies based on the type of bill and the issue being considered. Specifically, on big issues that are important to the party leadership, the whip organization will find out what rank-and-file members are thinking very early, before taking any other steps:

LEADERSHIP STAFFER: If we know way ahead of time that this big issue is coming down, we will start doing what you could call focus groups. Basically, you get groups of members together, and sometimes it can be regionally oriented, sometimes it can be because they are already organized as a caucus, and kind of hear them out.[50]

On major legislation, whip organizations typically allocate far more time and resources to gathering intelligence. Along with holding focus groups, whips go directly to members to find out what they are thinking on specific issues and specific legislation.

LEADERSHIP STAFFER: I spend a good amount of time coming in and saying, "Congressman so and so," if it's to the congressman or congresswoman directly, or if it's to the staff who are responsible for educating that member directly on the issue, "I understand your problem with it," or "tell me what the problem is."[51]

Of course, lawmaking is fluid and dynamic and requires that the whip organization constantly reacts to changes in the political environment and alterations to legislation and continue to collect information and adapt its strategies. As deals are struck among major players or as the

leadership adjusts the time-line for consideration of the bill, the procedure for gathering intelligence changes:

> LEADERSHIP STAFFER: A lot of times things get compressed. The whip of-
> fice moves at the speed of agreement or disagreement, and that happens
> pretty radically. . . . Sometimes because of the political pressure that we
> might be feeling because a recess is coming up and members want to have
> something to go home and talk about, that can be condensed to a [one-]
> day whip.[52]

And sometimes, despite the best-laid plans, issues and bills are simply difficult to get a read on. Legislation may be so broad and the politics
so unpredictable that the whip office, and thus the party leaders, might
not be sure what their caucus is thinking or only have an educated guess
about certain members. As one staffer put it, bluntly: "There's going to
be some issues you come across that are going to be so nuanced that
you're not going to know."[53]

Other times issues are significantly altered by the political context,
and the whip organization is forced to throw out what they know about
an issue's dynamics within the caucus and learn anew:

> LEADERSHIP STAFFER: Once in a while a piece of legislation would come
> up that we wouldn't think would really cause that much trouble, and then
> something obscure would come up that we weren't aware of that would af-
> fect a member's district and then the flow would be from the member to
> the whip's office. That way we would learn and would know of that next
> time something would come around that was trade related or that was wa-
> ter related. We knew that in that district it would really affect that mem-
> ber no matter who sat in that seat.[54]

The whip organization is constantly trying to keep a read on things,
looking for early signs of trouble down the road. Contentiousness on an
issue at the committee level may signal a bigger fight on the floor; so
might public statements by members of Congress or attempts by outside
groups to get involved. Whips and their staffers keep an eye on these
developments and adjust their intelligence gathering accordingly. Generally speaking the whip organization, as the dedicated eyes and ears
of the majority party leadership, is constantly seeking the thoughts and
preferences of members of their party caucus and reporting back to the

leaders so they can develop the right legislation and the right legislative strategies.

Even though they rely heavily on their whip apparatus, the rest of the majority party leadership, including the Speaker and the majority leader, and leadership staffers also spend time learning about their rank and file's opinions, preferences, and potential actions. They do this largely through direct contact with members and subcaucuses, using both formal, expected lines of communication and informal means. The leadership spends a good amount of time calling and talking with key members or key groups in its caucus. Generally the leaders will employ tactics much like those used by the whip organization and by committee staff. They will bounce ideas around and get a feel for the response to different things. On major issues and bills coming before the chamber, the leaders will often hold meetings where they can brief the entire caucus and also seek feedback. Much like the meetings committee chairs and staff hold with staffers from member offices, these often enable the leadership to find out if pitfalls are likely to emerge during the legislative process.

Meetings like these will also occur between the majority leadership and subcaucuses within the majority conference. These discussions can include a bit of back-and-forth, but the leadership's goal is to find out how a group of members might react. A leading staffer with one such subcaucus gave an example of this kind of interaction:

> CAUCUS STAFFER: We pitched to them an idea of what the next continuing resolution should look like, and they called and said, "You know, we got some feedback on that. We have a variation on it, what do you think?" And so we were talking it through and it sounded pretty good, actually.[55]

But as before and as with committees, this is not about leaders seeking tacit approval for their plans, it is about making sure what they are putting forth sounds good in principle and that the bill they will eventually bring to the House floor is not likely to stir up controversy but is salable, at the very least, within their own caucus.

Both committee and majority party leadership offices commit significant resources to gathering information on rank-and-file members' opinions and potential reactions concerning legislation being written and considered. The ultimate purpose of these exhaustive efforts is to de-

cide how to proceed with action on a bill. Sometimes the consequence
is a changed bill—what a former whip office staffer described as a "policy fix." He gave an example from a stimulus bill considered during his
tenure:

> LEADERSHIP STAFFER: The bill was to give rebate checks to taxpayers, and
> there was a huge concern among a group of members in my caucus about
> rebate checks going to people who are undocumented. . . . There the pol-
> icy solution was to put in a statement, what we call a "rule of construc-
> tion," in the bill that basically said that no checks shall go to undocu-
> mented people, blah, blah, blah, blah, blah, and penalties will be enforced
> if any undocumented people, or what not, were to receive checks unlaw-
> fully or whatever, blah, blah, blah, blah.[56]

Other times the majority party leadership does not have a formulated
plan for the bill and instead whips the caucus membership for ideas of
how the bill should be written so it will pass.

> LEADERSHIP STAFFER: We normally call that process "whipping to write."
> Meaning that you whip your members on certain issues, find out where
> the collective masses are, and then write that policy. That's not always the
> best policy, but it's the policy that passes.[57]

In instances like these the leadership decides that the simplest and
most effective solution to a potential problem with the bill is to write or
change the bill to address the problem. Sometimes the best course of action for a committee or for the majority party leadership is to acquiesce
to the preferences of a subset of their rank and file, or the opposition to a
bill, to guarantee a winning vote coalition in committee and on the floor.
This is what occurred with the Bart Stupak (D-MI) amendment regarding abortion funding in the Affordable Care Act during the 111th Congress. The majority leadership could not keep the issue of abortion from
surfacing during consideration of the bill, so it allowed an amendment,
sponsored by a member of its own caucus, to be considered and passed
on the floor of the House restricting funding for abortion services.
    Instead of changing the bill to please the rank and file, particular in-
terest groups, or potential opponents, another option is for leaders to
use what they have learned to push the bill they want to advance. With
knowledge of the dynamics around the bill and what it would take to ob-

tain the support of lawmakers and interest groups, leaders can work to sell bills, amendments, and legislative provisions to their rank and file, disseminating messages meant to undercut potential opposition and convince lawmakers to stick with their partisan inclinations and support their party or committee leaders. The tremendous staff resources that party and committee leaders employ to gather information can also be used to provide the information their rank and file may need, but in a way that reflects positively on the bill.

Leaders as Vendors of Information

Ideally, the intelligence gathered throughout the early legislative stages helps leaders identify what groups within their caucus may need more convincing on a bill or provision and suggests how to convince them. Further, leaders will ideally have learned what aspects of a bill might be controversial and will need to be framed, downplayed, or obscured, and what type of messaging may make the package as a whole sound palatable. Armed with this useful information, legislative leaders also use their significant resources to become vendors of cues and information in the chamber and to influence how their rank and file view legislation and policy proposals. By doing so they hope, first, to supply members of their caucus with leadership-approved information that will reinforce their partisanship while convincing them that supporting their leaders' position is the right move, and second, to undermine the efforts of the opposition and outside groups to cast legislation supported by the majority's leaders in a negative light.

Committee Chairs and Staff

Committee chairs and staff have both formal and informal means for transmitting information to the committee's rank-and-file members and staffs as they try to sell their legislation. Formal means include methods of distributing the bill and literature on the bill, as well as regular meetings among staff or among members of the committee. Informal means include phone calls, e-mails, and face-to-face exchanges between leaders and the rank and file in the halls of Congress.

Ahead of markup meetings, committee chairs and staff are compelled to provide their rank and file with information on the bill to be considered. However, the committee has great leeway over exactly what it supplies and when.[58] Sometimes a committee provides just a report on the bill; other times it might provide the actual draft. Although this can vary from bill to bill and from committee to committee, what might be referred to as "supplemental materials" are circulated to the offices of committee members on nearly every bill. Typically these documents include a memo providing general background on the issues being addressed, a brief summary, sometimes a brief legislative history, and sometimes a section-by-section memo summarizing the chairman's mark one section at a time. Committee staffers carefully prepare these materials to present the bill in a favorable light.

Just as important as the information in these documents is how that information is presented. Careful thought and planning go into what will be said about the bill. The goal is to sell the bill and downplay details that might be controversial, so some points are likely to be emphasized while others are minimized, with some made very clear while others are obscured by technicality. One staffer explained how this can be done:

> RANK-AND-FILE STAFFER: There will be some information given out about the bill that is more detailed and less accessible. On things they might not want you to understand because you might vote against it, they will be less clear. And on things that they are full-throatily behind they will be more clear.[59]

An example of this information tweaking can be seen in the management of H.R. 3199 by the Committee on Science, Space, and Technology in February 2012. Nearly a week ahead of its scheduled markup, committee staff distributed the bill text to the staffs of lawmakers on the committee, along with a background memo and a section-by-section memo. This was presented by the committee's majority staff as a noncontroversial bill directing the Environmental Protection Agency (EPA), in conjunction with the National Academy of Sciences (NAS), to conduct a study of the effects of using midlevel ethanol blend gasoline in motor vehicles. The section-by-section memo noted that this study was to be completed within eighteen months, before the EPA approved any midlevel blends for public use.

The materials suggested this bill was designed simply to ensure that the EPA did its scientific due diligence before approving the use of gasoline containing more than 10 percent ethanol (the legal limit at the time). But just as important is what was left unsaid. While the section-by-section memo noted that the report was to consider all available scientific evidence, the bill itself directed the EPA and NAS to consider some specific studies and government reports, including a previous EPA report that emphasized the potential negative effect that midlevel ethanol blends could have on older cars. Furthermore, the bill directed the EPA and NAS to analyze the effects of midlevel blends on all cars, even though EPA regulations and the planned policy changes allowed the use of such blends only in newer and lighter vehicles, since the engines of older and heavier vehicles were known to sustain damage when exposed to ethanol blends of any type. Both of these directives, not mentioned in the memo, were included in the bill to help ensure that the mandated study would return a generally negative assessment of the use of midlevel ethanol blends. Perhaps the most significant aspect of the bill not emphasized by the committee's memo was the implications of the eighteen-month timetable. By giving the EPA and the NAS eighteen months to complete the study, the bill ensured that no midlevel ethanol blend gasoline would be approved for the market for another year and a half. Even then, if the report was negative, it might derail pending regulations by the EPA that would allow newer, lighter vehicles to use midlevel blends.[60]

Ultimately, what the committee chair and majority staff portrayed as an objective, good-government bill was really a ploy to delay and potentially kill the EPA's proposed plans to permit these blends to enter the market. Even though lawmakers from midwestern and corn-growing states had political reasons to support an increase in the use of ethanol in gasoline, the bill was reported unamended by the committee by a party-line vote, nineteen to seven. The skewed information provided by the committee staff, a trusted source for majority Republicans on the committee, kept majority lawmakers in line on a bill that many of them could have found political reasons to oppose. In addition, with the bill presented as relatively uncontroversial, many members of the minority elected not to attend the vote, instead focusing on their upcoming primary elections.[61]

In addition to memos, committee staff circulate other materials they believe will be beneficial. For example, committees often circulate or publish on their websites lists of outside groups that have endorsed a bill, along with copies of the letters of endorsement. These endorsements can send rank-and-file members persuasive signals that not only does their committee leadership support the bill, but so do numerous political interests that may be important to them and their districts. Sometimes the committee also distributes data about the proposed policy's effectiveness or the need for the policy change. These data might be broken down by district to show members how the bill will benefit their constituents. For example, the data may show how much a lawmaker's district stands to gain in new federal funds.

Closer to the markup, the committee is likely to distribute material presenting the chair's position on proposed amendments to the bill. Sometimes the information is detailed and persuasive, explaining why the committee supports or opposes certain language. Other times it may just be a list of amendments along with the chair's position and no explanation. One rank-and-file member of Congress described what he typically received about proposed markup amendments:

> RANK-AND-FILE MEMBER: On a markup the chair might put out a paper with a description of each amendment and the chair's position. Other committees don't print out anything but the chair makes his position known as the amendment is offered.[62]

Often this information is provided informally, by e-mail, or simply expressed by the chair during the markup after the amendment is formally proposed.

All this information is of course carefully crafted by majority staff for maximum effect. Sometimes the information in the documents has its genesis in committee hearings on the subject. As noted above, committees carefully plan hearings to create a record of support for their legislative proposals. With each hearing, the witnesses invited, the questions asked, and the information culled from the testimony is aimed at fostering a strong case for what the committee chair and staff want to do.[63] Typically the majority staff will circulate a memo to their rank and file ahead of each hearing, proposing topics of discussion and sample questions members may want to ask the witnesses, hoping to influence what is asked and discussed throughout the hearing. If successful, the committee chair and majority staff will have cultivated a good amount of expert testimony to reuse as they sell the bill before a markup. Again, the Energy and Commerce Committee's work on ACES is a prime example. After releasing a rough draft of the bill, Waxman and Markey held four days of hearings, inviting industry and environmental groups to testify in support of the bill as a whole or specific provisions. They hoped to show hesitant members of the majority that there was broad support for the policies they were crafting.

In addition, a committee's majority staff will use formal briefings to inform committee members' staffs. These are the same briefings committee staffers use to gather feedback from members of the committee, but they can also be opportunities to deliver information:

> COMMITTEE STAFFER: There is a process that the majority conducts where they will call in all the associate staff of the subcommittee on a bipartisan basis and brief them on the contents of the bill.[64]

Rank-and-file staffers see attending these briefings as a must, although they know the information they get will be limited. Committee staffers are unlikely to delve into details of legislation that they may consider sensitive or that may arouse disapproval from the minority or some other faction on the committee. Generally the information given is fairly prosaic. One staffer provided a fairly adept analysis:

> RANK-AND-FILE STAFFER: There is usually a formal briefing held once a week by the committee staff. Usually they read you something and ask if there are any questions. And if you ask questions they won't give you a real answer. If you actually had important questions, you couldn't ask them in that forum anyway because it's a bipartisan briefing. These meetings are set up in a way not to answer questions. Sometimes you have to ask just on general principles, but you know you're not going to get any answers. Usually it's, "We're working on it and we're going through negotiations with leadership." You could have predicted it, but you had to ask.[65]

As this staffer suggests, part of the reason the information provided is so mundane is the presence of minority staff. The committee leadership certainly does not want to share anything more than the basic details of legislation in front of a group who are inclined to oppose it. However, in meetings among majority staffers only, the information isn't much better. The same staffer describes what happens to a majority staffer who asks tough questions during a bipartisan briefing:

> RANK-AND-FILE STAFFER: Sometimes staffers will ask tough questions during the bipartisan briefing, and then afterward, in the majority-only meeting they will get castigated for asking tough questions.[66]

The committee leaders think that majority members and staffers should not be asking probing questions about the committee's decisions. They should listen to what the chair and the majority staff are telling them about why they should be on board. Rank-and-file staffers often leave these meetings with little new understanding of the specifics of the legislation, but with plenty of information about why they should support it.

Some committee chairs, though not all, hold similar meetings with the rank-and-file members of the committee before a markup. These meetings are generally partisan, with the chair meeting with the majority members only. Some minority ranking members do the same with the minority members if they have any information to share. How often these meetings occur depends on a number of things. For some committees, their large membership makes these meetings impractical, so the meetings are more likely to be held by subcommittee chairs before the subcommittee markups. Whether these meetings occur can also depend on the chair's personal style. Some chairs are more inclined than others to hold this type of face-to-face meeting.

Of course rank-and-file committee members, and their staffs, are not fools. They know the information the committee gives them can be inadequate, biased, and crafted to sell the bill, but it is often the best they have. As described above, lawmakers typically have to rely on biased sources, and the information coming from committees may be the most trustworthy and detailed they can obtain. One member of Congress offered a telling description of how lawmakers must rely on committee information. While personal staffers provide their own analysis of the situation to their lawmaker, committee materials are often the basis of that analysis:

> RANK-AND-FILE MEMBER: I rely a lot on material the committee produces. . . . On my major committees my staff provides unique analysis. They use their judgment on whether the committee materials are accurate or complete.[67]

The key to getting better information from committees is to be persistent: to let the committee know something is really important to them or their boss and then follow up. Better information comes from asking things directly of the committee staff. Being direct and persistent often makes staffers more forthcoming, but following up and being persistent will not be possible for most lawmakers on most bills, given their limited time and resources. The rest of the time, lawmakers must rely on what is given them, and as one legislative staffer almost admiringly put it, "It's amazing how much the chairman of the committee can change the shape of information."[68]

As imperfect as it may be, the information committees offer may be the best and most persuasive available to lawmakers as bills move through this stage of the legislative process.

The Majority Party Leadership

The majority party leadership also actively supplies information to its rank and file, though it is different in nature and content from that supplied by committees. As with information gathering, the whip organization is deeply involved. The onus falls on that apparatus, but the rest of the majority party leadership take part as well. Some of the communication between leaders and their rank-and-file lawmakers is informal and initiated by the members looking for information.

> RANK-AND-FILE MEMBER: Members would go to the whip organization and raise the issue. A whip organization is important not only for vote counting, but also to be a source of information for rank-and-file members. We always had a local whip who would reach out to me, typically on general issues.[69]
>
> LEADERSHIP STAFFER: A lot of times members are looking for information. They want to answer the questions they are getting back in their districts.[70]

But more often than not, leaders actively provide information to their members rather than waiting to be asked. From a strategic standpoint it is important for the majority leadership to fill the information airwaves with their messages to set the tone of the debate over the bill, provide the information that assures their rank-and-file members that they can support the bill, and push rhetoric that undermines the opposition's messages.

One whip staffer was especially forthcoming about this information strategy. The way he explained it, the leaders can take advantage of their members' needs by "cherry picking" the information they relay:

> JC: Do you take some leeway in what information you provide your members?

LEADERSHIP STAFFER: Sure. Absolutely. You have a 1,500 page bill—
members aren't going to read through it. You can certainly cherry pick
what you give to them. Maybe that's intellectually dishonest or something,
but you really don't have the benefit of time if this thing is moving quickly.
So you need to get out the information you want them to know. . . . We often cherry pick the information.[71]

This pattern is not entirely leadership-driven. As this same staffer
clarified, the rank and file expect the information they get from the
leadership to be short and sweet. If they had time for longer or more
complex analysis, they would do it themselves. They are turning to their
leaders precisely because they do not have this kind of time:

LEADERSHIP STAFFER: They want to know what's in it and why it's good or
bad. And they are not going to do the homework on their end. They have
a lot less resources than the leadership does. They are relying on us to give
them that information, and it usually falls to the whip office to give them
the most timely and accurate information and certainly the other leadership offices do a good job of disseminating information as well.[72]

The leaders also have formal, regular methods for relaying their information and message to rank-and-file lawmakers. Leadership staffers
host weekly "whip meetings" where they brief staffers from each member of their caucus on what the leadership is working on, what legislation is coming up soon, and anything else it feels its lawmakers should
know. From time to time the leadership will also hold special meetings—
sometimes hosted by the whip's office, sometimes by the conference
chair, and sometimes by other members of the leadership—where information about specific bills or provisions is given directly to majority
lawmakers or their staff and some questions are fielded. One staffer described this procedure:

COMMITTEE STAFFER: On major bills, there's a chief of staff meeting every
Friday and a whip-staff meeting and a press secretary-staff meeting every Monday afternoon. . . . We get information about the schedule and
what's coming up this week and next week. And we get the political lay
of the land. There's a lot they won't have. But in terms of getting the ba-
sics on, well, this is in the bill and this is out. You know, they'll sort of
give a layout. And when they can they'll say, "Week three is going to be

a jobs week, so we might do unemployment extension or something else."
So they'll just give you sort of an idea.[73]

Beyond these formal meetings, the whips and the whip staffers will
actively seek out members from the start of the policymaking process.
As with information gathering, the whip office often knows ahead of
time which members, or group of members, may need more convincing.
Sometimes these appeals last right up through the vote:

> LEADERSHIP STAFFER: In the majority you whip them right up to and possi-
> bly during the votes. The best example of that would have been Medicare
> Part D prescription drug coverage for seniors. That vote was whipped all
> the way up to the vote, during the vote, and for three hours during that
> vote on the floor.[74]

Activity on the floor is more important than it might seem. Even on
important legislation, some members of Congress come to the floor either ambivalent or unsure of what they are going to do regarding amendments and sometimes even the final vote (Behringer, Evans, and Materese 2006). A whip organization can be very influential here. Members
crave information about what is going on, and whips and their staff are
happy to oblige.

In providing this information, leaders will appeal to their members by
emphasizing things that make their decision to support the leadership's
position easier. This can mean explaining certain tradeoffs in a bill so
that their members see the final product as more good than bad or demonstrating how the policy proposal is popular with the voting public or
with key interest groups:

> LEADERSHIP STAFFER: Sometimes you provide both straightforward infor-
> mation and tailored information. The first job is to say, "Let me give you
> the technical answer to your question." And then you say, "But I think it's
> important to understand why it ended up this way, the tradeoff with X," or
> "Doing this allowed us to get the following ten things you're really excited
> about," or "We wrote it that way because the alternative didn't work with
> the CBO," etc. . . . So you always want to answer members technically, but
> I think part of the job is selling it a bit.[75]
> LEADERSHIP STAFFER: You're trying to provide them, and we do this in the
> minority too, with public polling and outside political expertise. This is

what Democrats were doing a lot during Health Care. You saw that the
bill was opposed by a majority of Americans. But then they would break
down certain issues so they could tell their members, "Well, preexisting
coverage polls at 75 percent." And they would break down the issues so
they could tell their members, "Yeah, this whole thing has been kind of
demonized, but when you break down the popular provisions and when
you go out and start selling that when it's being implemented and people
realize that they are getting this new benefit it's going to be quite popular." So public opinion polling, that stuff, is quite beneficial.[76]

Ahead of the consideration of a bill on the floor, party leaders will
also seek out endorsements from allied interest groups and stakeholders.
In distributing the lists of these supporters, along with copies of their letters of endorsement, leaders hope to demonstrate to their members that
there is substantial support for a bill from groups likely to be important
to them and that they should support the bill too.

From the interviews, it appeared there were a variety of opinions
among rank-and-file members of Congress and their staffs about the
quality of information they received from the leadership. Some said it
was pretty straightforward but usually not very deep:

RANK-AND-FILE MEMBER: The information is pretty good. They have meet-
    ings and hand out sheets with information. They don't always give us all
    the information. You need to ask them. But they were promoters.[77]
RANK-AND-FILE STAFFER: With the stuff that comes to the floor, the leader-
    ship gives more information through caucus meetings and whip meetings.
    Those are two places that members get a lot of updates on what's included.
    That's not always the case. Not every piece of legislation is brought up in
    the course of those meetings. A lot of times major legislation will be.[78]

This same staffer indicated that the quality of information varied
quite a bit depending on the bill. On some bills the information is top
line, basic, or unsatisfactory. Other times the leadership feels the need
to go into some detail about the legislation to keep the caucus on board.
Basically, the information is tailored to the situation, to motivate as
much support as possible. During consideration of the Affordable Care
Act during the 111th Congress, the majority leadership felt that more detail would ease the minds of their caucus members:

RANK-AND-FILE STAFFER: In the case of the health care bill in the last Congress [the leadership] went through section by section of the bill explaining what each section does, and members could ask questions throughout. If you add it up, there were days of just caucus meetings where they went through and talked about the bill after all the committee meetings had occurred on it. A lot of times it will be just a summary of the legislation. At times there's guidance as to where leadership thinks you should be on certain legislation.[79]

Many lawmakers and staffers, such as the ones quoted above, find information from the leadership somewhat adequate, even if they wished they had more. Other members are much more skeptical. They often describe such information as inadequate, misleading, or biased:

RANK-AND-FILE MEMBER: I am always suspicious of the information that comes from the party.[80]

RANK-AND-FILE MEMBER: Mostly vote recommendations and talking points; less substance.[81]

RANK-AND-FILE MEMBER: One of the biggest complaints you run into is that whip materials sometimes turn out to be inadequate and even sometimes misleading. Without a partisan bent on this, it happened on a number of occasions when Mr. DeLay was whip, although I generally was very positive on the whip organization. I think the same complaint was levied against the whip organization under the Democrats in the last few cycles I was in Congress.[82]

RANK-AND-FILE MEMBER: The leadership offices or committee leaders do not intentionally mislead, but they may omit items that do not fit their messaging.[83]

Some of these lawmakers characterized leadership information as little more than talking points that they could not always even use back in their districts. These members suggested that the information was especially unhelpful for representatives in moderate or swing districts, and that it had such a partisan slant that it was probably helpful only to the most partisan lawmakers. This raises a larger point about the limits to leaders' abilities to sell their bills and their positions to their rank and file. Even though all lawmakers need information, some may be more skeptical than others. Generally the most orthodox members of a party caucus from the most orthodox districts can most afford to trust their leadership's priorities and positions, since they probably fit fairly well with their own. Those members who represent swing districts or otherwise are outside the party's mainstream need to be the most skeptical. They know that a partisan position and partisan talking points may not be effective in their districts, so they may not be as easily swayed by the their leaders' tactics. Subsequent chapters explore this and other limitations in more detail. Chapter 7, in particular, focuses on this subject.

Nonetheless, whether or not the rank and file finds the information the majority party leadership supplies extraordinarily useful, it may be the best, or only, information available during the short period when some bills are considered. Consequently, most members of Congress will have no choice but to pay attention to what their leaders are telling them and consider it when casting their votes. If the leaders are successful, they will keep the majority together during the vote.

Conclusion

Information, as the staffer quoted at the start of chapter 2 put it, is very valuable in Congress, so much so that lawmakers and staffers of all types—rank and file or leadership—work long and hard to obtain and use it so they can make the best decisions. With limited time and resources, typical lawmakers cannot comprehensively analyze legislation or gather all the insights they would like. Instead, they rely on cues, readily available sources, and their own predispositions to make decisions efficiently.

Knowing how information can shape the decisions of their rank and file, legislative leaders work to shape the information environment in the chamber. Both committee leaders and the majority party leadership use their substantial staff resources to stay in close contact with rank-and-file offices and gather intelligence about what lawmakers might support in a bill, what they might oppose, and what might motivate them and other political actors to vote with the chair or the leadership. They work to obtain a clear picture of the political dynamics around a bill or issue, then leverage this knowledge to supply the messages, cues, data, and other information they believe will reinforce support among their rank and file and undercut the effectiveness of opposition to the bill.

Legislative leaders thus try to dominate the flow of information within the House of Representatives. They want to know as much as they can about what other actors, inside and outside the chamber, are thinking, planning, or wanting. They also strive to be the most prominent and effective voice circulating information and messages as the legislative process unfolds, influencing what their lawmakers consider when considering legislation, and strongly influencing the preferences they develop and the decisions they make. These efforts are constant. On every important bill, leaders are working to shape the information passing through the chamber.

These efforts are a crucial part of legislative leaders' information strategies. However, at times leaders take additional steps. As the next chapter describes, on bills of particular importance they use tactics to restrict the information available about the legislation, making rank-and-file lawmakers rely on them even more. This is a source of power that legislative leaders can use strategically and effectively.

CHAPTER FOUR

Turning Out the Lights

Restricting Information

For leaders in congressional policymaking, power stems in part from their ability to influence what information is available, when, and to whom. For typical members of Congress, good information is a valuable resource but all too scarce. By contrast, legislative leaders can accrue an abundance of valuable and usable information. But leaders often keep their rank and file in the dark throughout as much of the legislative process as possible so that at crucial stages, such as during committee markups and floor consideration, leaders are the most credible voice, if not the only voice, providing information about what to support or oppose and how to vote.

Even though they have significant procedural control over the floor and their committees, party leaders and committee chairs can find their legislation imperiled if information falls into the wrong hands or if they lose control of the policy debate. Most significant legislation is complex, addressing numerous issues and engaging a multitude of political interests. The final language often reflects carefully fashioned compromises among a handful of important players in Congress, the private sector, and the administration. If opponents can raise a controversy or otherwise publicize unpopular aspects of a bill, or if rank-and-file lawmakers focus on information that may push them toward opposition, these delicate compromises could be derailed, jeopardizing passage of the bill.

What leaders hope to avoid is illustrated by the defeat in the early 1980s of a bipartisan effort, led by President Ronald Reagan and Representative John Dingell (D-MI), to amend the Clean Air Act. Dingell, then chairman of the House Committee on Energy and Commerce, with support of the Reagan administration, intended to ram through his committee a bill that would have reduced emission standards under the Clean Air Act of 1970. The bill, with broad support from American industry, important leaders in both parties, and a powerful Democratic chairman, looked like a sure bet for passage. But a coalition of members led by Representative Henry Waxman (D-CA) was able to stir up enough controversy to eventually kill it. Waxman, representing smog-filled Los Angeles, had a strong interest in blocking the legislation and was willing to allocate significant time and resources to its defeat. Since he was chairman of Energy and Commerce's Subcommittee on the Environment, Waxman's staff had strong ties with the Environmental Protection Agency. A key moment came when his staffers obtained a leak of the Reagan administration's draft recommendations for the bill that contained severe and unpopular cuts to clean air protection (Waxman and Green 2009, 80). Waxman and his allies spread this information to other members of the committee and ultimately forced Dingell to remove the bill from the agenda.

Successful information control might have kept Waxman and his allies at bay and aided the passage through Congress of the once broadly supported bill. By restricting access to information, leaders achieve two benefits. First, they hamstring the opposition. By keeping the specific contents of the bill under wraps, they take away ammunition from opposition lawmakers and groups trying to attack it. Second, they keep their own rank and file in line. By limiting what information is readily available and focusing their own messaging on reasons to support the leadership's position, they minimize the likelihood that their rank and file will find reasons to defect and oppose the bill.

However, leaders cannot restrict access to information on every important bill that comes before the chamber or their committees. On some bills it simply would not be possible, and on others it may be politically unwise. To give an idea of how frequently leaders restrict information, table 4.1 shows how frequently three such tactics analyzed in this chapter—restricted layover, self-execution, and bill complexity—were used by majority party leaders on important bills between the 106th and 111th Congresses.[1] Considered together, about half of the 518 bills analyzed were subject to at least one such tactic. Thus, while these tactics are prevalent, leaders do not and cannot employ them on every bill.

The theory and evidence presented in the previous chapters provide some clear expectations about when leaders are likely to use these tac-

TABLE 4.1. **Use of information-restricting tactics, 106th to 111th Congresses**

Tactic	Percentage of important bills
Restricted layover (twenty-four hours or less)	29.5
Self-execution	19.7
Complexity (one standard deviation above the mean)	12.7
Any of the three	48.6

tics. First, using them should further leaders' goals. As theorized in chapter 2 and demonstrated in chapter 3, legislative leaders concentrate on passing big-picture, partisan legislation. If these tactics are at all useful, they should help them achieve this key goal. As such, we should find these tactics used on legislation that leaders identify as a priority.

Second, information should be restricted when there is a clear need to keep it under wraps. If it makes little sense to go to great lengths to limit access, leaders can allow the legislative process to unfold in a more open, deliberative way and claim they have allowed the House to "work its will." But when openness may endanger a bill, restricting information is a necessity. For leaders, the more interest there is in a bill across the political spectrum, the greater the need to restrict. When there is a great deal of interest in a bill, it is likely that more groups will oppose aspects of it and work to alter its contents or undermine its passage. Since lawmakers typically vote with their leaders unless there are compelling reasons not to, legislative leaders have an interest in making it less likely that their rank and file will hear divergent viewpoints. Consequently, leaders will be more likely to keep everyone in the dark when the potential for outside influence is high, and we should find them more likely to use these tactics when there is more interest group interest in a bill.

This chapter draws on both interview evidence and evidence from the dataset of important legislation considered by the House from 1999 to 2010 (as described in the introduction and appendix B) to analyze the information-restricting tactics used by both party and committee leaders and test these expectations about their use. To do this I apply several unique measures, including issue-based measures of leadership, priority legislation, interest group interest in legislation, and the public salience of legislation. Although both party and committee leaders use information-restricting tactics, the quantitative analyses in this chapter are limited to their use by party leaders, since data are not available about their use in committees. Nonetheless, information restricting in committee is still evaluated qualitatively.[2] The evidence presented demonstrates that legislative leaders use such tactics to significant effect in the House of Representatives.

Restricting Information in Committee

Committee chairs and their staffs can limit the information lawmakers have during the committee stages of bill consideration and beyond. Using the intelligence they have gathered, committee leaders know how tightly information on a bill will need to be kept under wraps. When committee leaders restrict information, they do so primarily by controlling the drafting of bills and the release of information about the resulting drafts.

The "Chairman's Mark"

All bills that either originate in a committee or are referred to it after introduction can be marked up by committee staff under the guidance of the chair. This power stems from standing rules that allow the committee chair to select the markup "vehicle," or the version of the bill to be marked up (Oleszek 2007, 100–101). This allows chairs to significantly influence or alter the contents of all bills referred to their committees, whether they are originally written by the chair or by any other lawmaker. The resulting draft is known informally as the "chairman's mark." Committee chairs and staff keep tight control over the drafting of the mark. Though there are few rules limiting how much the chair can alter a bill through the mark, it would be unusual to change the core concept of the bill. Nevertheless, chairs can and do exercise significant influence over mark language and have the authority to add and subtract provisions to bills written by other members in order to bring the proposed policies in line with party interests or their own. Furthermore, major or important legislation often originates with chairs and their staffs.

Generally, very few individuals are brought into conversations that direct the drafting of the mark. With bills that originate within committee (as opposed to bills introduced by rank-and-file lawmakers and referred to the committee), discussions over draft contents primarily involve the committee staff, key personal aides to the chair, and the chair. One committee staffer described it this way:

> COMMITTEE STAFFER: The way it usually works is staff will develop recommendations for both policy and funding, and then we will sit down with whoever the chairman is for a long time—this takes a while, it's over the course of several weeks, each staff member will come in and talk about their part—and go over all the major policy issues, all the funding levels, and get sign-offs from him or changes if he wants something changed.[3]

A personal aide to an Appropriations subcommittee chair described it very similarly:

> COMMITTEE STAFFER: Prior to drafting we spend two hours for every component agency. It could be, in some cases, more than two hours where subcommittee staff and I will be with him going through line by line what we call out in terms of dollar amounts in the bill. All the grant programs, administrations, any other issues, earmarks of course. So we'll go through that and he'll sign off on amounts that we call out in the bill and the report. And we go through that through all of the portions of the bill. So that is prior to putting the legislative language together. Obviously [the committee staffers] come here with recommendations. So they'll have a packet of recommendations for the amounts for each account, and we'll go through all of those. And sometimes there'll be minor tweaks here or there. . . . Then he'll eventually see all the report language before the end of the process.[4]

If the bill was introduced by a lawmaker other than the chair, that representative will also play a major role in these draft discussions. The intelligence gathered by committee staffers will tell if there are other intensely interested rank-and-file members who should be brought into the intimate fold. But the more people who are brought into the discussions, the harder it is to control information about what is being discussed and what is being drafted. Unlike bills originating within the committee, bills proposed by rank-and-file members and drafted in a member's office before being referred to the committee entail a loss of control over information from the start. According to a staffer of one rank-and-file member:

RANK-AND-FILE STAFFER: Most bills that originate in the Science Committee come from members of that committee. And if that's the case, I usually know what's going on with the bill a fair amount in advance. And as
the bill is being written I will talk to [my] congressman. And if there are
points that he'd like to make in the bill I will work with the committee
staff and other offices to get them in there before it becomes public in a
markup form. So usually by the time it comes up at a markup we've talked
about it, he knows about it.[5]

From the perspective of the chair and the committee staff, the more
people who are involved in the drafting process the tougher it is to control.
With more principals, it is harder to ensure secrecy; the fewer principals
involved in drafting a bill, the easier it is to keep information under wraps.
In these instances, compromises are easier to negotiate, and information
can more easily be restricted. In general, committee chairs and their staffs
try to control the drafting as much as possible and will work to keep the
contents of the chairman's mark as private as possible. For bills that originate outside committee offices, information management depends to a
degree on the cooperation of the additional representatives involved. The
more control the committee can maintain over the drafting, the easier it
will be to control what information is released after the draft is completed.

Release of Draft Contents

Eventually the contents of the mark have to be released, but when this
moment arrives most committee chairs and staff still jealously guard
copies of the bill. In fact, committee staffs go to great lengths to control
the release of bill contents, if they are ever made fully available. From
the perspective of the chair and the staff, such action is necessary. Un-
restricted release could put a mark in the hands of the wrong lawmakers
or outside groups. If the opponents of a bill are able to analyze draft language early in the legislative process, they can begin developing effective legislative and communication strategies to build opposition to the
bill or support for changes—a calamity for committee chairs trying to
craft bills that meet their legislative goals. As one committee staffer explained it, "It's purely a matter of, once you let somebody walk out of
here with that paper, it's out there."[6] Once someone else has the text,
committee control of the bill is over.

To rank-and-file lawmakers and their staffs, however, the tight control committees keep on drafts can be frustrating. Especially when in the majority, members are concerned with seeing that bills being marked up address issues in a way that meets their interests and those of their constituents. At the very least, they want to avoid being blamed down the line for supporting a bill containing a provision unpopular in their districts (see Arnold 1990). Limited time and access to draft contents can make it difficult for lawmakers to vet the legislation adequately and can make it tricky to offer an amendment.

Each committee has specific rules and norms governing the release of information about items to be considered in committee meetings. Table 4.2 summarizes the formal rules of each committee during the 109th and 110th Congresses. Specifically, it shows how long before markup meetings each committee was required to make the mark available to committee members and how long before these meetings rank-and-file members had to submit proposed amendments.[7] There is substantial variation in these formal requirements.[8] Some committees have no requirements at all regarding the release of draft contents. Some committees, such as the Committee on Agriculture, are willing only to require the chair to announce the agenda of upcoming meetings as far in advance as is reasonably possible and provide no requirements for the availability of bill text. Rule language like this gives committee chairs and their staffs significant leeway over when and how they release information about draft contents and exactly what information is released.

Other committees have formal requirements among their rules but qualify them. During the 110th Congress, for example, the Committee on Natural Resources required that information on bill contents be made available to committee members forty-eight hours before any markup sessions; however, the rules also state that only a "summary of the major provisions" need be made available. The Committee on Science, Space, and Technology likewise had a forty-eight-hour requirement during both the 109th and 110th Congresses, but this rule just needed to be followed "to the maximum extent practicable." Other committees, like the Committee on Homeland Security during the 110th Congress, allowed chairs to unilaterally waive these requirements when necessary.

Only a few committees listed completely unqualified requirements among their official rules; however, all committees have a propensity to bend or ignore their standing rules when necessary and exercise broad interpretations of the meaning of "availability of contents." It seems that

TABLE 4.2. **Rules regarding the timeliness of bill text and amendment availability before markup**

Committee	Time before markup bill text must be made available		Time before markup amendments must be submitted	
	110th Congress	109th Congress	110th Congress	109th Congress
Standing committees				
Agriculture	none	none	24 hours	24 hours
Appropriations	3 days	3 days	none	none
Armed Services	none	3 days	none	none
Budget	6 hours	4 hours[9]	none	none
Education and Labor	48 hours	48 hours	"timely manner"	"timely manner"
Energy and Commerce	none	36 hours	none	none
Financial Services	2 days	2 days[9]	none	none
Foreign Affairs	24 hours[1]	24 hours[1]	none	none
Homeland Security	24 hours[2]	none	none	none
House Administration	none	none	"when requested"	"when requested"
Judiciary	none	none	none	none
Natural Resources	48 hours[3]	48 hours	none	none
Oversight and Government Reform	3 days	3 days	none	none
Rules[4]	—	—	—	—
Science, Space, and Technology	48 hours[5]	48 hours[5]	24 hours[5]	24 hours[5]
Small Business	none	none	none	"when requested"
Standards of Official Conduct[6]	—	—	—	—
Transportation and Infrastructure	48 hours[7]	48 hours[7]	none	none
Veterans Affairs	none	none	none	none
Ways and Means	2 days	2 days	none	none
Select committees				
Intelligence	none[8]	none[8]	"timely manner"	"timely manner"
Energy Independence and Global Warming	none	—	none	—

Source: Published committee rules for each committee during each Congress.

[1] Rule qualifies this requirement with "whenever possible."

[2] Requirement can be waived by the chair with advance notice to the ranking minority member.

[3] Rule refers specifically to making available a "summary of the major provisions" of a bill.

[4] Since the Rules Committee does not typically consider original legislation, its entries are left blank here.

[5] Rule qualifies this requirement with "to the maximum extent practicable."

[6] Standards of Official Conduct has unique procedures because of its unique jurisdiction.

[7] Can be unilaterally waived by the chair.

[8] The Select Committee on Intelligence has lengthy and varying rules regarding the availability of sensitive materials.

[9] Can be waived by the chair with concurrence from the ranking member.

a fairly typical method for releasing bill contents is to make a copy of the committee's report on the bill, and sometimes the full bill text, available for review by rank-and-file staffers for a limited number of hours, usually the day before the markup is scheduled. Copies of the report, the bill, or both often can be viewed in a subcommittee or committee office but are not to be removed. Personal staffers can come in and look at the documents and take notes, but that is as far as it goes. Several staffers described this procedure:

> COMMITTEE STAFFER: His subcommittee always makes everything available to staff before markup. They can't take it out of the room, but they'll say, OK, starting the morning of the markup, or sometimes the day before, at that time you'll have access. Every office has their own copy of the bill and a copy of the report and it's marked. It's not supposed to leave the room. You can take whatever notes you want and go.[9]
>
> COMMITTEE STAFFER: Probably a day before the subcommittee markup we will have staff in here and give them probably not the actual bill and report, but we will make it available for them to look at. . . . So we will make it available for them to check things they are interested in and have a chance for them to ask questions of staff about what's in there.[10]
>
> COMMITTEE STAFFER: We usually make the bill and reports available for associate staff to view and members if they'd like to, the day before the subcommittee markup. But only in the subcommittee offices; they can't take it back with them. So they'll be given a number of business hours before the subcommittee markup to view the product and to see the particular priorities that their boss has and be able to brief their boss on what is included in the bill before the subcommittee markup.[11]
>
> RANK-AND-FILE MEMBER: Usually we would have an opportunity to review a chairman's mark the day before legislation was brought forward.[12]

The lengths committee staffers sometimes go to in keeping bill reports and drafts from escaping borders on comedy. Staffers will often be placed at all doors to the committee office to make sure no one tries to slip out with a copy under an arm or hidden in a jacket. Other staff will be assigned to watch incoming staffers closely to make sure everything is kosher. As the first quotation above indicates, each copy of the bill and report is marked with the name of the office it is intended for so that if a copy is missing at the end of the day, the culprit can be identified.

While this method appears to be standard practice, a few committees seemed to be more liberal about distributing bill drafts. A staffer for one member of Congress described a more open procedure:

> RANK-AND-FILE STAFFER: We're normally notified by an e-mail saying that the legislation has been posted to the website, or they will send it internally. . . . Typically [we get] the full text in that time frame. Sometimes we'll get a report or a summary a little bit earlier, and then we'll get the final text. But normally we get the final version within twenty-four hours.[13]

Nonetheless, this method still describes a very controlled release. Although the actual contents are posted and fully available to the members, it is still done very late before markups, giving rank-and-file lawmakers little time to analyze the bill and giving opponents little time to develop strategies.

Even when bills are electronically distributed, committees will sometimes use, or misuse, technology to their advantage. An example I observed during the 112th Congress is illustrative. The day before the Committee on Transportation and Infrastructure began a marathon markup on H.R. 7, the American Energy and Infrastructure Jobs Act of 2012, the committee announced that it had made several changes to the original chairman's mark of the bill and distributed a PDF of the new draft to members of the committee by e-mail. Unfortunately, unlike most modern PDF files in which the text of the document is electronically searchable, this PDF was a grainy photo image of the bill that was neither searchable nor easily read. This left committee members' staffs with less than a day to scan a new draft of nearly nine hundred pages that had been altered and reorganized to both assess the changes made to the bill and redraft the amendments so they would be in order during the impending markup.

Most of the interviews with rank-and-file members of Congress or their staffs showed that they find this method of releasing drafts frustrating and troublesome. The transcription below was typical of the interviews conducted with rank-and-file legislators and their staffs:

> JC: For the typical amount of time you have between when you might receive the draft of the bill and the markup, is it an adequate amount of time to acquaint yourself with its contents?
> RANK-AND-FILE STAFFER: In general, no.[14]

As a staffer quoted in the previous chapter described it, ultimately lawmakers have to make judgment calls about legislation using the information available. But the controlled and restrictive release of bill contents can make obtaining useful information difficult. If the draft contents are not public, interest groups and other actors that lawmakers may want to hear from may not formulate an official opinion until after the markup. Even if these groups do have an official stance on the chairman's mark, it may not be possible for lawmakers to get in touch with relevant groups in time. Ultimately, when bill contents are restricted, the limits on lawmakers' time and resources for gathering information are exacerbated.

Restricted access to bill contents can also make drafting amendments and getting them accepted at markup difficult if not impossible. Drafting an amendment that fits appropriately within a bill's text is time consuming. Members of Congress and their staffs have to find where their amendment can fit in the bill, draft proposed language, then turn that draft over to the Office of Legislative Counsel for technical editing so the language is in order. Although a lawmaker's office might have an idea of what kind of amendment it would like to offer, it cannot formally create one before seeing the legislative language. Several members and staffers lamented this problem during the interviews:

> RANK-AND-FILE MEMBER: Sometimes drafts come up less than twenty-four hours before the markup. It makes it very hard to offer amendments.[15]
> JC: Were there any instances where you had intended to offer an amendment to a bill and because of the short time frame you were not able to?
> RANK-AND-FILE STAFFER: Yeah. There certainly were.[16]

One staffer shared an anecdote about a bill before the Committee on Science, Space, and Technology that exemplifies how committee chairs and staff can control the release of bill drafts to keep the bill they have crafted intact:

> RANK-AND-FILE STAFFER: After the oil spill, a bill came forward addressing natural resource policy, and the rules say drafts have to become available forty-eight hours before markup—they gave it to us fifteen hours before. We had an amendment ready to go, but it was already obsolete—the deadline [for amendments] is twenty-four hours. We got it to them in two hours

and they pushed back. They said, you know, we don't have enough time to work through this. So that is what can be frustrating for a personal office.[17]

The impression made in many of the interviews was that occurrences like this were not out of the ordinary. The way committees take control of the consideration of bills makes it very hard for rank-and-file members to have significant influence. Committee chairs and staffs do not want to jeopardize their bill's chances of moving smoothly through committee and onto the floor. The staffer quoted above even noted that because of these dynamics sometimes he could get information quicker from the other party's committee staff:

RANK-AND-FILE STAFFER: The fact that I have to go to the other party to get early drafts of the bill is reprehensible. And it isn't always because there are bad people operating it that plan to deprive you of information. A lot of time they are told to stall because negotiations are taking so long internally on their side that they don't want to share it and complicate things. And often negotiations don't start until there is a deadline for markup. So everything pushes back against the markup, and things may have become worse as negotiations go on with the minority party and so on, so things take longer and longer. Personal staff, as a result, are the last to know. . . . [The committee's] reaction is to say no and to not do anything to make it easier for people to change the bill that they've written and the compromises they have carefully made.[18]

Some of those interviewed suggested that control over information varied based on the chair's personality. Some chairs were dedicated to a more open process, whether because of their legislative philosophy or because the issues they were dealing with required it. As one rank-and-file staffer succinctly put it, "It all depends on the chairman. And a lot of times the staff will reflect the chairman and the way that the chairman wants to operate."[19] One former member of Congress singled out former Appropriations Committee chairman Jamie Whitten (D-MS):

LEADERSHIP MEMBER: They really didn't want everybody to fully understand what was going on. When Jamie Whitten was chairman of the Appropriations Committee he spoke with a deep Mississippi accent and people clearly could not understand what he was saying, and I think he used

that to his advantage. But I remember one time he came into the Rules
Committee and he really wanted us to understand what he was saying and
spoke very clearly. I understood every word that he was saying when most
of the time you couldn't understand him because of his accent.[20]

A staffer was equally critical of certain chairs, specifically noting
Representative Bill Thomas (R-CA), who chaired the Committee on
Ways and Means from 2001 to 2006: "Chairman Thomas was very much
in the camp of 'my product is perfect and I'm working in the tax code
and therefore you shouldn't be doing anything to it.' There are times we
pushed back on that. I still have scars from him yelling at me."[21] This
serves as a reminder that just how much information is controlled by the
committee is a function not just of the bills being considered, but also of
the person in charge.

All together, it is clear that committees go to great lengths to control what information about their marks is released and how, and that
these efforts affect the ability of rank-and-file lawmakers to be equal
and influential participants in the legislative process. From the moment
a bill is referred to a committee, or is begun in a committee, the process is controlled. Information on legislative language is held tightly by
just a few principal actors until very late, and even then efforts are sometimes made to obscure the information. The process is not necessarily
any more open outside committee. The majority party leadership also
restricts access to information.

Party Leaders Restricting Information

The majority party leadership has a number of procedures to restrict the
information available about legislation before the House, but controlling
information is not as easy for party leaders as for committee chairs. By
rule, the versions of bills reported by committees and placed on one of
the House calendars have to be made public, usually within three days.
Additionally, any member of the chamber can pick up copies of reported
bills from the committees, and typically the reported text of the legislation is made available in electronic form through the Library of Congress, the Government Printing Office, the committee's website, and by
other means. Simply that the bill has gone through a committee process means more details about the bill are going to be known than when

it was sitting in a committee office before markup.[22] Party leaders thus cannot obscure or hide its contents or keep their rank and file in the dark the way committee leaders can. Nevertheless, they still have numerous tactics available, including restricting bill layover, self-executing bills in the Rules Committee, and taking advantage of the complexity of some legislation.

Restricting Bill Layover

One way the majority party leadership can restrict information is to limit the time legislation is available for review before it is considered on the floor. House rules state that bills and resolutions must be made available to lawmakers for three calendar days before they can be considered (Rybicki 2006). Generally this rule is interpreted to mean that a bill should not be brought up for floor consideration until three calendar days have elapsed after each committee of jurisdiction has either reported the bill or has had the bill bypassed or discharged from its consideration. This rule seems to limit party leaders' abilities to accelerate the legislative process, but this requirement is far from restrictive for several reasons. First, "three calendar days" does not mean seventy-two hours. If a bill is reported by a committee at 1:00 a.m., with the House adjourning shortly after and reconvening at 6:00 a.m. the same morning, one calendar day is considered to have passed. Thus, three calendar days can pass in much less than seventy-two hours. But more important, layover requirements are almost always waived through language in the special rules providing for the consideration of the legislation. Whether the special rule is open, closed, or modified, language similar to this is nearly always included at the start of the rule:

> Resolved, That upon the adoption of this resolution it shall be in order to consider in the House the bill (H.R. 3996) to amend the Internal Revenue Code of 1986 to extend certain expiring provisions, and for other purposes. All points of order against consideration of the bill are waived except those arising under clause 9 or 10 of rule XXI.[23]

The language above effectively sidesteps layover requirements. If a member of Congress were to raise a point of order against the consideration of H.R. 3996 on the basis that it had not laid over for three calendar days, the point of order would be overruled because the special rule waived "all points of order against its consideration." As one former leadership staffer explained it, "The leadership had finessed the rules so that it wasn't that you could make a point of order against the rules."[24]

Layover requirements are frequently bypassed on important legislation. Figure 4.1 presents layover times for important legislation considered from 1999 to 2010.[25] The first thing to note is that layover times vary considerably in length. While some bills lay over for less than a minute, others lay over for several thousand hours (or hundreds of days). The second is that a significant proportion of bills lay over for less than seventy-two hours. More than 50 percent of these bills laid over for less time than House rules intend. More important, almost 30 percent of bills laid over for less than twenty-four hours. Among these are numerous major pieces of legislation including the Medicare Improvements for Patients and Providers Act of 2008, which made significant policy changes to mental health and low-income Medicare programs, the Children's Health Insurance Program Reauthorization Act of 2009, which enacted new programs, incentives, and funding for children's health coverage through Medicaid, the USA PATRIOT Act of 2001, which made sweeping changes to laws governing law enforcement, immigration, government surveillance, and counterterrorism, and both the 2001 and 2003 Bush tax cut bills, which made extensive changes to the federal tax code.

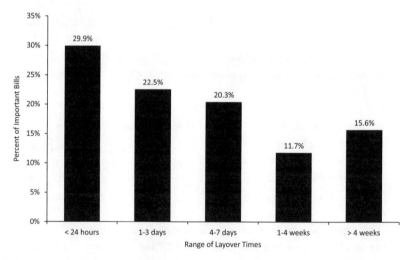

FIGURE 4.1. Layover times for important legislation, 106th to 111th Congresses. $N = 511$.

For rank-and-file members of Congress, less layover time makes it even more difficult to adequately analyze bill contents. Many of the rank-and-file members interviewed lamented the difficulty of doing their job under such time constraints:

> RANK-AND-FILE MEMBER: There were a number of occasions when we voted on things on the floor and there were details included that we were not properly exposed to.[26]
>
> RANK-AND-FILE MEMBER: Without going through regular order you have to do a lot more work. It was a lot more difficult.[27]
>
> RANK-AND-FILE STAFFER: Yes, especially on issues we haven't dealt with yet this session. When the process is sped up it makes it much more difficult. We pull it off, but it's pretty hectic.[28]

For minority party members and the minority leadership it is most difficult. With less time to analyze the bill, it becomes harder to orchestrate effective opposition to it, challenge some of its provisions, or conduct a public relations campaign against it. As a minority leadership staffer put it:

> LEADERSHIP STAFFER: Where we can be given notice of a bill, and sometimes a pretty substantial bill, that is coming to the floor the next day, we get that notice the night prior, sometimes at midnight or something like that. In that case we're really scrambling. So the information that we are coming up with, one, we don't have access to it, two, we don't have time.[29]

Consequently, this staffer continued, the minority can present only a rather general stance against the bill rather than something more specific or effective: "So we're usually using a tactic that's much more generalized with our members. We're saying, 'Well, we know there are tax increases in this bill so it's a tax increase bill, it's a job killer'—stay top of the line with your members with the message. But you can't get it as specific in that case, and that's really the minority's burden."[30] Basically, there is no time for opposition leaders to develop a comprehensive and organized set of talking points for opposing the bill. Instead they give their members some basic information to attack the bill with and hope some other actors or outside groups may have something more effective.

We can evaluate the expectations about when the majority party leadership will restrict information by looking at the variations in lay-over time for different bills. To assess whether leaders are more likely to restrict layover on priority legislation, priority bills must be identi-fied in a way unrelated to how the leadership handles that legislation. In other words, to understand how a bill's importance affects the way leaders handle it, bills cannot be deemed important, or a priority, *be-cause* of how the leadership handles them. The coding must be exoge-nous, and there are two ways to do this. The first references the bills in-serted into the first ten bill slots during each Congress. The first ten bill numbers (H.R. 1 to H.R. 10) are reserved for the Speaker of the House to use as he or she sees fit. The bills in these slots are a good indica-tor of what issues are most important to the majority party leadership. For each Congress the issue content of these bills is assessed. All bills primarily addressing any of these issues during that same Congress, in-cluding the first ten, are designated *majority leadership priority* bills.[31] The bills identified using this method reflect anecdotal knowledge of pri-ority legislation in each Congress. In the 110th Congress, for example, the bills identified include all the bills on the Democrats' "Six for '06" agenda.[32] However, they also include a number of other bills, including legislation addressing amendments to the Federal Intelligence Surveil-lance Act, other renewable energy bills, other higher education bills, and legislation addressing national security issues including the War on Ter-ror and the war in Iraq.[33] One alteration made to this coding is the use of H.R. 11 as one of the "first ten" bills during the 111th Congress. Unlike the previous Congresses, during the 111th Congress H.R. 11−20 were not reserved for the minority leader to use, as is typically the case, but were used by the Democratic leadership to introduce the Lilly Ledbet-ter Fair Pay Act of 2009, a key priority for the Democratic leaders and the White House.

The second measure of leaders' priority legislation recognizes the president's importance as a party leader and legislator-in-chief. The president is a major agenda setter for Congress, especially during times of unified government. As explained in chapter 2, legislative leaders in the House have numerous incentives to become champions of the pres-ident's agenda or to lead the opposition. One way to identify *presiden-tial priority bills* is through the issue content of statements made during State of the Union addresses. The Policy Agendas Project codes each sentence in each address for its issue content. For each year, the num-ber of times each issue topic was mentioned during the address was calculated. Each bill was then coded as a presidential priority based on the number of times the issue topic it primarily addresses was mentioned during the speech. This coding scheme conforms to our common understanding of the president's priorities. For example, in his 2009 address, President Obama mentioned issues related to the national budget and debt (issue code 105) thirty-one times, about 13 percent of the statements made during his address.[34] Both majority leadership priority bills and presidential priority bills should be more likely to be subjected to information-restricting tactics than other bills.[35]

These two measures are admittedly noisy. Among bills addressing the same topic within the same year, these measures cannot determine which ones might be higher or lower priorities. Generally, both measures are probably overly generous in their coding, erring on the side of coding as priorities bills that may not have been as important to the leadership. For the analyses conducted here, this is favorable. Because some nonpriority legislation is likely included in the group, any findings probably understate how greatly priorities drive the use of information-restricting tactics.

Figure 4.2 assesses the bivariate relationship between these measures and layover times for important bills that received floor consideration from 1999 to 2010. The data show that bills prioritized by the majority party leadership have layover times that are on average just 57 percent

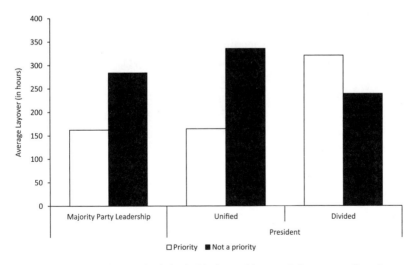

FIGURE 4.2. Layover times and priority legislation, 106th to 111th Congresses. $N = 461$.

as long as those not prioritized. To analyze presidential priority bills, the measure of State of the Union mentions was dichotomized so that bills receiving any mention in the most recent address were labeled a priority. During periods of unified government (when the House and the presidency were controlled by the same party) presidential priority bills had layover times averaging less than half the length of those for other bills. During divided government, the pattern is reversed, with priority bills receiving longer layovers. While all these differences are substantial, only the difference between presidential priorities and nonpriorities during unified government is statistically significant ($t = 1.49$; $p = 0.06$).

To assess whether leaders are more likely to restrict layover when there is more interest in a bill, a measure of *interest group interest* in each bill is needed. One way to measure interest group interest is to measure how much money groups potentially interested in a bill spend on political influence each year. The Center for Responsive Politics records the annual spending of interest groups organized into more than one hundred industries. To make these data usable for this study, the one hundred industries were matched to the Policy Agendas Project's nineteen major issue areas based on the issues each industry should be most concerned with influencing. Most of the industries were assigned to just one issue topic, but thirty industries were coded as having a strong interest in two major issue areas. The proportions of all interest group spending by industries concerned with each issue topic (in each year) are assigned to each bill based on *all* the major issue topics it addresses.[36] For example, if a bill dealt with both health care and education in 2006, the proportion of all interest group spending during 2006 by industries concerned with either health care or education—roughly 19.5 percent—would be assigned to the bill. These values serve as proxies for interest group interest in each bill analyzed.[37] For more details on matching the issue coding to the issue industries, see table B.3 in appendix B.

Figure 4.3 assesses the bivariate relationship between interest group interest and layover times for the same set of important bills. The graph shows only a modest negative correlation between the two measures ($r = -0.08$). Generally speaking, while bills that draw more attention from interest groups are likely to have slightly shorter layover times, the relationship is not dramatic.

In short, restricting bill layover is one way the majority party leaders restrict access to information on legislation. In doing so they give rank-and-file members of Congress less time to find reasons to dislike

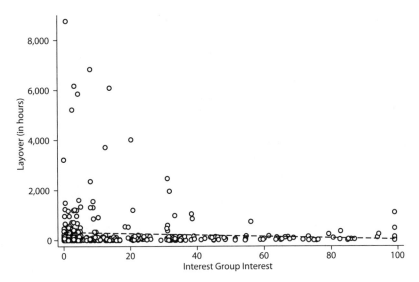

FIGURE 4.3. Layover times and interest group interest, 106th to 111th Congresses. $N = 461$.

the bill and ideally make them rely more on the information the leaders give them. Furthermore, restricting layover gives opponents less time to develop effective ways to oppose the legislation. However, restricting layover is just one tactic that party leaders use.

Self-Executing Rules

Another tactic the majority party leadership uses is to self-execute, or change the contents of bills through the Rules Committee. It works like this: The leadership-controlled Rules Committee will report a special rule that, along with setting the rules and procedures for floor consideration of a bill, will include, either in the rule's text or in a report accompanying the rule, one or more legislative amendments along with instructions that on the special rule's approval on the floor of the House, those amendments are "self-executed" into the original bill text.[38] In other words, self-execution allows the leadership to leverage its control over the Rules Committee to alter the contents of legislation by a procedural vote immediately before the bill is considered on the floor.

Self-execution provides two benefits for the majority party leadership. First, it allows them to almost unilaterally amend legislation. While it is true that self-executing provisions are adopted only on chamber passage of the special rule that contains them, on special rules votes, as on most procedural votes in Congress, it is considered heresy to help defeat your own party. As Sinclair (2000, 134) puts it, "Defecting from your party on procedural issues is considered a greater offense than defecting on substantive issues." This facet of partisanship in Congress has been readily understood for decades (see, for example, Jones 1964; Froman and Ripley 1965; Rohde 1991, 53; Cox and McCubbins 2005; Jenkins, Crespin, and Carson 2005; Theriault 2008) and has been growing in intensity since the 1970s (Schickler and Rich 1997).

Second, self-execution lets the leadership further exploit their informational advantages in several ways. First, special rules are written in private by the majority staff of the Rules Committee at the direction of the majority leadership. As such, the specific contents of the rule are not known until the Rules Committee markup. Second, self-executing provisions are typically not written with readability in mind. Rather than a series of amendment-like provisions that would strike and insert text at different points in the bill, self-execution often occurs as a single provision that strikes everything and replaces the entire bill. This type of editing makes it much more difficult for lawmakers to assess what changes have been made and to what effect, since they must analyze all of the new draft to identify the alterations. Third, while the resulting "Rules Committee Draft"—the name for the draft of the bill as amended by the special rule—is typically posted on the Rules Committee's website after the markup, bills are often brought to the floor mere hours after the Rules Committee reports its rule. Among the 387 bills in the important bills dataset considered on the floor under a special rule from 1999 to 2010, 83 percent were brought up for consideration within twenty-four hours of the special rule's being reported from the Rules Committee. Among the 103 bills self-executed, 90 percent came to the floor within twenty-four hours of the special rule's being reported, and all but three were considered on the floor within two days.

Self-execution is not a new development in congressional lawmaking, but its use has increased dramatically since the 1980s. As one former leadership staffer explained, "It started out harmlessly enough many years ago as just a way to make corrections without having to have a formal amendment to vote on it. But then the Democrats, when they were in the majority, especially under Jim Wright, would use that more and more to make substantive changes in the bill."[39]

Figure 4.4 presents the frequency of use of self-executing rules from

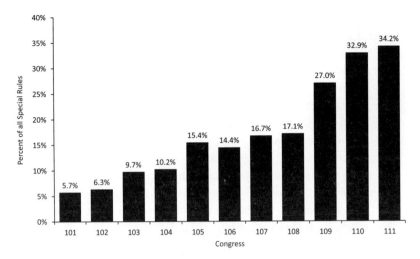

FIGURE 4.4. Percentage of special rules containing self-executing provisions, 101st to 111th Congresses. Source: Data on the use of self-executing provisions taken from the "Survey of Activities of the House Committee on Rules" published biennially in the United States Congressional Serial Set.

the 101st to the 111th Congress.[40] In the 101st Congress fewer than 6 percent of all special rules included self-executing provisions. By the 111th Congress more than one-third of all special rules included at least one self-executing provision.

Self-execution is not used solely as a means of amplifying the information asymmetries in the chamber. It is sometimes a way of "fixing" legislation to make it more palatable to the majority caucus before it gets to the floor:

> LEADERSHIP STAFFER: I think it's usually a matter of having late warning in the game, so it couldn't be corrected at the committee level anymore, and how do we correct something so we don't have this political problem on the floor. So, it was usually done with that in mind. It wasn't premeditated before the committee of jurisdiction reported.[41]

These types of fixes are sometimes done at the behest of the chair of the committee of jurisdiction, but other times the majority leadership use the ability to self-execute to make significant changes to a bill so that it better reflects their desires, with the added benefit of leaving little time for other lawmakers to respond. This same leadership staffer continued:

"It's usually with the complicity of the chairman of the committee. Although, Lee Hamilton . . . has said when he was Foreign Affairs Committee chairman he would take a little ten-page bill to the Rules Committee and it would emerge a thirty-page bill because they would self-execute other stuff into it."[42] Another party leadership staffer put it bluntly:

> LEADERSHIP STAFFER: Until you bring that bill to the floor you can change it as much as you want to, and you can change it for the betterment of certain members. . . . You know, not only do you have the schedule as a real advantage there because you're controlling the information in the majority, but you also have the legislation itself that you're controlling in your hands and you can it tweak as much as you want until the moment it's brought to the floor, basically.[43]

Another longtime member of Congress described self-execution as a tactic leaders use to advance legislative provisions that likely would fail in a more deliberative process such as through a committee vote or an amendment on the floor:

> RANK-AND-FILE MEMBER: They couldn't get something out of their committee if they allowed open votes, and so they would go through the Rules Committee.[44]

For rank-and-file members of Congress, self-execution can obviously be troublesome, especially if it is extensive. It often means they will be coming to the floor to vote on something they do not have full information on and that has been in their possession only a short time. Even if members had a good idea of what the bill was doing before self-execution, they may have little idea afterward:

> RANK-AND-FILE MEMBER: It makes it much more difficult to have information, because you don't really know what's in the final bill. . . . So while the bill may have been out there for a long time and the committee may have been doing a lot of work in public, when it's rewritten you don't really know the details.[45]

The expectations about when the majority party leadership restricts information can be evaluated by looking at which bills the leadership

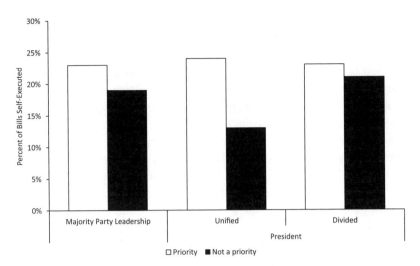

FIGURE 4.5. Self-execution and priority legislation, 106th to 111th Congresses. $N = 518$.

self-executes. Figure 4.5 shows how the likelihood of self-execution differs between majority leadership and presidential priority bills and all other bills. Generally, priority bills are more likely to be self-executed. Namely, 23 percent of majority leadership priority bills were self-executed compared with 19 percent of other bills. During unified government 24 percent of presidential priority bills were self-executed compared with 13 percent of nonpriority bills ($\chi^2 = 6.22$; $p = 0.01$). During divided government, the difference between presidential priority and nonpriority bills is much less stark. Similarly, there is a relationship between interest group interest and self-execution. Among bills that were self-executed by the leadership, the average interest group interest value was 25 percent, while among all other bills it was just 16 percent ($t = -3.59$; $p < 0.01$).

Ultimately, self-execution significantly empowers party leaders because it allows them to draft new bill content behind closed doors and amend existing legislation almost unilaterally at the very end of the legislative process. With little time to independently analyze the changes to the legislation, rank-and-file lawmakers must rely on their leaders for information. Doing all this in a condensed time span helps the leadership keep control of the legislative process and maintain the support of majority lawmakers on the floor.

Bill Complexity

The majority party leadership can also exploit the complexity of legislation considered in the House. Legislation considered in Congress
varies in how easily its contents, intent, and implications can be understood. All else equal, complex bills make lawmakers depend even more
on cues and information from knowledgeable sources like their leaders. With simpler bills, these cues and information are likely to be less
crucial, since it takes less time and policy knowledge to read and analyze the bill and fully understand its intent and implications independently. Lawmakers will still seek information from other sources, but
it will be more supplemental than critical. Understanding a bill that
is especially long, dense, or technical may require expertise from lawmakers or their staffs and more time for consideration than is usually
allowed. Since lawmakers typically specialize on only handful of issues, this situation will empower those in the know, including legislative leaders.

Leaders in the House can take numerous steps to make legislation
more complex, then exploit the resulting informational imbalance. They
can package legislation in an omnibus bill that is hundreds of pages long,
deals with a multitude of issues, and is time consuming for rank-and-
file lawmakers to process. Committee chairs and party leaders can also
draft legislation to be more difficult to read, using more technical jargon
than is necessary, writing provisions in a way that is less than straightforward, or burying the lead by including significant provisions toward the
end. Since chairs and leaders are involved in drafting most major legislation considered by the modern House, there are ample opportunities to
use these strategies.

The rank-and-file lawmakers and staff interviewed suggested that
complex bills are more difficult to fully digest. As one lawmaker noted,
even if you had time to sit down and read the bill from beginning to end,
it was no guarantee that you would totally understand it:

> RANK-AND-FILE MEMBER: There was usually enough time [to read the
> bills]. . . . But it was like reading a computer program. The language is
> dense and hard to understand.[46]

Another former member noted that she probably voted on a number of
things during her time in office that she did not fully comprehend:

RANK-AND-FILE MEMBER: Large, omnibus appropriations bills were a problem. You could only look at the parts that you cared about to look for
problems. . . . I'm sure there were some instances when the legislation was
so complicated that I couldn't quite grasp it all.[47]

Several lawmakers and staff noted that expedited consideration and
bill complexity were a lethal combination. When a bill is particularly
technical, complex, or lengthy, or covers an issue that has not been extensively legislated on before, an abbreviated period of consideration is
not always enough:

RANK-AND-FILE STAFFER: In the case of massive pieces of legislation [it was
not enough time]. In a lot of cases, while we might not have had the final text, we knew pieces that were going to be incorporated into it be-
forehand, and a lot of times we're using language that has been previously
used and we know that's going to be there, so we can start before we have
the final version. But it would certainly be more helpful to have notices
more than twenty-four hours in advance.[48]

RANK-AND-FILE STAFFER: It depends on the size of the bill. It also depends
on if the bill is something we have gone through before. If so, less time is
needed to understand it.[49]

RANK-AND-FILE MEMBER: It's like going to a neurosurgeon and asking for
brain surgery and him saying it will take ten hours and you asking him if
he can do it in thirty minutes![50]

One leadership staffer agreed that complex bills were more difficult
for most lawmakers to adequately dig into on their own and that this
provided an opportunity for leaders to nudge their rank-and-file in a
particular direction:

PARTY LEADERSHIP STAFFER: Even if you could read a bill you wouldn't understand it. So this whole "read the bill" stuff is almost a little bit disingen-
uous, because reading five lines referencing some part of the code isn't going to help you at all unless you are a committee staffer that wrote the damn
thing. So they are relying on us for those big pieces that are moving to tell
them exactly what's in the bill, and if you're in the minority, why it's bad.[51]

At least one former lawmaker also agreed. In discussing how quickly
some major bills were considered during his time in office, he noted that

it was under these conditions that there were opportunities for abuse by the leadership:

> RANK-AND-FILE MEMBER: For the way, particularly . . . I mean, it depends on the subject matter. If you're talking about a tax provision, sometimes this would be really pushing it. If you're talking about a broad Social Security policy or a broad human resources issue, probably it was enough time to consider. . . . If it requires a great deal of detail—an extended appropriation, a major deregulation or reauthorization—and if it's brought to the floor on an expedited basis, that typically creates problems. That's probably the case where if it's being brought to the floor for the first time as an issue, this is probably the area where you are most likely to find abuse and members not being given enough time to consider the details.[52]

As with layover and self-execution, the expectations about when the majority party leadership will restrict information can be evaluated by looking at bill complexity. The complexity of each bill in the dataset of important bills can be measured using an index of each bill's size, scope, issue complexity, and readability.[53] Bill size is measured as word length, and scope as the total number of the Policy Agendas Project's nineteen major issue areas the bill addresses. Issue complexity is measured by categorizing the complexity of the issue primarily addressed by each bill. Following Canes-Wrone and de Marchi (2002), regulatory issues (business, financial, energy, environment, trade policy) are treated as high-complexity, while social policy issues (abortion, crime, civil rights, civil liberties, drug control, school prayer) are treated as low complexity. Other matters, such as social welfare issues (education policy, Medicare, Medicaid, Social Security) and foreign policy issues are treated as moderately complex, given that these issues often include elements that are both easy and hard (table B.4 in appendix B provides the full categorization). Readability is measured using the Flesch Reading Ease metric (Flesch 1948).[54] Each measure is standardized and ordered so that larger values correspond to more complexity, and an additive index is created.[55] The index ranges from roughly −5.5 to 11 with the mean just above zero.

Figure 4.6 shows the relationship between the bill complexity index and the measures of party and presidential priorities. Among important bills considered from 1999 to 2010, majority leadership priority bills were more complex than nonpriority bills ($t = -2.76$; $p < 0.01$). Similarly, during unified government presidential priority bills were significantly more

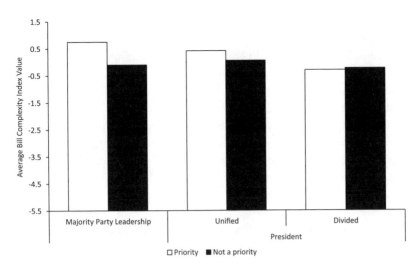

FIGURE 4.6. Bill complexity and priority legislation, 106th to 111th Congresses. $N = 518$.

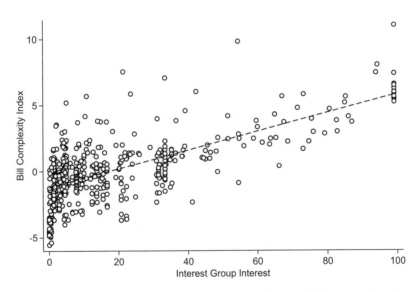

FIGURE 4.7. Bill complexity and interest group interest, 106th to 111th Congresses. $N = 518$.

complex than nonpriority bills ($t = -1.34$; $p = 0.09$), though the difference is erased during divided government. Figure 4.7 similarly shows the relationship between the bill complexity index and interest group interest for each bill. The figure shows there is a fairly strong positive relationship, since bills that are more complex attract much more attention from interest groups.

Generally, by using complex language or developing massive omnibus packages, legislative leaders can exacerbate and exploit the informational disparities in the chamber and make rank-and-file lawmakers even more dependent on them for information.

Multivariate Analyses of the Decision to Restrict Information

The evidence above suggests that the decision to use information-restricting tactics may be strategic—to advance priority legislation or to protect legislation from outside influence. However, the bivariate analyses cannot consider other factors that may influence the use of these tactics, including factors that may limit leaders' abilities or willingness to restrict information. For this reason several multivariate analyses of the use of each tactic assess how these strategic factors drive their use.

Other Factors in Decisions to Restrict Information

A number of other factors may influence leaders' decisions to use the tactics available to them. First, the *public salience* of a bill or issue may limit their ability to restrict information. Rank-and-file members of Congress, concerned with their reelection, are more cautious and engaged in making decisions on legislation addressing topics salient with the public. Salience among their constituents is likely to motivate lawmakers to commit the time, attention, and resources—asking questions, seeking additional information, and being persistent with committee and leadership staff—to become informed on a bill early in the legislative process (Hall 1996). As discussed in chapter 3, such motivation and investment of time can help lawmakers overcome their informational disadvantages on particular bills. The more lawmakers are motivated to engage in a bill, the more difficult it will be for leaders to control information about it. If a bill is salient only to a small subset of the public or

just a handful of lawmakers, leaders will be able to involve these mcm-
bers and accommodate their views. However, a bill or an issue that has
widespread or national public salience is likely to attract most lawmakers, if not all, to commit significant resources. With many lawmakers' interests primed, it will be more difficult for the leadership to broadly restrict access to information and limit the direct input of many rank and
filers. In these circumstances, members will remain in tune with the bill
as it moves through the stages of the legislative process and be persistent
in asking questions and demanding answers from committee and party
leaders and their staffs.

One method of measuring public salience uses newspaper articles and
editorials to estimate the importance of issues (Epstein and Segal 2000;
Binder 1999).[56] Research shows that the public's attention to political issues is strongly related to their coverage in the news (Iyengar, Peters,
and Kinder 1982; Page and Shapiro 1992, 12–13; McCombs 2006). Mayhew (1991) and Binder (1999) both use *New York Times* editorials to determine the salience of issues. I similarly rely on *New York Times* editorials, specifically a sample of 10 percent of all signed and unsigned
editorials each year that appeared in the *Times* from 1999 to 2010. Each
editorial was coded for one of the 225 issue topics it most directly addressed (using the Policy Agendas Project codebook). For each year, I
calculated the proportion of sampled editorials containing identifiable
issue content that address each issue topic, then assigned each bill a
value based on the salience of the issue it primarily addressed. For example, in 2008, eight editorials in the sample addressed the "U.S. banking system and financial institution regulation" (issue code 1501). A total of 116 editorials sampled for that year were coded as containing issue
content. Consequently, all bills in 2008 that primarily addressed the
banking system and its regulation were assigned a value of 6.9 percent.

In addition to public salience, several factors internal to Congress
may influence the use of information restriction. One factor that may
be important is the polarization of key lawmakers on each bill. Conditional theories of party leadership influence suggest that leaders are
given more leeway to employ aggressive procedural tactics on legislation
on which the parties are highly polarized (see, for example, Aldrich and
Rohde 2000). *Polarization of key lawmakers* measures the polarization
of the lawmakers from each party who are most likely to have an interest in each bill. Committee memberships provide rough indicators of

which members of Congress will be especially interested in certain topics and bills, because lawmakers' issue specialties and interests correlate strongly with their committee seats (Hall 1996; Adler and Lapinski 1997). To assess the degree of polarization, I calculated the absolute difference between the median first-dimension DW-NOMINATE[57] scores of the majority and minority members of the committee the bill was referred to. If the bill was referred to multiple committees, I calculated the averages of the median scores for each majority and minority committee membership, then assessed the absolute difference. The larger the value of this measure, the more polarization is likely present on the bill in question.

In addition to the polarization of lawmakers, committee chairs may be important to the majority leadership's restricting of information. As Sinclair (2012) notes, most leadership-driven policymaking efforts include relevant committee chairs in the discussion. Potentially, the use of these tactics may be sensitive to the degree of policy agreement between the majority leadership and the chairs of the committee(s) of jurisdiction. *Committee chair relative ideology* measures the difference between the majority party leadership's ideology and the ideology of the committee chair of the bill's committee of jurisdiction. I measured the ideology of the majority leadership by averaging the first-dimension DW-NOMINATE scores of the Speaker of the House, the majority leader, and the majority whip, then calculated the difference to demonstrate by how much each chair is more moderate than the majority leadership. In other words, chairs who are more liberal (conservative) than the leadership during Republican (Democratic) majorities would produce positive values on these measures, while chairs more different in the opposite direction would produce negative values. This measure allows the tests to distinguish if the leaders are more concerned about extremists in their own party or about chairs who would attempt to pull policy in a moderate direction.[58] If a bill was referred to one committee, the measure is simply the difference between the majority leadership's averaged DW-NOMINATE score and the DW-NOMINATE score of the chair. If the bill was referred to multiple committees, I averaged the DW-NOMINATE scores of the chairs before assessing the difference.

Finally, a few other factors may influence the use of information-restricting tactics. For one, *appropriations bills*, because they have historically been considered under more open and deliberative procedures, should be less likely to be subject to these tactics. The *number of com-*

mittees a bill was referred to may also be important. According to Sinclair (2012), multiple referrals tend to produce more unorthodox legislating, including leadership domination of negotiations and procedures. Given this finding, these tactics may be more commonly used with bills referred to multiple committees. Bills *considered under suspension of the rules* are typically considered very quickly and may have shorter than average layover times, but they should be less likely to be complex.[59] Additionally, bills passed in response to the September 11 attacks in late 2001 were considered under extremely expedited procedures.[60] Finally, temporal factors may be important as well. Specifically, the number of *days left in a Congress* when a bill is placed on the legislative calendar (after being reported, bypassed, or discharged from its committees) may influence the likelihood that any of the tactics will be used. With less time less to legislate, layover times may be shorter, self-execution may be more likely in order to avoid delays, and bills may be more complex as legislation is compiled into large omnibus packages.

Results of the Analyses

Table 4.3 presents the results of analyses predicting the use of each tactic. The first column in the table presents the results of a Cox Proportional Hazards (CPH) regression model assessing the effect of the variables on layover time. CPH models are a type of duration model that assesses how variables affect the likelihood that an event will occur as time progresses. These models are common in medical studies, modeling the likelihood that patients will die. For this reason they are often termed "survival models," since they literally test how long a patient survives. In recent years duration models have been used in political studies to analyze numerous political phenomena such as congressional retirements (Box-Steffensmeier and Jones 1997) and policy adoption and repeal (Berry and Berry 1990; Ragusa 2010). These models are useful for testing layover times, since they literally test the effect of variables on the time that bills lay over before floor consideration begins.[61]

The results in column 1 strongly indicate that bills prioritized by the majority leadership are more likely to have short layover times. The coefficient for majority leadership priority bills is statistically significant in a positive direction.[62] With CPH models, a positive coefficient indicates that a variable increases the likelihood that duration will be short. For this analysis, positive coefficients can be understood to indicate that an

TABLE 4.3. **Predicting the use of information-restricting tactics, 106th to 111th Congresses**

	Model 1: Restricted layover	Model 2: Self-execution	Model 3: Bill complexity
Majority leadership priority bill	0.305**	0.011	0.699**
	(0.143)	(0.338)	(0.198)
Presidential priority bill	0.006	0.007	0.014
	(0.010)	(0.023)	(0.014)
Presidential priority bill × Divided government	<0.001	0.018	0.048**
	(0.015)	(0.034)	(0.022)
Interest group interest	0.006**	0.017**	0.064**
	(0.002)	(0.005)	(0.003)
Public salience	−0.009	0.094	−0.074*
	(0.030)	(0.067)	(0.043)
Committee chair relative ideology	0.090	−0.522	2.625**
	(0.406)	(0.994)	(0.566)
Polarization of key lawmakers	0.368	1.140	−5.103**
	(0.800)	(1.633)	(0.973)
Appropriations bill	0.366**	−0.769**	1.092**
	(0.125)	(0.339)	(0.167)
Number of committees	0.105**	0.136**	0.301**
	(0.035)	(0.069)	(0.046)
Considered under suspension of the rules	0.943**	—	−0.496**
	(0.165)		(0.219)
September 11 bill	1.740**	—	—
	(0.536)		
Days left in a Congress	0.001*	< 0.001	< −0.001
	(<0.001)	(0.001)	(<0.001)
107th Congress	−0.048	−0.193	0.748**
	(0.170)	(0.411)	(0.224)
108th Congress	−0.057	−0.744	1.299**
	(0.177)	(0.493)	(0.241)
109th Congress	−0.087	−0.340	1.808**
	(0.181)	(0.440)	(0.242)
110th Congress	−0.077	−0.180	1.934**
	(0.177)	(0.409)	(0.237)
111th Congress	−0.137	−0.193	2.161**
	(0.194)	(0.453)	(0.259)
Constant	—	−2.241	−0.972
		(2.200)	(1.293)
	$N = 501$	$N = 501$	$N = 501$
	BIC = 4957.386	ePCP = 0.701	Adj. R^2 = .647

Note: Significance tests are two-tailed; standard errors are in parentheses
*$p < 0.10$
**$p < 0.05$

increase in an independent variable increases the likelihood of a truncated layover time. Hazards ratios can be calculated from the coefficient
estimates. Here, hazard ratios can be interpreted as percentage changes
in the likelihood that a bill will have a reduced layover time. The hazard
ratio for majority leadership priority bills is 1.368. This means that bills
prioritized by the majority leadership are, on average, 37 percent more
likely than other bills to have reduced layover times.

Although presidential priorities do not appear to influence the leadership's use of reduced layover as a tactic, interest group interest in a bill
does. Bills that attract more interest group interest are significantly more
likely to have abbreviated layover periods. The predicted hazard ratio
for a 1 percent increase in interest group interest is 1.006, which can be
understood as a 0.6 percent increased likelihood of a reduced layover
for each 1 percent increase in spending by interested groups. This seems
small, but as figure 4.8 demonstrates, the magnitude of the effect can become quite large as the full range of interest group interest is considered.
Notably, an increase of one standard deviation in interest group interest
(about 23 percent) nets a 14 percent increased likelihood of a truncated
layover time.

These results hold despite the influence of several other factors. Con-

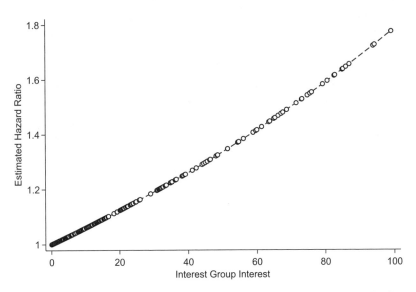

FIGURE 4.8. Predicted hazard ratio for interest group interest on bill layover. Hazard ratios
are derived from regression results in column 1 of table 4.3.

trary to expectations, appropriations bills appear more likely to be considered after a reduced layover. Appropriations measures are, on average, 44 percent more likely than other bills to have a reduced layover. This result likely reflects the increasingly partisan atmosphere surrounding spending bills. Additionally, bills referred to more committees are more likely to have reduced layover times. Specifically, each additional committee results in an 11 percent increased likelihood of an abbreviated layover. This reflects Sinclair's (2012) assertion that leadership influence over bills is more likely when bills are referred to more than one committee. Bills considered under suspension of the rules are also likely to be expedited. These bills are, on average, 2.5 times more likely than other bills to have a reduced layover. Finally, the days remaining in a Congress influences layover, but in the opposite direction than expected. Bills are actually more likely to have reduced layover early in a Congress. This may reflect the consideration of bills late in a session that have been on the calendar for months. It may also reflect the recent trend of frontloading the legislative agenda, with majorities in the House calling up and quickly passing key pieces of legislation in the first few weeks.[63]

Column 2 in table 4.3 presents the results of a logistic regression analysis predicting the likelihood that a bill will be self-executed. The results of this analysis indicate that the legislative priorities of neither the president nor the majority party leadership factor significantly into the decision to self-execute. The coefficient for majority leadership priority bills is in the expected direction, but it is not statistically significant. The same is true for the measures of presidential priorities. By contrast, the interest of outside groups appears to strongly and significantly influence the likelihood that a bill will be self-executed. Figure 4.9 presents the influence of interest group interest on the likelihood of self-execution. The predicted likelihood increases substantially as interest group interest becomes more intense. While the likelihood of self-execution is less than 20 percent when interest is low, bills subject to the most intense group interest appear to have a better than 40 percent likelihood of being self-executed.[64] These findings indicate that the decision to use this tactic is responsive to the threat of involvement of outside groups rather than to the planned priorities of the leadership. When the leaders believe the widespread political interest in a bill threatens their control and could focus lawmakers' attention on reasons to oppose it, they will alter and manage the bill through self-execution in ways that could not be done through an open and deliberative process.

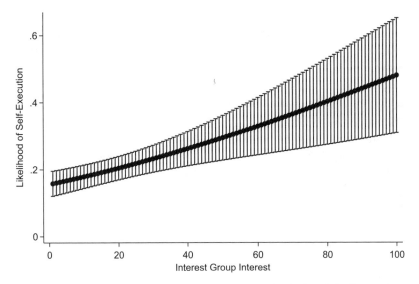

FIGURE 4.9. Predicted impact of interest group interest on the likelihood of self-execution.
Predicted likelihoods are derived from regression results in column 2 of table 4.3.

Two other factors also appear to influence the likelihood of self-execution. Appropriations bills are far less likely to be self-executed: the model predicts that appropriations bills will be 47 percent less likely than other bills to be self-executed. In this way, at least, the consideration of spending bills remains more traditional than with other legislation. Self-execution is more likely on bills referred to multiple committees. Bills referred to just one committee are predicted to have a 19 percent likelihood of self-execution. However, additional committees increase this likelihood at a rising rate. For example, bills referred to three committees have a 23 percent likelihood, and bills referred to six committees have a 30 percent likelihood of being self-executed. This again confirms Sinclair's (2012) assertion that the majority leadership is likely to use unorthodox tactics on bills referred to more than one committee.

Column 3 in table 4.3 presents the results of an OLS regression analysis predicting the complexity of each bill. The results confirm that majority leadership priority bills will be significantly more complex than other bills. Since the dependent variable is an index, substantive interpretation of the coefficient is difficult. However, its magnitude, 0.699, represents an increase in the index of almost one-third of a standard deviation. This is a fairly meaningful effect. The results also indicate that presidential priority items tend to be more complex. A truncated regression model without the interaction with divided government reports a positive, statistically significant coefficient of 0.033 for presidential priority bills.[65] Substantively, this coefficient indicates that an increase of one standard deviation in the number of mentions of an issue in the State of the Union address (about seven mentions) results in a 0.23 increase in the bill complexity index.

The interactive model provides more nuance to this relationship. Figure 4.10 plots the marginal effect of State of the Union mentions separately during unified and divided government. Note that most of the bills (about 58 percent) dealt with issues that did not receive attention in the State of the Union address, so any mention during the speech is relatively meaningful. The plot demonstrates that for issues mentioned a handful of times (less than seven mentions) bills are statistically more likely to be more complex during unified government than during divided government. However, as the number of mentions rises, the effect on bill complexity blurs between periods of unified and divided government, with the size of the confidence intervals swelling. These results show that presidential influence over the complexity of legislation is in-

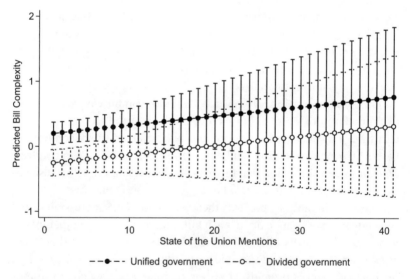

FIGURE 4.10. Marginal effect of presidential priority on bill complexity: unified vs. divided government. Predicted effects are derived from OLS regression results in column 3 of table 4.3.

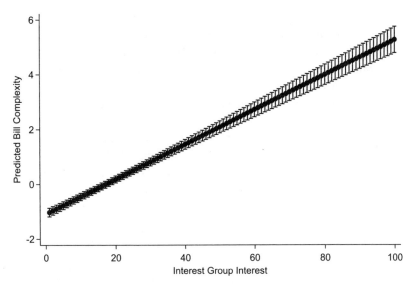

FIGURE 4.11. Predicted effect of interest group interest on bill complexity. Predicted effects are derived from OLS regression results in column 3 of table 4.3.

fluenced by party control of the House, but the issues presidents prioritize the most are treated similarly—at least in regard to bill complexity—during unified and divided government.

The results also show that interest group interest drives bill complexity. The coefficient is statistically significant and positive. Figure 4.11 presents the predicted effect of interest group interest on bill complexity. The figure shows that bills subject to substantial group interest are likely to be substantially complex. Specifically, bills attracting an average level of interest group interest (roughly 18 percent) are predicted to be around the mean of bill complexity (about 0.2 on the bill complexity index). However, bills subject to interest group interest one standard deviation above this average (roughly 41 percent) are predicted to have values of about 1.5 on the bill complexity index, more than half a standard deviation increase in the index.

Notably, this finding holds even after controlling for the number of committees each bill is referred to. While the larger number of issues addressed in many complex bills (as noted above, scope—the number of issue areas addressed in a bill—is one of the four factors in the bill complexity index) should attract more interest groups, controlling for the number of committees a bill is referred to, which is also related to the number of issues a bill addresses, does not wash out the significant influence of interest group interest. Neither does explicitly controlling for each bill's scope. The analysis was replicated controlling separately for each bill's scope, but the impact of interest group interest remains positive and statistically significant. This indicates that the influence of outside interests on a bill's complexity reflects more than just the number of issues it addresses.[66]

Several other factors also influence the complexity of legislation considered in the House. Unlike the other models, a bill's public salience significantly influences bill complexity: more salient bills tend to be less complex. This suggests that on issues attracting significant public attention bills are crafted so the meaning and intent are easily understood, perhaps to provide clear signals about the party's efforts to address issues of significant public concern. Additionally, polarization matters, but the relationship is the opposite of that expected. The more polarized the key actors are, the less complex the legislation. Moderate committee chairs, however, relate to increased bill complexity. Appropriations bills are also predicted to be more complex, probably reflecting the particular way appropriations measures are written. Not surprisingly, bills considered under suspension of the rules tend to be less complex. This reflects the contemporary use of the suspension calendar to pass relatively simple and noncontroversial pieces of legislation.

Additionally, the results indicate that bill complexity is increasing over time. The indicators for each Congress show that, all else equal, the typical bill is becoming more complex with each passing Congress. This result is not surprising, given the increased use of omnibus bills for major legislative achievements (see Krutz 2001; Sinclair 2012). However, since omnibus legislation encompasses only two of the four factors in bill complexity (size and scope), it is possible that this increase also reflects a tactical shift on the part of legislative leaders toward crafting important legislation to be more difficult to read, though this assertion is not tested here.

Although the results presented here generally support expectations about party leaders' strategic use of information-restricting tactics, results vary from tactic to tactic. While interest groups interest drives the use of all three tactics, majority leadership priorities influence a bill's layover and complexity but not its propensity to be self-executed. Similarly, presidential priorities significantly influence only the complexity of bills, not their layover or likelihood of self-execution. The variation may be due to the noise inherent in each measure. While the measures of majority leadership and presidential priorities generally capture which issues these leaders are focused on, as discussed above, they are somewhat noisy in that they, by design, capture all important bills addressing those issues. As such, these measures may understate the influence of leadership priorities. To this point, it is worth noting that these variables are always in the expected direction, even if they are not statistically significant. In short, while the variables do not have statistically significant results in every instance, the general thrust of the findings indicates that information restriction is used strategically to pursue leaders' goals and protect their interests.

Conclusion

Over the course of the conversations I had with members of Congress and their staffs, one person summed up the use of these tactics rather well:

> LEADERSHIP STAFFER: Now, they tend to go along, the majority does, with their leadership when a decision like that is made. "Well, we've got to get this done before such-and-such a date," or "There's a deadline and we didn't have the time to go through the full process." But other times I think it's, frankly, done to make sure people don't have too much time to look at it. It's an old political trick. If you've ever attended even a Young Democrats or a Young Republicans meeting and the leadership of that organization wants to put something through quickly, they don't give their members a day or even a few hours to look at something they're going to put to a vote. They'll pass it out and say, "Oh yeah, by the way, here's an amendment, any discussion?" You know, people are trying to read it the same time they're asking for discussion. But it's an old trick—the element of surprise.[67]

Restricting information widens the informational disparities between leaders and their rank and file. Lawmakers are already strapped for time and resources, and obtaining the information they need to make decisions is already difficult. The tactics described in this chapter make it harder and increase lawmakers' reliance on their legislative leaders.

By keeping the drafting under lock and key and controlling the release of information about the chairman's mark only late in the game, committee chairs can restrict what information is available about their committees' bills. Likewise, party leaders have a variety of tactics for limiting access: they limit the time rank-and-file members have to read and analyze legislation by reducing layover times, self-executing, and using bill complexity as a weapon. All these actions keep rank-and-file lawmakers in the dark throughout the legislative process, dependent on the information their leaders provide, and less likely to find reasons to oppose the bills their leaders push.

Legislative leaders in the House recognize that these tactics can help them achieve their goals and move legislation through the chamber. The multivariate analyses presented in this chapter demonstrate that they use these tactics strategically. The use of the tactics on priority legislation demonstrates that leaders are restricting information so as to achieve a key leadership goal—passing big-picture, partisan priority bills. Their use in response to significant political interest in a bill demonstrates that leaders use them to protect bills by heading off others' attempts to damage or kill them.

That leaders pick and choose when to use these tactics also suggests that they cannot be used without limit or on every bill. On some legislation it is unnecessary to aggressively restrict information. Leaders may believe they can let the process play out in a more open or deliberative manner yet achieve the same outcome. For members of Congress who want to have input, a process like this is more satisfying. Similarly, political conditions may force a less restricted approach. If a bill has broad public and lawmaker interest from the start, leaders may be forced to open up the process or at least be more forthcoming with information throughout. Nonetheless, as shown in table 4.1, leaders employ these tactics often—on about half of the important bills analyzed in this chapter.

Ultimately, by restricting the information available to rank-and-file lawmakers, the minority party, and other actors in the political sphere, legislative leaders are taking control of the legislative process and working to aid the passage of their priority legislation the way they have worked to craft it. The interview evidence presented in the previous chapters indicates that typical rank-and-file lawmakers find such tactics interfere with their ability to gather the information they need to make independent decisions and to become as involved as they might like. Generally, this study has suggested that lawmakers should be more likely to vote with their leaders on legislation when there is less information available, because they will have more trouble finding reasons to oppose the position their leaders have taken. The next chapter turns to the task of testing this assertion.

CHAPTER FIVE

Leadership-Driven Partisanship

The amount of information a member wants depends on how much they want to go against the leadership. Generally, most Democrats and Republicans know that they are going to vote with their party most of the time.—Rank-and-file member of Congress[1]

At 3:47 a.m. on June 26, 2009, the House Committee on Rules reported H.Res. 587, a special rule providing for the consideration of the American Clean Energy and Security Act of 2009 (H.R. 2454), a nearly 1,100-page bill that had been marked up and reported in May by the Committee on Energy and Commerce. The rule, which included two self-executing provisions, essentially took a hatchet to the version of the bill approved by the committee and replaced it with a bill the Democratic leaders believed would pass the House, achieve their policy goals, and represent a win for the party. The first self-executing provision struck the entire text of H.R. 2454 and replaced it with H.R. 2998, a newly introduced energy bill that had been negotiated and drafted by Henry Waxman (D-CA), chairman of the Committee on Energy and Commerce, Edward Markey (D-MA), chairman of the Select Committee on Energy Independence and Global Warming, and the Democratic leadership. The second provision was a 300-page amendment making various changes, big and small, throughout the text of H.R. 2998. It aimed primarily at winning the votes of midwestern and moderate Democrats unhappy with the committee's version of the bill by undercutting their reasons for opposition.

Combined, what the provisions made in order for consideration on the floor was a shell of H.R. 2454 with the text of H.R. 2998 inserted into it, along with a 300-page amendment. Because the changes were made so late and done in two separate self-executing provisions, no single integrated copy of the bill text was available. Instead, lawmakers would need to read the new 1,200-page bill for differences from the old 1,100-page text, while following along with the changes made by the 300-page amendment. Adding to the chaos, the Democratic leadership notified the chamber that the special rule would be considered on the floor later that morning and the bill would be debated and voted on by the end of the day, ostensibly so Democrats could claim victory on energy policy before heading home to see their constituents during the Fourth of July break. Under such severe time constraints, Democratic lawmakers would have to rely on Waxman, Markey, and their party leaders to explain why the changes resulted in a bill they should support. Republicans would have to turn to their leaders for a different argument.

Undoubtedly, only lawmakers deeply involved in the negotiations over the bill's final language could possibly have read the entire text or understood and considered each of its provisions before the vote. At least one Democrat, Representative Neil Abercrombie (D-HI), admitted to reporters that he did not have a chance read the bill and that "you'd have to have hours and hours and hours to be able to do all that, but we're well aware of the main items." He added, "Well, I think the overall goals of the bills need to be supported."[2] The 219 other lawmakers (all but eight were Democrats) who supported the bill must have felt the same. The information they had on the bill was enough to give them the confidence that the behemoth energy bill was something that they should support, or at least that they had no reason to oppose. Republicans, similarly limited in their ability to read the bill, clearly felt the opposite. Representative John Boehner (R-OH), then minority leader, spoke for an hour on the floor expressing his outrage. Boehner ultimately summed up his feelings, telling *The Hill* that the bill was a "pile of shit."[3] The GOP lawmakers who turned to Boehner's leadership offices for information on the bill were clearly not interested in voting for a mound of fecal matter.

The evidence in the previous chapters suggests that legislative leaders' informational tactics make rank-and-file lawmakers more dependent on their leaders for information and thus less likely to find reasons to oppose them. This chapter conducts several quantitative analyses of final passage votes on important bills considered from 1999 to 2010 to further test this relationship. The findings suggest that when party leaders use the information-restricting tactics identified in chapter 4—restricted layover, self-execution, or bill complexity—the final vote becomes more partisan, with majority members more likely to vote in favor and minority members more likely to vote in opposition.

Alone, the quantitative analyses presented in this chapter cannot establish the direction of causality between information-restricting tactics and the partisanship apparent on final passage votes or the specific votes cast by individual lawmakers. In other words, despite controlling for various independent variables that should predict the level of partisanship on each vote, these analyses cannot fully rule out the reverse causal story: that the leadership employs these tactics when they expect the vote to be particularly contentious. However, it is important to consider the results below in concert with the interview evidence presented in the previous chapters about how legislative leaders can control the information lawmakers have and thus influence how they view the legislation being considered. Combined, the quantitative and qualitative evidence at least suggests that these tactics contribute to the partisan nature of roll-call outcomes.[4]

The analyses below focus on party leaders largely because similar analyses are not possible on committee votes. As described in the chapter 4, committee leaders' uses of informational tactics are not publicly recorded. Without knowing when and how committee leaders use these tactics, their effects cannot be analyzed. Nevertheless, there is no reason to believe that when they are used the effects are any different. Without information, lawmakers will need to turn to their committee leaders and staff for insight. If anything, the effects should be more pronounced in committee.[5]

Ultimately, the polarizing effects of information restriction by the majority party leadership suggests that leaders can use such tactics to secure votes by keeping their own rank and file from finding compelling reasons to vote with the opposition. This helps party leaders induce their caucuses to act like responsible, programmatic parties; however, it raises important questions, discussed at the end of the chapter, about the quality of representation and deliberations in congressional policymaking.

Information Restriction and Partisan Voting Behavior

There are several ways to assess how much restricting information increases partisan voting on the floor of the House. Here I present the results of two sets of tests. The first set uses each bill in the dataset of important legislation as the unit of analysis. Three dependent variables are analyzed. The first is the Rice index of party difference on the final passage vote for each bill (Rice 1928). This measure captures the absolute difference between the proportion of the majority and minority parties voting in favor of passage. The bigger the value, the more polarized the vote. The next two dependent variables are dichotomous indicators of party votes on final passage: the first indicates if more than 50 percent of each party voted against the other, and the second if at least 90 percent of each party voted against the other. Combined, these three dependent variables identify the how greatly information-restriction drives partisanship on final passage votes.

The primary independent variables for these tests are the measures of each tactic: restricted layover, self-execution, and bill complexity. For these tests, layover time is log-transformed to reflect the expectation that there is probably a decreasing effect for each additional hour of bill layover. In other words, a change from ten to one hundred hours of layover likely has a larger effect on the ability of the typical lawmaker to become informed on a bill than a change from 3,010 to 3,100 hours. The other tactics are measured the same way as in chapter 4. In addition, layover time and bill complexity are interacted in the analyses to test for the possibility that the effects of bill complexity are more pronounced when lawmakers have less time to consider the bill, as some of the interviewees suggested.[6] The use of each of these tactics is expected to increase the likelihood of a party vote, and the degree of difference between the parties, on final passage votes.

Included in these tests are a number of bill-specific control variables that may also predict partisan voting. The first indicates if a bill was a *majority leadership priority bill*, as defined in chapter 4. On priority bills it is likely that the majority leadership pushes members harder to vote with the party than on other bills. The indicator of *presidential priority bills*, as defined in chapter 4, is included as well. Lee (2008) shows that congressional parties are systematically more polarized on presidential agenda items. The tests also include the measure of the *polarization of key lawmakers* used in chapter 4, since issues that polarize the lawmakers most likely to be engaged on the issue are likely to be more polarizing in general. An indicator for *appropriations bills* is included, since spending measures have historically found more consensus on the House floor than other measures. Bills *considered under suspension of the rules* also typically result in more consensus, since they require a two-thirds majority for passage. In addition, the *number of commit-tees* a bill is referred to may influence the likelihood of a party vote. On one hand, if the bill was considered by several committees, more members of Congress may feel they have a stake in its passage. However Sinclair (2012) notes that multiple referral tends to lead to more unorthodox lawmaking procedures, including committee bypass and leadership domination of policymaking. Under these conditions a party vote may be more likely.

Temporal considerations may be important as well. The number of *days left in a Congress* when a bill is placed on the calendar may be important, since lawmakers on both sides of the aisle may feel more pressure to support a bill later in a session because they decide something is better than nothing. Finally, since the parties have become increasingly polarized over the period studied here, dichotomous indicators for the Congress in which each bill is considered are included (with the 106th Congress excluded). Since each Congress since the 106th has been more partisan than the last, partisan voting should be more likely in later Congresses than in earlier ones.[7]

The second set of tests assesses each individual vote cast by each member of Congress on final passage on each bill in the dataset. The purpose is to determine if restricting information increases the likelihood of lawmakers' voting for or against a bill, controlling for both bill-specific and lawmaker-specific influences. Tests are run separately for members of the majority and minority parties at the time of each vote. The dependent variable is coded as one if lawmakers voted in favor of passage and zero if they voted against passage. Missed votes and "present" votes are not included. The primary independent variables, bill-specific variables, and temporal variables are the same for these analyses as for the bill-level analyses.

Additionally, two lawmaker-specific variables are included in these analyses to control for major factors in vote choice. The first is each lawmaker's voting tendencies, measured as the absolute value of each one's first-dimension DW-NOMINATE scores. Controlling for this factor is crucial to demonstrate that information-restricting tactics influence voting irrespective of each lawmaker's place in their party's "ideological" spectrum. Since the absolute values are used, higher values indicate members on the extreme ends of each caucus. Second, the partisan character of each lawmaker's district is controlled for as well. Lawmakers from more moderate districts or swing districts should be less likely, on average, to consistently vote with their party. *District partisanship* is measured using the percentage of the two-party vote won by the presidential candidate from each lawmaker's party in the most recent presidential election. In the resulting measure, larger values indicate the district is more partisan in favor of the lawmaker and should predict an increased likelihood that majority lawmakers will vote for any bill and a decreased likelihood that minority lawmakers will vote for any bill.

The results of each analysis are presented below. First, table 5.1 presents OLS regression analyses predicting the Rice index of party difference on the final passage votes for each bill in the dataset that received such a vote. The first three columns show results with indicators for each of the information-restricting tactics separately, then they are combined in column 4. As a whole, the results suggest that more complex bills and self-executed bills produce significantly more divisive splits between the parties. The models in both columns 1 and 4 indicate that a one-unit increase in the bill complexity index scale increases the Rice index by almost three points (on a scale of 0 to 100). More to the point, an increase of one standard deviation in bill complexity (roughly 2.5 units) increases the Rice index by more than seven points. The more complex the bill, the more divided the parties are on the final passage vote.

Similarly, the results indicate that when the majority leadership chooses to self-execute legislation, it injects more partisanship into the proceedings. The results in column 4 suggest that self-executed bills produce final passage votes that are, on average, seven points higher on the Rice index of party difference scale. When the majority leadership uses the Rules Committee to change the contents of a bill at the last second, such as with the American Clean Energy and Security Act of 2009, rank-and-file majority lawmakers become dependent on their leaders' messages about the changes and are more likely to vote in favor of the bill. Minority lawmakers, similarly, rely on their leaders for information on why the bill is horse manure and are more likely to vote against it. Contrary to expectation, layover time does not appear to significantly influence the degree of disagreement between the parties. In the results presented in columns 2 and 4, layover time is in the expected direction (with longer layover times producing less partisanship), but the effect is not statistically significant. The interaction between layover time and bill complexity also does not produce a significant effect. Although the significance test for the interaction term in the regression is not a reliable indicator of the actual significance of the interaction (Brambor, Clark,

TABLE 5.I. **Predicted Rice Index, 106th to 111th Congresses**

	1	2	3	4
Information-restricting tactics				
Bill complexity index	2.920**	—	—	2.644**
	(0.678)			(0.821)
Layover hours (logged)	—	−0.291	—	−0.455
		(0.480)		(0.478)
Self−execution	—	—	9.698**	7.062*
			(3.737)	(3.767)
Bill complexity index × Layover hours (logged)	—	—	—	0.024
				(0.164)
Bill-specific variables				
Majority leadership priority	2.300	4.514	5.181	2.096
	(4.331)	(4.424)	(4.346)	(4.392)
Presidential priority	0.425*	0.629**	0.594**	0.408*
	(0.240)	(0.240)	(0.238)	(0.240)
Polarization of key lawmakers	83.746**	60.561**	59.898**	80.014**
	(20.389)	(20.152)	(19.979)	(20.450)
Appropriations bill	−14.492**	−10.008**	−8.330**	−13.016**
	(3.740)	(3.664)	(3.693)	(3.830)
Number of committees	1.762*	2.619**	2.446**	1.548
	(1.040)	(1.044)	(1.035)	(1.050)
Considered under suspension of the rules	−41.995**	−44.581**	−40.211**	−41.678**
	(4.728)	(5.208)	(4.933)	(5.224)
Days left in a Congress	0.005	0.004	0.005	0.005
	(0.008)	(0.008)	(0.008)	(0.008)
Congress				
107th Congress	−12.582**	−11.408**	−11.526**	−12.440**
	(4.760)	(4.852)	(4.815)	(4.755)
108th Congress	−10.807**	−7.153	−6.778	−9.818*
	(5.183)	(5.237)	(5.193)	(5.199)
109th Congress	−8.002	−2.606	−2.631	−7.743
	(5.366)	(5.324)	(5.286)	(5.390)
110th Congress	5.342	11.081**	11.003**	5.134
	(5.102)	(5.027)	(4.976)	(5.120)
111th Congress	8.261	13.836**	13.201**	7.875
	(5.576)	(5.531)	(5.495)	(5.578)
Constant	−31.119*	−14.601	−18.058	−28.336
	(18.774)	(19.094)	(18.718)	(18.981)
	$N = 453$	$N = 453$	$N = 453$	$N = 453$
	$R^2 = 0.289$	$R^2 = 0.259$	$R^2 = 0.270$	$R^2 = 0.291$

Note: Coefficients are estimated using OLS regression; significance tests are two-tailed; standard errors are in parentheses.
*$p < 0.10$
** $p < 0.05$

and Golder 2006; Ai and Norton 2003), a plot of the predicted effects of bill complexity varying with layover time confirms that there is no substantive interactive relationship.[8]

The null findings with the layover measure may be a consequence of its noisy nature. Compared with the measures of self-execution and bill complexity, the measure of layover time is less precise. As constructed, the measure may at times overestimate how much time lawmakers have to review legislative language, while at other times it likely underestimates it. For example, the measure conceptualizes layover as the number of hours that elapse between the time when the final committee reports the bill, or otherwise has it discharged, and when floor consideration begins. However, the full text of legislation is rarely made available immediately after a committee finishes its work. There is often a lag, and the length of that delay can vary. At the same time, on some bills the leadership may distribute bill language to its members before the bill is officially placed on the House calendar. That the coefficient is in the expected direction suggests that a more precise measure may have had a statistically significant effect.

Ultimately, the results show that when leaders restrict access to information there is more partisanship on final passage votes. The next two sets of analyses provide additional support for this conclusion. Table 5.2 presents the results of logistic regression analyses predicting a 50 percent party vote, and table 5.3 presents the results of similar analyses predicting a 90 percent party vote on final passage of each bill. Regarding a 50 percent party vote, the results in column 1 and column 4 both indicate that complex bills increase the likelihood of such a vote. Specifically, while bills one standard deviation below the mean of bill complexity have a 34 percent chance of receiving a 50 percent party vote on final passage, bills one standard deviation above the mean of bill complexity have a 61 percent chance.[9] This is equal to a 79 percent increased likelihood.

The amount of time a bill lays over also influences the likelihood of a 50 percent party vote. In column 2 and column 4, shorter layover times predict more partisanship on final passage votes: bills with layover times one standard deviation above the mean of layover (logged) have a 41 percent chance of a 50 percent party vote, while bills with layover times one standard deviation below the mean have a 56 percent chance. This is equal to a 37 percent increased likelihood. The interaction between bill layover and bill complexity appears statistically significant in

TABLE 5.2. **Predicted likelihood of a 50 percent party vote, 106th to 111th Congresses**

	1	2	3	4
Information-restricting tactics				
Bill complexity index	0.207**	—	—	0.348**
	(0.057)			(0.089)
Layover hours (logged)	—	−0.078*	—	−0.134**
		(0.041)		(0.048)
Self−execution	—	—	0.276	0.124
			(0.278)	(0.292)
Bill complexity index × Layover hours (logged)	—	—	—	−0.037**
				(0.017)
Bill-specific variables				
Majority leadership priority	0.090	0.178	0.252	−0.005
	(0.333)	(0.332)	(0.326)	(0.341)
Presidential priority	0.042**	0.052**	0.052**	0.036*
	(0.020)	(0.020)	(0.020)	(0.020)
Polarization of key lawmakers	8.685**	6.442**	6.612**	8.699**
	(1.824)	(1.665)	(1.676)	(1.852)
Appropriations bill	−0.682**	−0.374	−0.326	−0.648**
	(0.285)	(0.267)	(0.270)	(0.293)
Number of committees	0.265**	0.296**	0.301**	0.221*
	(0.115)	(0.111)	(0.111)	(0.113)
Considered under suspension of the rules	−4.009**	−4.286**	−3.801**	−5.147**
	(0.687)	(0.703)	(0.664)	(0.945)
Days left in a Congress	<−0.001	<0.001	<−0.001	<0.001
	(0.001)	(0.001)	(0.001)	(0.001)
Congress				
107th Congress	−1.001**	−0.795**	−0.834**	−0.966**
	(0.377)	(0.367)	(0.367)	(0.377)
108th Congress	−0.908**	−0.570	−0.599	−0.901**
	(0.395)	(0.381)	(0.380)	(0.400)
109th Congress	−0.971**	−0.504	−0.533	−0.929**
	(0.406)	(0.384)	(0.383)	(0.413)
110th Congress	−0.019	0.364	0.395	−0.175
	(0.393)	(0.374)	(0.373)	(0.403)
111th Congress	0.482	0.857**	0.846**	0.497
	(0.449)	(0.431)	(0.431)	(0.461)
Constant	−7.883**	−5.933**	−6.459**	−7.380**
	(1.677)	(1.570)	(1.573)	(1.698)
	$N = 453$	$N = 453$	$N = 453$	$N = 453$
	ePCP=0.653	ePCP=0.649	ePCP=0.645	ePCP=0.661

Note: Coefficients are estimated using logistic regression; significance tests are two-tailed; standard errors are in parentheses.
*$p < 0.10$
**$p < 0.05$

TABLE 5.3. **Predicted likelihood of a 90 percent party Vote, 106th to 111th Congresses**

	1	2	3	4
Information-restricting tactics				
Bill complexity index	0.359**	—	—	0.367**
	(0.063)			(0.092)
Layover hours (logged)	—	0.026	—	<0.001
		(0.044)		(0.049)
Self-execution	—	—	0.923**	0.573*
			(0.288)	(0.313)
Bill complexity index × Layover hours (logged)	—	—	—	−0.009
				(0.019)
Bill-specific variables				
Majority leadership priority	−0.240	0.106	0.110	−0.175
	(0.389)	(0.359)	(0.357)	(0.399)
Presidential priority	0.040**	0.056**	0.053**	0.039**
	(0.019)	(0.018)	(0.018)	(0.019)
Polarization of key lawmakers	6.796**	3.558**	3.470*	6.645**
	(2.024)	(1.808)	(1.828)	(2.061)
Appropriations bill	−0.714**	−0.182	0.020	−0.557
	(0.363)	(0.337)	(0.350)	(0.379)
Number of committees	−0.070	0.060	0.024	−0.088
	(0.094)	(0.084)	(0.090)	(0.101)
Considered under suspension of the rules	−3.030**	−2.713**	−2.454**	−2.899**
	(1.078)	(1.044)	(1.038)	(1.191)
Days left in a Congress	0.001*	0.001	0.001*	0.002*
	(0.001)	(0.001)	(0.001)	(0.001)
Congress				
107th Congress	−0.843*	−0.630	−0.583	−0.785
	(0.501)	(0.483)	(0.482)	(0.502)
108th Congress	−0.644	−0.194	−0.117	−0.559
	(0.498)	(0.474)	(0.481)	(0.505)
109th Congress	−0.994*	−0.238	−0.241	−0.910*
	(0.514)	(0.476)	(0.484)	(0.520)
110th Congress	−0.749	0.041	0.009	−0.730
	(0.477)	(0.437)	(0.445)	(0.487)
111th Congress	−0.199	0.531	0.456	−0.181
	(0.480)	(0.441)	(0.452)	(0.487)
Constant	−7.895**	−5.575**	−5.752**	−8.001**
	(1.944)	(1.797)	(1.791)	(2.007)
	N = 453	N = 453	N = 453	N = 453
	ePCP=0.763	ePCP=0.732	ePCP=0.740	ePCP=0.766

Note: Coefficients are estimated using logistic regression; significance tests are two-tailed; standard errors are in parentheses.
*$p < 0.10$
**$p < 0.05$

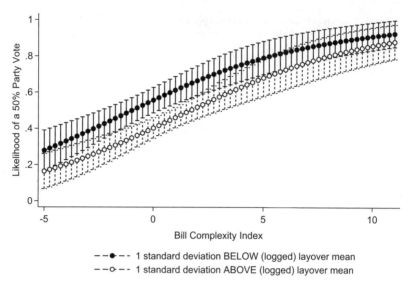

FIGURE 5.1. Interactional effect of layover and bill complexity on the likelihood of a 50 percent party vote.

the results presented in column 4, and a plot of the predicted effects confirms an interactive relationship. Figure 5.1 presents the predicted effect of bill complexity on the likelihood of a 50 percent party vote separately for bills with short layovers (one standard deviation below the mean of layover) and those with relative long layovers (one standard deviation above the mean), along with 95 percent confidence intervals. The results indicate that while at low and high levels of complexity there is no significant difference in voting behavior between bills with short and long layovers (owing to the overlap of the confidence intervals), around the mean of bill complexity (0.05) the predicted effects are statistically different. This suggests that for moderately complex bills, layover can magnify the effects of bill complexity, causing lawmakers to be even more likely to cast partisan votes. By contrast, among simpler bills layover is not a problem, and among the most complex bills it does not appear that any amount of time is sufficient—lawmakers are likely to vote in a partisan way regardless.

Unlike bill complexity and layover, self-execution does not increase the likelihood of a 50 percent party vote, though the coefficient is in the predicted direction. However, as shown in table 5.3, self-execution significantly increases the likelihood of a 90 percent party vote on the final passage of a bill. Specifically, the model in column 4 predicts that self-executed bills have a 24 percent chance of a 90 percent party vote on final passage, while all other bills have just a 16 percent chance. This is a 50 percent increased likelihood of a highly partisan vote. Again, complexity is important: the analysis presented in column 4 predicts that bills one standard deviation below the mean of complexity have a 9 percent chance of a highly partisan floor vote, while bills one standard deviation above the mean have a 31 percent chance. Layover time, by contrast, does not appear to significantly affect a bill's likelihood of a highly partisan vote on final passage. Similarly, the effect of bill complexity is not conditioned by layover.[10]

Across these analyses there is substantial evidence that restricting information on important bills increases the partisanship apparent on final passage votes. Among the tests of the Rice index, the results suggest that bill complexity and self-execution both increase the difference apparent between the parties. For the tests predicting the likelihood of a 50 percent party vote, complexity and reduced layover increase the likelihood of a final passage vote split along partisan lines. For the tests predicting the likelihood of highly partisan votes (90 percent party votes), the results indicate that complex bills and self-executed bills are more likely than other bills to result in strict party-line voting on final passage.

Bill complexity has the most robust effect on partisanship, with every test indicating that more complexity results in more partisanship. On highly complex bills lawmakers turn to their leaders for information, providing the majority leadership with opportunities to encourage their rank and file to support the bill on the floor. Self-execution influenced partisanship in two of the three sets of tests. When changes are made through the Rules Committee late in the legislative process—almost always immediately before floor consideration—rank-and-file lawmakers have to rely on their leaders to tell them what changes have been made and what they mean. The partisan information they are provided ultimately produces more partisanship on the final passage votes. Layover time influences partisanship in one of the three sets of tests. Specifically, short bill layover increases the likelihood of a 50 percent party-line vote on final passage. When there is little time for lawmakers to understand a bill's contents and implications, it appears that many of them default to their partisanship or turn to the information their leaders provide in deciding how to vote.

These results hold despite controlling for numerous predictors of party voting, including several that had significant effects in the tests. Across all the tests, the polarization of key lawmakers was important. The more polarized these key actors, the more polarized the final votes on the floor of the House. Bills addressing issues given priority by presidents in State of the Union addresses also typically received more partisan final passage votes. This confirms Lee's (2008) finding about the polarizing effect of presidential involvement in policymaking. Additionally, on every test, votes on bills considered under suspension of the rules were less partisan, as were appropriations bills.

While these results demonstrate the polarizing effect of restricting information, they do not provide details about the dynamics of this effect. In other words, the tests described above cannot determine if the increased likelihood of partisanship is caused by increased cohesion among just majority lawmakers, among just minority lawmakers, or on both sides. They also cannot determine if these functional dynamics vary depending on the tactic employed. However, tests assessing the effect of information-restricting tactics on the vote choices of each lawmaker on each bill can uncover these dynamics. Generally speaking, each tactic should increase the likelihood that majority lawmakers will support a bill on the floor of the House and decrease the likelihood that minority lawmakers will support it.[11]

Table 5.4 presents the results of analyses predicting the likelihood that majority lawmakers will vote yea on each bill in the dataset that received a final passage vote. The results generally indicate that restricting information increases support among majority lawmakers. As with the bill-level analyses, the results are presented with each tactic analyzed individually and then combined. The results in column 1 provide some evidence that bill complexity increases majority lawmakers' likelihood of voting yea. The coefficient is positive and statistically significant, but the substantive effect is small. Majority lawmakers, on average, have a 92.5 percent likelihood of voting yea on bills one standard deviation below the mean of bill complexity, but a 93.5 percent likelihood on bills one standard deviation above the mean. Again, this predicted change is small, but it is necessarily so. Majority lawmakers, on average, were tremendously likely to support all the bills analyzed here. Specifically, from the 106th to the 111th Congresses, majority lawmakers voted yea more than 93 percent of the time, so there is limited room for improvement. The majority party leadership is often working at the margins in trying to persuade their rank and file to support legislation. The

TABLE 5.4. **Likelihood of voting yea, majority lawmakers, 106th to 111th Congresses**

	1	2	3	4
Information-restricting tactics				
Bill complexity index	0.032**	—	—	0.006
	(0.006)			(0.009)
Layover hours (logged)	—	−0.036**	—	−0.035**
		(0.005)		(0.005)
Self-execution	—	—	0.108**	0.103**
			(0.032)	(0.033)
Bill complexity index ×	—	—	—	0.007**
Layover hours (logged)				(0.002)
Bill-specific variables				
Majority leadership priority	0.778**	0.769**	0.814**	0.753**
	(0.046)	(0.046)	(0.046)	(0.047)
Presidential priority	−0.001	0.001	0.001	−0.002
	(0.002)	(0.002)	(0.002)	(0.002)
Polarization of key lawmakers	−0.210	−0.541**	−0.476**	−0.317
	(0.190)	(0.184)	(0.183)	(0.192)
Appropriations bill	0.143**	0.190**	0.211**	0.161**
	(0.035)	(0.033)	(0.034)	(0.035)
Number of committees	−0.115**	−0.114**	−0.109**	−0.120**
	(0.007)	(0.007)	(0.007)	(0.007)
Considered under suspension	0.570**	0.441**	0.607**	0.503**
of the rules	(0.060)	(0.063)	(0.061)	(0.064)
Days left in a Congress	0.001**	0.001**	0.001**	0.001**
	(<0.001)	(<0.001)	(<0.001)	(<0.001)
Lawmaker-specific variables				
DW-NOMINATE	−2.540**	−2.540**	−2.539**	−2.542**
(absolute value)	(0.093)	(0.093)	(0.093)	(0.093)
District partisanship	0.037**	0.037**	0.037**	0.037**
	(0.002)	(0.002)	(0.002)	(0.002)
Congress				
107th Congress	−0.046	−0.027	−0.038*	−0.047
	(0.042)	(0.042)	(0.042)	(0.042)
108th Congress	0.283**	0.332**	0.329**	0.307**
	(0.047)	(0.046)	(0.046)	(0.047)
109th Congress	0.237**	0.299**	0.297**	0.224**
	(0.049)	(0.047)	(0.047)	(0.049)
110th Congress	−0.003	0.039	0.062	−0.033
	(0.053)	(0.051)	(0.051)	(0.054)
111th Congress	−0.337**	−0.288**	−0.279**	−0.376**
	(0.057)	(0.056)	(0.056)	(0.058)
Constant	1.740**	2.138**	1.889**	1.950**
	(0.196)	(0.196)	(0.193)	(0.199)
	$N = 90{,}947$	$N = 90{,}947$	$N = 90{,}947$	$N = 90{,}947$
	ePCP=0.873	ePCP=0.873	ePCP=0.873	ePCP=0.873

Note: Coefficients are estimated using logistic regression; significance tests are two-tailed; standard errors are in parentheses.
*$p < 0.10$
**$p < 0.05$

goal is to secure 218 votes, and often the leadership is targeting a vote total right around that number, so the addition or subtraction of just a few
votes can be significant.

Layover time also influences the votes of majority lawmakers. Specifically, the results in columns 2 and 4 both show that the longer a bill lays
over, the less likely it is that a member of the majority party will vote for
it. Specifically, majority lawmakers have an average 92.3 percent likelihood of voting for bills with layovers one standard deviation above the
mean, but a 93.7 percent likelihood for bills one standard deviation below the mean. When bills are available for less time, majority lawmakers are less likely to find reasons to oppose a bill and more likely to go
along with their party and support it. The results in column 4 indicate
there might be an interactive relationship between bill complexity and
layover, and analysis of the predicted effects confirms this finding. Figure 5.2 shows the predicted effect of bill complexity on the likelihood
of majority lawmakers' voting yea for bills with short and long layovers.
The graph indicates that for all except the most complex bills, those with
shorter layovers are even more likely than those with longer layovers to
induce majority support. The two tactics intensify each other's effects,
but when bills are exceptionally complex, no amount of layover appears

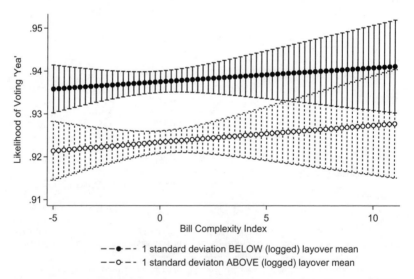

FIGURE 5.2. Interactional effect of layover and bill complexity on the likelihood of a majority lawmaker's voting Yea.

to mute the effect. Finally, self-execution also appears to increase majority support for bills on the floor: majority lawmakers have a 93.5 percent
likelihood of voting for self-executed bills, compared with a 92.8 percent
likelihood of voting for all other bills.

Once again, the substantive impact of these tactics does not look impressive, but it is important to recall that using informational tactics on
any bill likely does more to keep majority lawmakers from voting *against*
the bill than to bring additional lawmakers on board. Since most lawmakers default to voting with their party in the absence of compelling
information to the contrary, the leadership's goal in using these tactics
is not necessarily to increase majority support, but to minimize defections. At the very least, these analyses demonstrate that when information is restricted, the majority is significantly less likely to have its members vote against the bill. In an era of small majorities, such as the one
studied here, this is a meaningful result. From the 106th to the 111th
Congresses, the majority averaged just 232 members in the House (a
fourteen-seat majority). Preserving even a few majority votes can make
the difference between success and failure.

Taken together, these results indicate that part of the way information-
restricting tactics increase partisanship on final passage votes is by preserving majority support. But this is only half of the story. The results
presented in table 5.5 indicate that restricting information saps minority support for legislation as well. Complex bills generally find less support among minority lawmakers on the floor. Specifically, minority lawmakers have, on average, a 60 percent likelihood of supporting a bill one
standard deviation below the mean of bill complexity, but just a 46 percent likelihood of supporting a bill one standard deviation above that
mean. In other words, members of the minority party are 23 percent less
likely to vote for a bill when it is relatively complex than when it is relatively simple.

Layover matters as well. Among bills that had layover times one
standard deviation above the mean, minority lawmakers had a 56 percent likelihood of providing support. But among bills with layover periods one standard deviation below the mean, that chance of support was
51 percent. Self-execution has similar effects: minority lawmakers have,
on average, a 46 percent chance of supporting self-executed legislation
compared with a 56 percent chance of supporting all other bills. There
is also evidence of an interactive effect between layover time and bill
complexity. The coefficient for the interaction is statistically significant,

TABLE 5.5. **Likelihood of voting yea, minority lawmakers, 106th to 111th Congresses**

	1	2	3	4
Information-restricting tactics				
Bill complexity index	−0.139**	—		−0.112**
	(0.004)			(0.005)
Layover hours (logged)	—	0.033**		0.043**
		(0.003)		(0.003)
Self-execution	—	—	−0.569**	−0.475**
			(0.020)	(0.020)
Bill complexity index × Layover hours (logged)	—	—	—	−0.005**
				(0.001)
Bill-specific variables				
Majority leadership priority	−0.226*	−0.286**	−0.338**	−0.195**
	(0.023)	(0.023)	(0.022)	(0.023)
Presidential priority	−0.016**	−0.023**	−0.022**	−0.014**
	(0.001)	(0.001)	(0.001)	(0.001)
Polarization of key lawmakers	−3.609**	−2.239**	−2.310**	−3.312**
	(0.121)	(0.114)	(0.116)	(0.122)
Appropriations bill	0.808**	0.603**	0.497**	0.708**
	(0.020)	(0.019)	(0.020)	(0.021)
Number of committees	−0.065**	−0.095**	−0.094**	−0.056**
	(0.006)	(0.006)	(0.006)	(0.006)
Considered under suspension of the rules	2.247**	2.316**	1.989**	2.229**
	(0.041)	(0.042)	(0.041)	(0.045)
Days left in a Congress	−0.001**	−0.001**	−0.001**	−0.001**
	(<0.001)	(<0.001)	(<0.001)	(<0.001)
Lawmaker-specific variables				
DW-NOMINATE (absolute value)	−3.085**	−3.037**	−3.070**	−3.124**
	(0.072)	(0.072)	(0.072)	(0.073)
District partisanship	−0.007**	−0.006**	−0.006**	−0.006**
	(0.001)	(0.001)	(0.001)	(0.001)
Congress				
107th Congress	0.876**	0.777**	0.829**	0.887**
	(0.027)	(0.027)	(0.027)	(0.027)
108th Congress	0.768**	0.564**	0.555**	0.719**
	(0.028)	(0.027)	(0.027)	(0.028)
109th Congress	0.745**	0.451**	0.460**	0.736**
	(0.029)	(0.027)	(0.028)	(0.029)
110th Congress	1.153**	0.861**	0.881**	1.220**
	(0.034)	(0.033)	(0.033)	(0.034)
111th Congress	0.258**	−0.029	0.012	0.299**
	(0.040)	(0.039)	(0.039)	(0.040)
Constant	4.841**	3.651**	4.073**	4.576**
	(0.122)	(0.120)	(0.120)	(0.125)
	N = 79,204	N = 79,204	N = 79,204	N = 79,204
	ePCP=0.599	ePCP=0.592	ePCP=0.596	ePCP=0.604

Note: Coefficients are estimated using logistic regression; significance tests are two-tailed; standard errors are in parentheses.
*$p < 0.10$
**$p < 0.05$

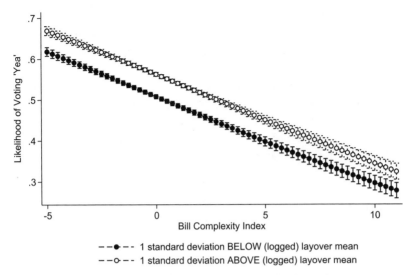

FIGURE 5.3. Interactional effect of layover and bill complexity on the likelihood of a minority lawmaker's voting Yea.

and analysis of the predicted effects confirms a strong relationship (see fig. 5.3). Across the range of bill complexity, bills with shorter layover periods garnered even less minority support.

In short, the degree of support for legislation on the floor of the House is substantially influenced by how much the majority party leadership restricts access to information. When less information is available, minority leaders can more easily line up their rank and file against the bill and establish a contrast with the majority. This suggests that restricting information is a double-edged sword for the majority leadership. By keeping things under wraps, they can keep lawmakers on their side of the aisle in line. However, there is a steep cost in terms of support from the minority. Ultimately, this dynamic suggests that the majority may be unable to use these tactics successfully when significant minority support is necessary for a bill to pass.

These findings hold despite controlling for several variables that strongly predict the vote choices of both majority and minority lawmakers, including their relative ideologies, the partisan leanings of their districts, and the emphasis placed on particular bills and issues by the majority party leadership and the president.[12] As a whole, these results paint a stark picture about the dynamics of how environments where information is manipulated affect the decisions made by individual lawmakers and by the House of Representatives as a whole. When typical lawmakers are faced with limited information about the bill they are considering, whether because the bill is difficult to parse and understand, because it is being considered quickly, because its contents were changed at the last minute, or because of some combination of the three, they become more partisan, either because they fall back on their partisanship to make a decision, because the information their leaders give them reinforces their partisan leanings, or both.

Conclusion

The regression results presented in this chapter, obviously, cannot by themselves prove that lawmakers' partisan votes are caused by information restriction. But taken in concert with the previous chapters, these findings strongly suggest that leaders can leverage their informational advantage to influence votes in the House. Recall that each of the tactics analyzed here is used by the majority leadership largely to advance key legislative priorities and to minimize the influence of other political voices that may threaten its goals. This suggests that by employing these tactics the leadership is able to ensure more majority support for these key items in these key situations. By limiting how thoroughly individual lawmakers can independently analyze the legislation before them and hear the viewpoints of a variety of sources, the leadership can keep more of the majority in line, minimizing the likelihood that members will find compelling reasons to oppose their leaders and vote against the party. These results suggest that legislative leaders can exercise impressive influence over congressional policymaking by using their procedural prerogatives to exploit the asymmetrical possession of information within the chamber.

These results also suggest that, to a degree, partisan polarization in the House of Representatives is related to the way leaders manage the legislative process. The more restrictive their tactics, the more polarized the parties on the final vote. Some of the polarized behavior is undoubtedly due to the issues and topics addressed by the bills they are used on. If leaders are using these tactics on the items they consider most important, these may be issues that already divide the parties. However, the analyses presented here control for the priority placed on each issue by the majority leadership and the president, as well as the polarization of key actors on each issue. Irrespective of these controls, restricting information leads to more partisan votes.

While these results are a boon for the leadership, they raise important concerns about the nature of policymaking in the House. On one hand, advocates of strong, responsible parties should be pleased. The leaders of each party can use these tactics to line up their rank and file on votes, establishing contrasts for the next election. In this way party leaders can get their caucuses to function like programmatic parties in a political system that has numerous impediments to such behavior. On the other hand, these results suggest that the majority leadership is able to diminish the deliberative nature of the House of Representative. By restricting information and accelerating the legislative process, leaders are minimizing the voices and influence on policymaking of representatives, interests, and ultimately constituents. The process becomes decisively top-down, driven by the goals and interests of those in leadership posts. Chapter 8 discusses this concern in more detail.

Ultimately, legislative leaders' abilities to manage the flow of information in the House and restrict access to information by members of Congress and groups outside Capitol Hill allows them to take control of policymaking and line up votes. Knowing these tactics are effective if they use them well in committee and on the floor, leaders can exercise great influence over how laws are crafted and what is passed into law.

CHAPTER SIX

Two Cases of Leadership

L egislative leaders use the tactics described here often and to great effect. The evidence gathered from my participant observation, interviews, and statistical analyses suggests as much. However, examining the use of informational tactics—gathering, providing, and restricting information—on specific bills can provide additional insight into this means of influence. This chapter, through two case studies, demonstrates how lawmaking in the House can be viewed and understood through a lens that posits significant information-based leadership influence. By supplying the context of the consideration of particular bills, these cases show how leaders try to achieve their goals by using specific tactics based on their informational advantages to drive the policymaking process.

The first case is the consideration of the American Clean Energy and Security Act of 2009 by the Committee on Energy and Commerce. The second case is floor consideration of the REAL ID Act of 2005. These cases are worthy of close investigation for a number of factors of theoretical importance. Each was a major bill in the eyes of the majority party leadership and the president at the time. Each also attracted significant interest group interest. Perhaps more important, in each case there was the potential for the majority party to become split. In other words, there was a real chance that ineffective control over information might have led to failure in committee or on the floor, giving the party and the leadership a black eye. Finally, one of the cases studies leadership under Democratic control of the House, while the other took place during Republican control. This underscores that both parties aggressively use these tactics as a form of leadership. Combined, these studies add context to our understanding of leaders' informational powers and of how lawmaking in particular cases can be understood as leadership driven.

The American Clean Energy and Security Act

The drafting and consideration of the American Clean Energy and Security Act (ACES) by the Committee on Energy and Commerce exemplifies how committee leaders can use their information power to craft and push legislation on their terms. ACES was a major bill by any standard, and arguably a top priority for the House Democratic leadership and President Obama at the start of the 111th Congress. The committee's leading duo—Henry Waxman (D-CA), chairman of the Energy and Commerce Committee, and Edward Markey (D-MA), chairman of the Energy and Commerce Subcommittee on Energy and Environment and chairman of the Select Committee on Energy Independence and Global Warming—would need to use significant informational tactics to advance it through committee and onto the floor. The bill would represent the primary effort by Democrats and the Obama administration to comprehensively alter the nation's energy policies, reduce the use of fossil fuels, and promote the development of renewable energy resources.

This was an issue that drew significant attention from various political interests, including the energy industry, environmentalists, business advocates, and consumer groups.[1] It also had the potential to divide the Democratic caucus. Before any action was taken on the legislation and before Markey and Waxman even released their proposal, it was clear that Democrats from districts relying heavily on coal and other carbon fuels to generate electricity would have reason to oppose legislation that aimed to limit their use. These divisions on energy policy had existed in the Democratic caucus for years and were not erased by the party's dramatic electoral victory the previous November.[2] Knowing caps on emissions would be part of any dramatic energy overhaul, "brown-state" Democrats began to push back even before the chairmen finished drafting their legislation.[3] Of course Waxman and Markey were well aware that these divisions would exist and that these midwestern, southern, and plains states Democrats might oppose any legislation that included carbon emissions caps or that might increase energy costs for ratepayers in coal-heavy districts and states. The chairmen would need to manage the creation and consideration of ACES in a way that would increase the likelihood that these brown-state Democrats would focus not on reasons to oppose the bill, but on reasons to support it.

Markey, specifically, was well aware of the political risk of proposing anything that would limit carbon emissions without including something to soften the blow for the carbon fuels industry and for consumers. Economists, academics, and many politicians agreed that a simple carbon tax was the most efficient and effective way to cut carbon emissions, making it more expensive to burn fossil fuels and creating an incentive to develop clean energy technologies. However, the 1993 Clinton-Gore proposal for such a tax (the so-called BTU tax), which Markey supported, had gone down in flames. In 2009 that failure still warned Democrats of the perils of pushing for too aggressive an energy policy. As Markey stated early in the 111th Congress, "I am aware of the economic arguments for a carbon tax, but politics is the art of the possible."[4]

These concerns—the importance of the bill to the Democratic Party, the enormous group interest in the bill, and the potential for a divided Democratic caucus—drove the steps Waxman and Markey took to influence, control, and restrict information as they drafted the bill, released it, and guided it through committee. Before and during the drafting, Waxman, Markey, and the staff of the Committee on Energy and Commerce worked behind the scenes to determine how they could craft a favorable energy policy that would retain the support of enough brown-state Democrats to pass, or at the very least keep enough of them from partnering with Republicans to kill it. Rick Boucher (D-VA), representing heavily coal-dependent southwestern Virginia, was quickly identified as someone Waxman and Markey would need to consult and work with to craft provisions, language, and messages that might appeal to other coal-state Democrats.[5] In 2009, Boucher was a subcommittee chairman, and the fourth most senior Democrat on the Energy and Commerce Committee (behind only Waxman, Markey, and John Dingell [D-MI]). He was widely recognized as an expert on energy issues, having helped craft a compromise energy proposal at the end of the previous Congress and having been a major player in fashioning the Clean Air Act Amendments of 1990. He was also known as an unyielding supporter of the coal industry, having resisted efforts to legislate on climate change for years. Further, he was firmly in the moderate wing of the party across an array of issues. Holding a perfect A+ rating from the National Rifle Association and having been a strong supporter of the war in Iraq, he was just the member moderate and coal-state Democrats might trust for information and cues, and as a congenial lawmaker he was well liked and trusted throughout the Democratic caucus. In short, he was exactly the type of lawmaker identified in chapter 3 as so involved and concerned with the policy at hand that the leadership had to bring him into the deliberations.

Discussions with Boucher made it clear that his priorities were protecting the utilities industry, in particular the coal industry, and protecting low-income, rural ratepayers from any harmful effects of the energy overhaul.[6] Nonetheless, Boucher's efforts during the 110th Congress to develop compromise legislation indicated that, at least compared with some other moderates on the committee, such as Dingell, Charlie Melancon (D-LA), or Jim Matheson (D-UT), he was committed to producing and supporting an energy overhaul bill. Dingell, while recently more amenable to helping advance climate change legislation, had spurned Democrats in the past, using his post as the top Democrat on Energy and Commerce from 1981 until 2008 to protect the auto industry from legislation that would require reducing emissions or increasing fuel efficiency. Melancon and Matheson were seen as far less friendly to the goals of the chairmen and the party on energy issues. Matheson, for example, was publicly critical very early on. A press release from his office the day Waxman and Markey unveiled their initial draft proposal was critical, calling it "problematic on several fronts."[7]

Having kept the drafting process behind the closed doors of the Energy and Commerce offices, on March 31, 2009, Waxman and Markey released their proposal in the form of a discussion draft. The bill broadly proposed a cap-and-trade program, developed numerous programs to promote the growth of renewable energy resources, and set targets of reducing carbon emissions by 20 percent by 2020 and 80 percent by 2050. Despite the dozens of hearings the committee had held on the topics of climate change and energy policy since the start of 2007, including eight during the first three months of 2009, the chairmen held four straight days of hearings on the draft, taking testimony from sixty-seven witnesses, to demonstrate support for a cap-and-trade program among numerous crucial interests. Witnesses at the hearing included a pantheon of power players from the executive branch, the energy industry, the scientific community, various interest groups, and from both political parties, affirming their support for the plan. Among others, these influential individuals included Secretary of Transportation Ray LaHood, a former Republican congressman; Chad Holliday, chairman of DuPont; Red Cavaney, senior vice president of government affairs for ConocoPhillips; Kevin Knoblach, president of the Union of Concerned Scientists; and David Manning, vice president of external affairs for National Grid. Even former chairman Dingell expressed support for the bill in his opening statement.[8]

As noted in chapter 3, chairs can use hearings to build a record of support for their legislation. Then, ahead of and during markups, the committee can remind its members of the broad political support for specific provisions or the bill as a whole and work to persuade potentially wayward members to stick with the chairman on votes. Waxman and Markey began by getting many diverse interests to provide at least tentative support for the plan, and in some cases overwhelming support. Chairs also use hearings to gain a sense of the tactics and messages that opponents of legislation will use, potential trouble areas that may provoke divisions within the majority, and general pitfalls that await them down the line. The discussion draft allowed Waxman and Markey to observe these reactions during the hearings as minority witnesses and Republican members of the committee trotted out their talking points against the bill.

Repeatedly, the most significant point of contention was the establishment and trading of emissions allowances. These allowances represented the "trade" part of the cap-and-trade policy. With a cap placed on carbon emissions, utilities and other carbon producers would be allowed to purchase credits, or allowances, permitting specific companies to produce emissions beyond the cap. The allowances would initially be sold or distributed by the government but then could be sold among energy producers, potentially easing the burden on heavy polluters but creating a market incentive by rewarding those who reduce emissions with the ability to sell their unused allowances for profit and punishing those who continue to pollute by forcing them to spend significant funds on allowances.

Numerous witnesses, while often supportive of other aspects of the bill, were concerned about the allowance policy. Paul Cicio, president of Industrial Energy Consumers of America (a manufacturing trade association), for example, noted that a favorable allowances policy was needed to protect his constituents.[9] Specifically, he argued that allowances needed to be distributed initially to protect against any dramatic rise in costs for production or consumption. James Rogers, chairman of Duke Energy, an energy producer in the southeastern United States heavily reliant on coal, noted that for his company to support the bill, the government would need to cover 100 percent of the initial costs of the allowances.[10]

Cap-and-trade policies had long been controversial in the United States, and the bill's details on allowances would likely play a major role in determining support or opposition among stakeholder groups and lawmakers. Markey and Waxman knew this was coming, so when their discussion draft was released, several sections of the bill dealing with allowances were intentionally left blank. Specifically, the way allowances would be distributed, their cost, and various other key aspects of the cap-and-trade proposal were unfinished. In addition, Subtitle D of Title 4 of the draft, which was to deal with consumer assistance during the transition to a clean energy economy, was also left entirely blank. Waxman and Markey thus avoided establishing any details on the two parts of the bill that were most likely to be controversial and would be crucial to obtaining the support of coal-state Democrats. By doing so they avoided setting specifics that opponents could drum up support against and that might result in a drop-off of support among Democrats.

It also allowed the chairmen to listen as utilities companies, manufacturers, consumer groups, and others expressed in their oral and written testimony what types of details they might be willing to support in these provisions and what details might engender opposition. In fact, a large share of the hearings focused on these issues of allowances and consumer protections. The second day of the hearings, for example, led off with a panel discussing the concerns that various organizations representing electricity providers had about potential options for distributing allowances. Other panels also featured lengthy discussions of allowance policies. Unable to discuss specific details, witnesses had to direct their testimony to pros and cons they found on a variety of policy options that they believed might be considered. The resulting testimonies revealed a variety of opinions, interests, and desires for the allowance policies. Some advocated allocating the allowances directly to producers, others to distributors. Some thought cost protections should be directed toward the energy industry, while others wanted them given directly to consumers. In general, the witnesses offered a litany of policy options and opinions, and the result was to present the industry as far from unified on policy details. The only consistent theme was that energy companies wanted assurances that the policies would neither hurt their profits nor increase rates for their consumers. Recall that these were exactly Boucher's priorities. It is no coincidence that the chairmen left these specific sections of the bill blank.

The omissions in the draft also allowed Waxman and Markey to sit back as Republicans and conservative groups tipped their hands, revealing talking points against potential allowances and consumer protection policies. Armed with this information and the information gathered from stakeholders, the chairmen could withdraw to their chambers to begin to amend their discussion draft, filling in these crucial details strategically before the markup took place. They could also begin to plan how they would advance the bill, what messaging they would use, and how they might be able to persuade their brown-state Democrats to stay on board.

On May 15, Markey and Waxman formally introduced H.R. 2454, the American Clean Energy and Security Act. The new bill, at 932 pages, was 284 pages longer than the discussion draft. The new text reflected work they had done to fill in the omissions in the previous draft and to address some of the concerns raised by lawmakers and stakeholders before, during, and after the hearings. As noted in chapter 3, control of the drafting does not mean other lawmakers will not be involved. In fact, several Democrats helped draft the final language. It does mean, however, that the involvement of other members of Congress is limited. Other lawmakers may be brought in and consulted on specific parts of the bills, but only the chairs and their staffs will be involved every step of the way. Waxman's statement at the opening of the markup on the bill describes the involvement of other key members of the Energy and Commerce Committee:

> Mr. Boucher crafted a compromise of the global warming title that bridged the differences between industry and environmental groups. Mr. Doyle and Mr. Inslee showed us the path for protecting our industrial heartland. Mr. Green and Mr. Gonzalez crafted revisions that addressed concerns of oil refiners. Mr. Butterfield and Mr. Rush have worked to protect the interests of low-income consumers. And Ms. Sutton developed an innovative cash-for-clunkers proposal.
>
> On issue after issue—protection of consumers, energy efficiency, investment in research and development, electric vehicles, transportation planning, international deforestation, and many others—members of this committee

proposed good ideas and pragmatic and effective solutions to difficult problems [emphasis added].[11]

The primary contribution of each of these lawmakers was on just part of the bill. Representatives Mike Doyle (D-PA) and Jay Inslee (D-WA) helped out on provisions to protect jobs from moving overseas, for example, but were not intimately involved in the rest of the bill. Furthermore, Waxman describes their involvement as having "proposed" good ideas. Even in a setting such as opening remarks to the consideration of a bill, which always include markedly reverent acknowledgments and thanks to all of those involved, Waxman limits his recognition of these lawmakers' contributions. Ultimately Waxman and Markey would decide whether to incorporate these proposals and exactly how to do so. Nonetheless, by bringing these lawmakers into the fold, the chairmen all but ensured their support throughout the markup on amendments and on the final vote. Because these lawmakers now had a stake in some part of the bill and in the opportunities for claiming credit that would come from its passage, Waxman and Markey would be able to count on their support.

The way Waxman and Markey managed the committee's consideration of the bill displayed effective use of the informational tactics available to committee leaders. It began with their unveiling the chairman's (or in this case chairmen's) mark. With the bill introduced on May 15 and the markup not scheduled to begin for three days, it might appear that members of the committee had ample time to read the legislation, interact with stakeholders and outside groups, and discuss the implications of the bill with their staffs. It also might seem to allow members on both sides of the aisle plenty of time to draft amendments to offer during the markup. But the timing of the release was more strategic than it seemed at first. The text of the bill as introduced was not available until late in the afternoon on May 15, a Friday, with the committee set to convene for markup at midday on Monday. With no votes scheduled in the House since about 4:30 p.m. the previous Thursday, most members of Congress were back in their districts when the bill was introduced and the text released. In fact, the House session on May 15 lasted just five minutes, allowing Waxman and Markey to formally introduce the bill at that time rather than earlier in the week or on the following Monday when more lawmakers would have been around.[12]

This timing meant that lawmakers and their staffs would have to try

to digest the massive bill over the weekend, when the lawmakers themselves were scheduled to attend events with constituents back in their
districts, and when it would be harder to get in touch with stakeholder
groups. To fill the information void, along with the bill text, the committee released a twenty-five-page memo summarizing and highlighting the
bill, and fifty-four pages of letters of endorsements from hundreds of organizations and businesses, including previously staunch opponents of
climate change legislation such as the country's top auto companies. In
addition, Waxman, Markey, and the committee staff worked to discuss
the bill with committee members to explain the hard work and delicate
compromises it reflected and how it was good for the country, good for
the Democratic Party, good for the new president, and something they
should stand together on and pass with minimal changes.

Even so, Waxman and Markey's efforts to use informational tactics
continued at the markup. After the session convened early in the afternoon on Monday and members of the committee offered their opening
remarks, Waxman formally called the bill forward for consideration and
immediately moved to offer an amendment in the nature of a complete
substitute. The substitution rather than the actual bill would be the vehicle considered for additional amendment for the rest of the markup.
This move provided numerous benefits for the chairmen. First, it allowed them to make last-second changes to the massive bill draft and
in fact expand it by sixteen pages. Although Waxman initially claimed
the changes were largely technical, he subsequently admitted there were
some substantive changes to the bill as well.

Second, it further limited the time lawmakers would have to digest
the bill and, more important, produce amendments for the markup.
While the minority staff on the committee had been informed that
the amendment would be introduced, like everyone else they had not
seen the actual text until it was distributed at the markup. And though
Waxman announced that the committee would conclude its business
for the day and reconvene the next morning to begin consideration
of amendments, this nonetheless left members of the committee with
less than twenty-four hours to digest the changes to the bill and draft
their amendments. Under these conditions they would have to rely on
the chairmen and the committee staff for information. In fact, ranking member Joe Barton (R-TX) voiced his displeasure with the way the
amendment was introduced and requested that the committee furnish
a summary of the changes. Waxman said he would oblige, but when

the summary appeared later that evening it was only one page long and short on details.

Finally, by moving to consider a substitute amendment to the bill for further amendment, Waxman reduced the amount of amendment activity possible during the markup. As on the floor of the House, only two degrees of amendments are in order during committee consideration of a bill. In other words, amendments can be offered to amendments, but no further amendment can be proposed to an amendment to an amendment. Since the substitute was itself an amendment, any further amendment language offered would be final, and there would be no opportunity to amend the amendments offered during the markup. This took away the minority's ability to offer amendments, hear objections from the majority, then tweak them to make them more appealing and try to siphon off votes or damage the bill.

The way Waxman and Markey managed the three days of amending also intensified informational disparities and benefited the chairmen. Waxman instituted a number of procedures at the start of the markup. First among them was requiring members to submit their proposed amendments to the clerk at least two hours before they would be offered. The goal of this requirement was not to give members of the committee time to review amendments before they were offered, but to give the chairmen and their staffs time to review each amendment, plan a defense if they did not like it, or negotiate with the sponsor if they thought it could be incorporated in some form. In addition, Waxman operated the session so that amendment texts would not be distributed to members of the committee until they were formally offered by the members at the markup. As a result, on any given amendment, the only people guaranteed to have seen it ahead of its offering were the majority and minority staffers of the committee (since the text would undoubtedly be shared among the staffs), the chairmen, and ranking member Barton. Consequently, members on both sides of the aisle would often be dependent on their leaders and the committee staff to provide information and cues as they endeavored to understand the amendment and decide how to vote while it was being debated.

In addition to the amendment procedure, the grueling schedule Waxman and Markey maintained for the markup would encourage absences from the proceedings and ultimately discourage the minority from offering a staggering number of amendments. The markup itself spanned thirty-seven hours over four days, with the last three days focused solely on amending. In each of these three days, the markup began in the morning and concluded late in the evening. Days two and three of the markup, for example, began about 10:00 a.m. and recessed about midnight. During these hours members of the committee would have various other responsibilities to tend to, including other committee meetings, constituent meetings, and votes on the floor. Although the committee would recess for floor votes, members may have often chosen to remain in their offices and monitor the committee's proceedings on television so they could get other work done or be briefed by their staffs. In fact, it was not uncommon for as many as ten members of the committee (about 17 percent) to be absent for an amendment vote.

The combination of these procedures (the two-hour rule, the last-minute distribution of amendment text, and the grueling schedule) produced confusion throughout the proceedings, especially among minority members of the committee. On several occasions the wrong amendment text was distributed. For example, during day three of the markup Representative Cliff Stearns (R-FL) offered an amendment regarding nuclear power; however, it was not until Stearns had finished his five minutes of introducing and discussing the amendment that someone noticed that the wrong amendment had been distributed. This created a bit of confusion as consideration of the amendment continued:

> [MR. STEARNS] Mr. Chairman, my staff has indicated that you might have the wrong amendment that you are talking about. Is it a possibility that the amendment that I have before me and which I have described, you don't have that same amount and we are not talking about the same thing? Because I think we—you recognize that you might have the wrong amendment.
>
> [THE CHAIRMAN (WAXMAN)] There has been a misunderstanding. But would you prefer the other amendment to be the—by unanimous consent would you—
>
> [MR. STEARNS] Yes—that out by unanimous consent so then you have the right amendment.
>
> [THE CHAIRMAN (WAXMAN)] So what we are proposing is that, by unanimous consent, the amendment by Mr. Stearns that will be in order for consideration at this point will be the amendment that will keep nuclear power—deal with nuclear power on the baseline question.
>
> [MR. STEARNS] Yeah. I am sorry for the confusion.

[MS. HARMAN] Mr. Chairman, I am asking which—is the amendment that was passed out the amendment that we are considering?

[THE CHAIRMAN (WAXMAN)] No. The amendment we are considering is the amendment that is now being passed out, and the amendment that members received is not the amendment we are considering.[13]

At other times members expressed general confusion about the proceedings, the bill, or what was happening at the moment:

[MR. BURGESS] Give me a page number, if you would. I have got so many bills in front of me, I don't know where I am. I am just a simple country doctor.

[THE CHAIRMAN (WAXMAN)] Well, first of all, you are in the Commerce Committee room in the Rayburn House Office Building.

[MR. BURGESS] Thank you for that.[14]

[MR. BARTON] I feel a little bit like, Mr. Chairman, I have gone to a church bazaar and bought the mystery package, not knowing what is in it.

[THE CHAIRMAN (WAXMAN)] Congratulations.[15]

As emphasized in chapter 3, disseminating information and messages is an important means for leaders to shape how their rank and file view the policies being considered and to influence the votes they cast. Throughout the markup, Waxman and Markey worked to disseminate their messages to majority members of the committee to keep them in line against harmful amendments. One message they repeatedly returned to was that the bill was the result of a carefully crafted compromise—a delicate balance—struck so as to encourage the growth of renewable energy resources while protecting the energy industry and consumers, and that any major change could topple the whole thing. On various amendments Markey or Waxman reiterated this defense. For example, in response to an amendment offered by Representative Mike Rogers (R-MI) to nullify the bill if China and India did not take steps to reduce greenhouse gas emissions in the near future, Markey stated: "We have carefully constructed in the legislation a set of protections for our industries that these industries have embraced as a group."[16] On an amendment offered by Representative Greg Walden (R-OR) to include old-growth forest materials within the definition of renewable biomass, Markey responded: "This [amendment] undermines the goals in many other parts of the underlying bill including wildlife and natural resource adaptation . . . what we have here is a balance that was struck."[17]

On an amendment offered by Representative Marsha Blackburn (R-TN) regarding changing the legal definition of carbon dioxide as a pollutant, Waxman argued: "And I don't think we ought to pass this amendment because I believe this amendment would negate the entire bill. It would say that carbon is not a pollutant and therefore need not be regulated."[18] On an amendment offered by Representative Phil Gingrey (R-GA) regarding the sale and distribution of emissions allowances, Markey responded: "So, in conclusion, I urge a no vote on the Gingrey amendment. It would unbalance something that has been very carefully constructed."[19]

Another common messaging tactic Waxman and Markey used was to refer to the support for the bill of various interest groups and stakeholders in the energy industry. This was especially common when the minority offered amendments they argued would keep the bill from harming those groups. Sometimes direct reference was made to the hearings held in April, when some of these industry leaders testified in support of the work being done by the committee. Other times the references were to groups that endorsed the bill as introduced. It seemed the chairmen were most aggressive in disseminating this type of message in response to amendments they viewed as real threats to be adopted, which would negatively affect the policy as they had crafted it. For example, perceived major threats to the bill were amendments addressing nuclear power. The bill built in protections for the nuclear industry but did not include it among the list of energy resources that would be subsidized. Republicans aimed to exploit this facet of the bill, since many Democrats on the committee were vulnerable on nuclear issues because they had nuclear plants in or around their districts. As Representative Stearns put it in debating his amendment:

> When I look at this list, Mike Ross has two nuclear power plants in Arkansas. Ms. Eshoo, there is four in California, and Ms. Harman. There is five, Representative Castor, in Florida. Mr. Barrow we have four nuclear power plants in Georgia. Bobby Rush has 11 in Illinois. There is two in Maryland, Mr. Sarbanes. Mr. Dingell has three. Mr. Pallone has four in New Jersey. Eliot Engel, you have six in New York. Mr. Butterfield, you have five in North Carolina. Mr. Doyle, you have nine nuclear power plants in Pennsylvania. Tennessee, there is three for Mr. Gordon. And, of course, in Texas, Mr. Green, you have three nuclear power plants. And Rick Boucher has four in Virginia.[20]

If these Democrats were to defect and support the various Republican amendments on nuclear power, it would damage the bill in the eyes of Waxman and Markey. For this reason, on the numerous amendments that addressed nuclear power, the chairmen were aggressive in noting the nuclear industry's support for the bill as written. On the Stearns amendment in question, Markey quoted from the press release of a major nuclear utility company in support of the bill: "In fact, Constellation Energy, which is one of the largest nuclear utilities in the United States is endorsing this legislation: 'Constellation Energy applauds the proposed climate change legislation as a promising first step in promoting greater investment in renewable technology, energy efficiency, and new nuclear.'"[21]

Regarding this same amendment, Waxman noted some of the various energy producers who supported the bill: "So we negotiated with and have the agreement with—this proposal—with Duke Energy, American Electric Power, Edison Electric Institute, Exelon, PG&E Corporation, FPL Group, Entergy Austin, Constellation Energy, Seattle City Light, Public Service Enterprise, and PNM Resources."[22]

On an amendment offered the next day by Representatives Walden and Fred Upton (R-MI) regarding the status of nuclear power, Markey responded similarly: "As the chairman already pointed out, our goal is not in this legislation to harm nuclear power. In fact, most of the major nuclear energy utilities in the United States have endorsed this bill."[23]

The chairmen levied this type of response on other issues as well, including those proposing to alter to the status of hydropower in the bill. On this issue, Markey noted: "And just so that all members can know that the language in the bill has been endorsed by the National Hydropower Association. . . . The National Hydropower Association in conjunction with the American Rivers Association drafted the language that is actually used for the production tax credit as well. So we try to work with groups that, you know, are out there and we believe that we reached a good formula."[24]

About the language in the bill regarding the distribution of emissions allowances, he noted: "Second, in terms of the allocation with regard to the utility sector, we worked with the Edison Electric Institute in developing this formula. This is a formula that was accepted across the full span of the Edison Electric Institute. It is something that was embraced by them and actually serves as a foundation to the legislation."[25]

In some instances the chairmen delegated the job of responding to amendments to other members of the majority. This was done strategically. Since they were both members of their party's liberal wing, Waxman and Markey apparently thought some of their messages would be more effective coming from more moderate Democrats or those representing districts that relied heavily on industries that Republicans were arguing the bill would hurt. For example, when Representative Tim Murphy (R-PA) offered an amendment that he argued would protect the steel industry from the damaging effects of the bill, Waxman yielded to Representative Mike Doyle (D-PA), who represented steel-heavy western Pennsylvania, to come to the bill's defense:

> I would like to start by quoting a letter that was sent to us by the International President of the United Steelworkers Union, Leo Girard, who represents all of the steelworkers who Mr. Murphy talks about and that mostly reside in [my district] where we have U.S. Steel's two active steel plants, Edgar Thomson in Braddock, and Mon Valley Works in West Smithland. This is from the International President of the Steel Workers: "Leo Girard, International President of the United Steelworkers Union, today praised the progress made by the U.S. House Energy and Commerce Committee in its work to pass comprehensive climate change legislation with the following statement.[26]

In another instance, responding an amendment offered by Representative Michael Burgess (R-TX) to prohibit the trading of carbon credit derivatives in the stock market, Waxman deferred to Representative Bart Stupak (D-MI), a respected expert on market policies and regulations, especially regarding the trade of derivatives. Waxman yielded to Stupak on another occasion as well, when Representative George Radanovich (R-CA) offered an amendment to dissolve Title 3 of the bill if electricity rates increased by 100 percent in any part of the country. This amendment coincided with messaging efforts by the National Republican Congressional Committee (NRCC) to argue that Democrats did not care about ratepayers or the cost of electricity. Stupak, a Democrat in a Republican-leaning district, spoke against the amendment as frivolous, said the message was misleading, and called on other moderate Democrats to hold the line with him:

> I am looking here at my BlackBerry, and since we started this mark-up I've received five attack messages from the Republican National NRCC communications, the latest one being last night at 10:29, saying that we are against

jobs, saying we are against America, saying we are for high prices. So you are absolutely right. This is just another message amendment and those of us on the committee who may be like in my case, a Republican-leaning seat but I am a Democrat, we can be assured there will be another press release so I have had five now in the first 2 days and I am sure when we are done with this mark-up, by the time we are done there will probably be at least three more, so these are just message amendments. They are not sincere. They are not really towards promoting good legislation or correcting or identifying a problem. It is just for message, so I hope we would stay united and vote no because I don't want to be the only one getting these emails.[27]

In a very effective moment, Waxman recognized Boucher, who had been quiet for most of the proceedings, to defend the provisions in the bill meant to protect the coal industry from an amendment offered by Representative John Shimkus (R-IL):

For the last month, I have been engaged in an intensive and ultimately successful negotiation with Chairman Waxman and Chairman Markey in order to address some core concerns, and these are exactly the same concerns that motivated the amendment that came from Mr. Shimkus. . . . I am very satisfied with the arrangements that we have made which are now reflected in the text of the bill that the committee is marking up.[28]

It is important to note again that these messages and arguments were not intended to dissuade Republican opposition to the bill or try to get Republican members of the committee on the Democratic side. Their purpose was to persuade Democratic members of the committee to stand with their chairmen. Open, deliberative processes like mark-ups are a challenge to legislative leaders trying to use their informational power. The minority has an opportunity to point out compelling reasons for members of the majority to oppose the legislation at hand— especially vulnerable members of the committee who may hold less than safe seats. In cultivating their responses, the chairmen (ideally as a more trustworthy source than the minority) are providing information that will help members of the majority feel safe voting with the party line. When amendments were offered, the chairmen would always respond to the Republican messages with their own messages, hoping to provide their lawmakers with reasons, or the cover necessary, to stay with them.

In general, Waxman and Markey's efforts were successful. The chairmen held the committee's Democrats together on most votes—at least enough to defeat every potentially damaging amendment. Notably, not a single amendment that the chairmen opposed was adopted, and on not a single amendment vote did more than five (out of thirty-six) Democrats defect.[29] In fact, of the fifty-six amendments offered by Republicans, only three were adopted, each by a voice vote owing to their noncontroversial nature, and each with the blessing of the chairmen.

In addition, of the eight members Waxman and Markey brought in to help draft key parts of the bill, each stayed on the party line on almost every vote. Among the thirty-eight roll-call votes taken during proceedings, in only one instance did any of them vote against the chairmen.[30] This result is impressive, given that among these members were lawmakers such as Boucher, Doyle, Representative Betty Sutton (D-OH), Representative G. K. Butterfield (D-NC), and Representative Gene Green (D-TX), who represented moderate districts that relied on coal and other nonrenewable energy sources and who could have found constituency-based reasons to support some of the Republican amendments. By giving these representatives even a small stake in the bill, the chairmen helped ensure the support of some key members on amendment votes and on passage.[31]

The bill passed committee by a vote of 33–25, with just four Democrats—John Barrow (D-GA), Matheson, Melancon, and Mike Ross (D-AR)—voting in opposition and one Republican, Representative Mary Bono Mack (R-CA), voting in favor. More important, the bill as crafted by the chairmen had survived four days of markup and emerged unscathed. Among the amendments adopted, many simply expanded on aspects of the bill as already established. For example, the first amendment adopted was one offered by Dingell, along with Inslee and Representative Bart Gordon (D-TN). This amendment created a new loan program for the development of new energy resources. Another amendment was the "cash for clunkers" program offered by Sutton, who had already worked out the details with the chairmen behind the scenes. Other amendments were minor or relatively noncontroversial, such as an amendment offered by Representative Peter Welch (D-VT) to create a certified wood-burning stove program. By any standards, the bill that was reported by the committee looked very similar to that proposed by Waxman and Markey.

To at least some degree, this success can be attributed to the way the chairmen used their information power. Through the hearings they built a record of support for the bill and encouraged opponents to reveal their talking points. During the drafting they involved key members of the committee they had identified, such as Boucher and Inslee, to present a united front during committee consideration. Through the timing of the bill's release, along with the last-minute introduction of the substitute language, they gave lawmakers little time to analyze the final legislative language and made them more dependent on committee-produced materials and information. In managing the markup, they ensured that they would have a response to every Republican amendment by requiring members to submit their amendment language at least two hours ahead of its offering. And in presenting their messages against Republican attacks on the bill, they were able to address potential concerns of moderate and brown-state Democrats, pointing to the support for the bill among industry leaders and other moderates in the party. Although congressional consideration of the bill was not over and much work was still to be done, this victory in the Energy and Commerce Committee paved the way for the final consideration on the floor of the House and ultimate passage of a bill favorable to the Democratic leadership.

The REAL ID Act of 2005

The consideration of the REAL ID Act of 2005 exemplifies how the majority party leadership can use informational tactics to secure passage on the floor of the House of a bill that might have been imperiled under more open, deliberative, and informed consideration. This bill presented Republican leaders with several challenges and ultimately required them to use a self-executing rule. Its consideration highlights how the majority leadership can use self-executing rules to amend bills so as to achieve their goals, while also influencing the information their rank and file consider when making voting decisions.

The REAL ID Act of 2005 had its origins in the 9/11 Commission's report and efforts by congressional Republicans to address the report's recommendations. Among other things, the report recommended that the United States make changes to its immigration policies that focused "on targeting terrorist travel through an intelligence and security strategy based on reliable identification systems and effective, integrated information-sharing, including the expansion and consolidation of the border-screening systems" (Grimmett 2006, 30). In 2004, Congress passed the Intelligence Reform and Terrorism Prevention Act (IRTPA), a key priority for both the House leadership and the White House, which addressed many of these recommendations. The bill as passed in the House, however, went further than its Senate counterpart and included provisions regarding federal identification card standards, modification of the amnesty process, and border security that were either stripped or heavily modified during conference negotiations. Representative James Sensenbrenner (R-WI), chairman of the House Judiciary Committee and author of those provisions, was promised that, in return for his supporting IRTPA on the floor, the leaders would support his push in the next Congress for a stand-alone bill addressing those issues.

On January 26, 2005, Sensenbrenner introduced H.R. 418, the REAL ID Act. Though the bill's title referred to its provisions setting federal identification card standards, it included language addressing all three provisions stripped from IRTPA two months earlier. First, it established and accelerated the implementation of national standards for state-issued identification such as driver's licenses. Second, it reformed existing amnesty laws to strengthen the ability of the Justice Department and the Department of Homeland Security to deport potential terrorists. Third, it made court challenges to the completion of a border fence along the Mexican border illegal.

For several reasons the REAL ID Act was far from guaranteed unified Republican support, or passage, on the floor. First, these policy proposals were stripped from IRTPA during conference negotiations because they lacked support from some Republicans in the Senate and some libertarian-leaning Republicans in the House. Coupled with strong Democratic opposition, there was little margin for error. Second, while much of the new bill's language mirrored the provisions stripped from IRTPA, it included several additional provisions that made the proposed policies even more aggressive than those Congress had rejected the previous year. For example, it included new language blocking from obtaining a visa and entering or traveling through the United States any foreign national whom the attorney general or secretary of homeland security determines has engaged, is engaging, or "is likely to" engage in terrorist activities, is or was affiliated with a terrorist organization, supports terrorist activity, or is the spouse or child of someone meeting any of these standards. Additionally, it included new, more stringent requirements for the federal recognition of state-issued identification cards, in particular temporary IDs provided to foreigners living in the United

States on visas. In some ways the proposals included in H.R. 418 went well beyond the recommendations of the 9/11 Commission, and even beyond the policies passed in the House version of IRTPA the previous fall. If the old language had engendered some Republican opposition, the new language might be even more likely to do so.

Third, in touching on immigration the REAL ID Act broached an issue that threatened to divide Republicans more fundamentally. During the 2004 campaign, and after his reelection, President Bush noted his support for substantial immigration reform, including policies such as a guest worker program that would allow illegal immigrants to stay and work in the country legally.[32] While some Republicans sided with the president, others strongly opposed anything but strong border security and a more aggressive deportation policy. As a *CQ Weekly* article on the Sensenbrenner bill put it at the time, "The move is likely to plunge Congress into a fierce debate over immigration policy and expose a rift in the GOP on the issue. Although President Bush is calling for legislation that would make it easier for immigrants to enter the country and take lower-skilled jobs unfilled by American workers, many in his party want the nation to tighten its borders and deport aliens who are in the United States illegally."[33] Sensenbrenner's bill seemed at odds with the direction the newly reelected president wanted to take and risked garnering a presidential veto threat, and consequently a loss of support from many moderate Republicans.

Further raising the danger of defections within the Republican ranks were the various interest groups that had come out in opposition to the bill. While the list of groups included numerous liberal or Democratic-affiliated interests such as the AFL-CIO, the Anti-Defamation League, Amnesty International, and the SEIU, it also included some groups that may have given Republican lawmakers pause, including the National Governors Association, the Gun Owners of America Association, the Republican Liberty Caucus (a libertarian group), and the American Conservative Union.[34] The bill also had opposition from various religious groups and organizations.[35] Republicans who typically aligned with these groups might find reasons to vote in opposition.

Finally, unified Republican support for the bill was challenged by a separate bill introduced by Representative Tom Davis (R-VA), a moderate Republican and chairman of the Committee on Government Reform. This bill included essentially the same proposal as H.R. 418 on identification standards, but it did not include the controversial language on amnesty laws or the border fence. This bill thus offered a more modest option that Republicans uncomfortable with some of Sensen-brenner's language could support instead.[36]

To get the bill passed through the chamber unharmed, Sensenbrenner and the Republican leaders would need to get their rank and file to view the bill in a way that made it easy to support. They would need to get House Republicans to focus on messages that painted the bill in a favorable light, and in a light that did not make it appear controversial. Largely, their strategy was to portray the bill as related to, and a continuation of, the work they accomplished in IRTPA and the recommendations of the 9/11 Commission. Both IRTPA and the 9/11 Commission's report had broad bipartisan support in Congress. The House-passed version of IRTPA had garnered the support of all but eight Republicans, as well as sixty-nine Democrats on final passage. The final, bicameral version of the bill passed with even broader support, 336–75, with the vast majority of each party voting in favor. In linking H.R. 418 to these actions, the GOP leadership hoped to recreate these winning coalitions and get a unified Republican caucus to vote alongside moderate Democrats to send the REAL ID Act to the Senate.

The leadership's messaging tactic was on full display as debate opened on February 9. Representative Pete Sessions (R-TX), a senior member of the Rules Committee, made several references to the 9/11 Commission and to the popular IRTPA:

> This legislation continues the reform mission begun by Congress in the 9/11 Recommendations Implementation Act. . . .
> Closing the asylum loopholes identified by H.R. 418 will provide greater security for the American people because as the 9/11 Commission staff report noted, "A number of terrorists . . . abused the asylum system." . . .
> . . . the 9/11 Commission and Congress have recommended and taken a number of appropriate actions that have made it more difficult for terrorists to enter the United States through the visa or other legal immigration process; and this bill will go even further toward attaining that goal.[37]

Representative Roy Blunt (R-MO), the majority whip, also referred to the 9/11 Commission during his remarks on the floor: "The bipartisan commission that looked into 9/11 dealt specifically with this issue, something that has been overlooked in much of our debate now, the almost-sanctified 9/11 Commission. That commission said travel documents are as important as weapons and urged the Congress to do something about travel documents that did not reflect the true status of individuals."[38]

Representative David Dreier (R-CA), chairman of the Rules Committee, in his floor statement on the rule governing the debate, addressed the tension between the president's support for immigration reform and H.R. 418. Noting his support for a guest worker program, he stressed that support for this bill was not counter to his or President Bush's position, and that in fact they were complementary efforts:

> I am supporting this effort on border security in part because I am convinced that we will be able to, down the road and I hope soon, address the immigration reform question. I happen to believe that it is important for us to identify the people who are here in this country illegally. And, yes, I am opposed to granting blanket amnesty, as is President Bush, but I do believe that moving in the direction of some sort of worker program is something that we must look at and must address. But we are taking a proper step in finally doing what we wanted to have incorporated in the 9/11 Commission package that we passed out of here, and I congratulate all my colleagues who have been involved in this.[39]

Generally, Republican leaders worked to present the REAL ID Act as a homeland security and antiterrorism bill rather than an immigration bill. Democrats worked to portray the bill as undoing some of the key provisions of IRTPA, actually hurting homeland security efforts, and ultimately nothing more than a thinly veiled attack on immigrants. Representative Jane Harman (D-CA), ranking member on the Intelligence Committee, spoke directly to this point, ultimately calling the REAL ID Act an "imposter":

> What H.R. 418 will do is undermine several key provisions of the Bipartisan Intelligence Reform and Terrorism Prevention Act, which Congress passed and the President signed into law just 2 months ago. . . .
>
> We dealt with this issue responsibly in the intelligence reform legislation. The law establishes tough minimum Federal standards for driver's licenses so that all driver's licenses have certain key security features. . . .
>
> [The provisions in IRTPA] are much stronger than what is being proposed by H.R. 418, yet H.R. 418 would repeal these critical new security upgrades.[40]

Getting the REAL ID Act passed in a way that pleased Sensenbrenner and the leadership would take more than just an effective message. After all, the message could simply be countered by the conservative-leaning groups opposed to its provisions. The leaders would need to find a way to focus Republicans' attention on what they were selling them, rather than on what others were urging. Their strategy had four parts. They would not be able to keep lawmakers completely in the dark on the bill's contents; after all, it was introduced a couple of weeks before floor consideration. However, they could expedite the legislative process to limit the scrutiny it received and try to get rank-and-file Republicans to see it as essentially the same as the policies passed the year before. So, first, the leadership bypassed all committee work on the bill. The bill as introduced was under the jurisdiction of three committees: Judiciary (chaired by Sensenbrenner), Energy and Commerce, and Government Reform. An open and deliberative process might have exposed the bill to the same attacks that had seen its provisions stripped from IRTPA, raised concerns about the new language in the bill, and exposed the divisions within the party on immigration. In bypassing this deliberative work, the leaders hoped to minimize the salience of these concerns.

Second, the leaders would need to ensure that Representative Davis was on board. A recalcitrant Davis would pose problems for the bill's prospects. Opposition from Davis, a well-liked, influential moderate from a swing district just south of Washington, DC, could spur opposition among any number of other moderate or vulnerable Republicans. Just as Waxman and Markey brought in Boucher to try to ensure moderate support for their energy bill, the leaders brought in Davis to ensure that he would be a part of its push for passage. Having introduced his own identification standards bill—an issue very much under the jurisdiction of his committee—Davis might have had reason to be displeased that the Sensenbrenner version was to get considered instead. The leaders made sure Davis was part of the rollout of the bill and that he would get some of the credit for the new policy. Davis would be involved in media outreach on the bill over the subsequent months and was even given floor time to manage during the debate on H.R. 418. However, just to be safe, the leaders ensured that his floor time would be restricted to the part of the bill under his committee's jurisdiction—the federal identification standards that he supported: "I want to use my time today to discuss the provisions contained in H.R. 418 that fall within the jurisdiction

of the Committee on Government Reform which I chair: security measures for Federal acceptance of state-issued driver's licenses and personal identification cards, commonly referred to as identity security."[41]

Davis repeated the leadership's talking points on the bill during his
floor remarks, noting that it was meant to implement the recommendations of the 9/11 Commission and that the policies included had been
passed the year before: "Before I recognize the next chairman, I wish
to respond to the gentlewoman's question of why are we doing this. We
are doing this because the 9/11 Commission Report asked that we do
it. They made it a priority. We are doing it because our committee, the
committee the gentlewoman sits on, the one I chair, authorized this last
year and the House overwhelmingly passed this last year."[42]

In short, Davis was given various perquisites to stand with the leadership on the REAL ID Act, a story consistent with perspectives on leadership power that emphasize control over and distribution of institutional resources. However, the leaders did this with just one member
of Congress in order to broadly bolster their control over the information environment in the chamber. By getting Davis to echo their message on the bill, they hoped to get other moderates to buy into that interpretation of the REAL ID Act. This informational effect would have far
broader benefits than pleasing Davis.

Third, the leadership needed President Bush's support. Bush's recent
statements and efforts on immigration policy made it unclear whether
he would support or oppose the bill as written. In fact, given his posture
on immigration during the election campaign, anything less than explicit
support might be seen to suggest opposition. At the time of the bill's introduction, Bush did not take a position, and as of late January it appeared there might be a major standoff on immigration between House
Republicans and the White House, since Sensenbrenner suggested he
"might not work to advance other immigration proposals, such as Bush's
guest-worker initiative, unless his provisions are enacted."[43] Not wanting
to jeopardize his plans for various immigration proposals, Bush agreed
to support the bill, and the White House issued a press release on February 9, just as debate began on the floor.[44] This let the leadership tout presidential support for the bill just as most members were turning their attention to it. Presidential support was crucial. Even if the leaders could not
convince members that the bill was an antiterrorism and national security
bill, they could point out that Bush, whom many of the moderates would
side with on immigration issues, supported the bill, so they should too.

Finally, the leadership and Sensenbrenner had one more tactic to ensure that the bill passed undiluted. Unlike most bills, H.R. 418 came to the floor for consideration under the auspices of not one special rule, but two. H.Res. 71 made the bill in order for consideration on February 9 for sixty minutes of debate but ordered that consideration would be suspended once debate time expired. During the debate, the Rules Committee was meeting to set the terms for the completion of consideration, including any amending. The rule that emerged that evening (H.Res. 75) included self-executing provisions making significant changes to the bill. These provisions did two things to help the majority leadership. First, it aimed to undercut attacks that focused on the bill's asylum provisions. By making it more difficult for refugees to obtain asylum in the United States, the bill garnered the opposition of numerous interest groups that advocate for asylum seekers and refugees.[45] In some ways the asylum provisions had quickly become the focus of the debate over the bill. A *CQ Weekly* article, for example, was titled "Lawmakers Spar over Asylum," and objections to its asylum provisions were mentioned repeatedly on the floor. For example, Representative Jim McGovern (D-MA), a member of the Rules Committee, stated: "I cannot believe that the United States Government would be that cruel and we would turn our backs on people who need asylum in order to truly be free from torture and persecution."[46] Representative Linda Sanchez (D-CA) similarly argued, "If the REAL ID Act is passed today, it will deny driver's licenses to those immigrants and slam the door shut on refugees seeking asylum from blood-thirsty regimes."[47] Representative Jerrold Nadler (D-NY), who would sponsor an amendment to strip the asylum provisions from the bill, stated: "Under the excuse of national security, for example, the asylum provisions in this bill completely gut the possibility of many legitimate victims of persecution to be granted asylum. Asylum law is supposed to be about protecting individuals, including women and children, from serious human rights abuses; it is not supposed to be about seizing on any possible basis to deny a claim or return people to persecution."[48]

The Republican leadership was clearly concerned that this opposition might endanger the bill's prospects. Consequently, the self-executing provision aimed to undercut this attack by eliminating a cap on the number of refugees who could obtain lawful permanent resident (LPR) status in the United States each year. At the time, just ten thousand refugees could obtain LPR status each year, keeping many asylum seekers from obtaining their full rights as residents of the United States and increasing their risk of deportation. The annual caps were greatly unpopular among refugee and asylum advocates. Eliminating them not only aimed at putting amnesty groups in a bind regarding their opposition to the bill but allowed the Republican leaders to disseminate the message to their rank and file that the changes to the bill should make it easier for *legitimate* asylum seekers to come to the United States and stay permanently and that members could tout this provision to explain their vote in favor of the bill to citizens and groups concerned about protecting the asylum process. In short, this provision was meant to give wavering Republicans the reason they needed to stand with the leaders.

Second, with this cover in place, the self-executing provision included several changes that made the core provisions of the bill even more aggressive. As it was put by Representative Alcee Hastings (D-FL), who managed the Democrats' time in opposition to the rule, "In the short time we have had to review this new language, it appears to be more controversial than the bill's original provisions."[49] Specifically, the bill made various changes to its asylum provisions that expanded the grounds on which judges were to determine the credibility of an asylum seeker's claims, including *any* discrepancies between refugees' oral statements to officers at the airport and their written applications. The new provisions also made it even easier for the government to deport refugees by, among other things, barring them from appealing orders of deportation on grounds of habeas corpus or mandamus and by putting the burden of proof on the refugees rather than the government. Finally, the self-executing provision further limited the ability of any government or citizen to object to the completion of the border fence, adding that it would be inadmissible not only for courts to hear objections to the construction of the fence, but for any "administrative agency, or other entity" as well. This change could be interpreted to mean that no challenge at all could be made to the completion of the fence.

These new provisions were aggressive, but lawmakers were given little time to digest them. In fact, the exact language of the self-executing amendment was available much later than every other proposed amendment that was submitted to the Rules Committee for consideration. Although the committee had required that all proposed amendments be submitted by 12:00 p.m. on February 8, the leadership bent the rules, and Sensenbrenner submitted the final language for the eighteen-page self-executing amendment much later in the day. Consequently the minority and everyone else had even less time to look at the amendment

ahead of the markup and understand the changes it made.[50] The final
text of the bill, the self-executing amendment, and other amendments
made in order were not posted by the Rules Committee until the night
of February 9, with final consideration and votes scheduled to begin the
following morning.

In these circumstances typical lawmakers who were relatively unfa-
miliar with asylum laws and procedures would have a hard time independently digesting the rather technical changes made to asylum procedures and their implications for the legal standing of asylum seekers and
their effect on US immigration policy in general. They would have to
rely on Sensenbrenner and the Republican leadership to explain how the
new language affected the underlying bill.

The leadership's message was simple. The self-executing provisions
made some minor, technical changes and otherwise provided straightforward substantive improvements to help the bill achieve its aims. And
contrary to the attacks of Democrats and other groups, it helped asylum
seekers by dropping the cap on how many could become permanent residents each year. Representative Sensenbrenner's floor statement summarized the message:

> The manager's amendment, which will self-execute upon adoption of this res-
> olution, makes technical changes to the bill as well as making a number of
> substantive improvements. One such modification will be to remove the an-
> nual cap on the number of aliens granted asylum who can become permanent
> residents each year. The current cap of 10,000 has resulted in a multi-year
> backlog that has caused unnecessary hardship to aliens already found to have
> been fleeing persecution. Hardly an anti-refugee provision.[51]

The use of the self-executing rule had another benefit. Specifically,
it worked to undermine a Democratic amendment to the bill that might
have been able to garner Republican support. The Democrats had their
best shot at undercutting the bill by an amendment sponsored by Representative Nadler. This amendment would have struck from the bill section 101, which included the controversial new provisions expanding the
government's ability to reject and deport immigrants through the asylum
process. With a number of groups opposed to these provisions, it might
have been tempting for some Republican lawmakers to defect and support the amendment. However, the self-executing amendment inserted
the new provision eliminating the refugee ceiling into section 101. Be-

cause Nadler had to submit his amendment before the language of self-execution provisions was known, he could not structure it to save this provision, which most Democrats and many Republicans supported. Consequently, the amendment as made in order by the Rules Committee would strike all of section 101 including this new provision. Ahead of the consideration of the amendment, Nadler asked for unanimous consent to alter his amendment to allow the new provision to stay:

> The rule makes in order virtually a new bill, which we did not get to see until after the deadline for submitting amendments to the Committee on Rules. There was no opportunity to draft our amendments to reflect the bill that we are now considering. My amendment would strike section 101 from the bill as amended by the manager's amendment. But the manager's amendment adds a provision to which we do not object, namely, raising the cap on asylum adjustments. This unanimous consent request would change my amendment so as not to change this good provision added at the last minute by the chairman. If we had seen the manager's amendment before the Committee on Rules deadline, this request would not be necessary.[52]

Representative Sensenbrenner objected to the request, effectively killing it, and later, during debate on the amendment, he was more than happy to point out that if adopted it would strike the new, popular provision: "Now, the bill as it is currently before us takes away the cap of 10,000 approved asylum applicants who are admitted to permanent residency every year. The Nadler amendment strikes that."[53]

By keeping everyone in the dark about what the self-executing provisions would contain (and that there would be self-executing provisions at all) Sensenbrenner and the Republican leadership made it difficult, if not impossible, for minority Democrats and those opposed to the bill to craft amendments that would siphon off Republican support and damage the bill. The amendment was ultimately defeated 185–236, with just ten Republicans voting in favor. In fact, the bill made it through floor consideration unfazed, with just three minor and consensual amendments adopted by voice vote.

In sum, the self-executing rule did everything for the leadership that the previous chapters suggest it should do. It created confusion by making various changes to the bill at the last second, so rank-and-file Republicans had to rely on their leaders for information, while simultaneously making it more difficult for Democrats to effectively oppose or amend the bill. Further, it allowed Sensenbrenner and the majority leadership to insert a provision lifting the LPR status cap to provide cover while they made the rest of the bill more aggressive. This gave the leadership an additional talking point to ease concerns in their caucus that many would view the bill as too harsh on refugees. In short, it reinforced the leaders' efforts to get their membership to view the bill as easy to support.

Due in part to the informational tactics Sensenbrenner and the Republican leadership used, the REAL ID Act was passed 261–161. Republicans overwhelmingly held the line on the bill, with just eight voting in opposition. Generally, Republicans were able to recreate the voting coalition that had passed the House version of IRTPA the previous year with forty-two moderate Democrats also voting for passage. In some ways the leaders did even better at holding Republicans in line than they did with IRTPA, despite the more aggressive provisions. Three Republicans who opposed the House version of IRTPA—Representative Ray LaHood (R-IL), a moderate, and Representatives Zach Wamp (R-TN) and John Duncan (R-TN), two notable libertarians—voted for passage of H.R. 418.

The Republican leadership was able to pass an aggressive bill while maintaining the support of Republicans and moderate Democrats. Without question, the self-executing amendment changed the bill to give the government even more authority to reject refugees, deport immigrants, and block legal challenges to the completion of the border fence. These changes cannot be understood as being made to broaden the appeal of the bill. If anything, taken as a whole, they should have done the opposite. The only concession the leaders made, and ultimately what they promoted about the self-executing provision—the removal of the refugee ceiling—was a fairly hollow one. If the government could more easily block and deport asylum seekers before they could apply for LPR status, the removal of the ceiling would not make much difference.

The REAL ID Act was the first major bill considered on the floor during the 109th Congress, and it was a win for Sensenbrenner and for a Republican leadership hoping to advance aggressive antiterrorism and immigration policies. In closely managing the process, distributing a clear message to their rank and file, and using a self-executing rule to exacerbate information asymmetries, they got the bill passed in the House in a way that otherwise might not have been possible.

Conclusion

The two cases presented here demonstrate how legislative leaders can leverage their informational advantages and use the tactics discussed in the previous chapters to craft legislation and move it through the chamber. There are a few takeaways worthy of comment. The first is the pervasiveness of leaders' involvement in House policymaking. In both cases, legislative leaders were involved in every step. With ACES, Waxman and Markey crafted the bill, negotiated with key players, structured and chaired hearings, developed effective messaging for the legislation, strategically managed the release of legislative language, and closely managed every step of the committee's markup. With the REAL ID Act, Sensenbrenner and the Republican leadership crafted the bill's language behind the scenes, bypassed committee consideration, developed and coordinated effective talking points and messaging, self-executed the bill in a strategic manner, and guided it through floor consideration. The act of legislating was leader-centric and leadership driven. Most other actors were reactionary. It is clear just how consequential leaders are to what legislation is considered, what actions lawmakers take, and what legislation ultimately passes.

Second, it is clear how central information is to the legislative process and the strategies legislative leaders adopt. Both committee chairs and party leaders rely heavily on informational tactics to advance their legislation. Waxman and Markey worked assiduously to gather intelligence about how lawmakers and interest groups would react to potential legislative provisions, while keeping everyone in the dark about what they would ultimately do. When they finally did introduce their bill, they accelerated the legislative process, and throughout the markup they provided their rank and file with reasons to stand with the leadership. Similarly, the Republican leadership worked to control the information environment throughout the consideration of the REAL ID Act, bypassing more deliberative processes, changing the legislation at the last second, and having their talking points repeatedly invoked on the floor of the House. These are the tactics introduced in the preceding chapters in action, and they are tactics legislative leaders use frequently and to great effect.

Of course, leaders' abilities to use these tactics are not limitless. As noted at times in the preceding chapters and illustrated in this chapter, leaders will have to involve the most deeply interested lawmakers (at least majority lawmakers). This is highlighted by Boucher's involvement on ACES and by the steps the Republican leaders had to take to appease Davis on the REAL ID Act. Furthermore, as hinted in previous chapters, lawmakers outside their party's orthodoxy, including moderates and those from swing districts, may be less susceptible to leaders' tactics because they will be more skeptical of what they are selling them. This can be seen in Matheson's and Melancon's persistent opposition on ACES. As the next chapter investigates, the use of informational tactics is somewhat limited by the trust rank-and-file lawmakers have in their leaders and the information they provide. Lawmakers who are less trusting may be less amenable to leadership influence and more frustrated by their use of these tactics.

CHAPTER SEVEN

Trust and the Limits to Leadership

If you don't trust the information [committees and party leaders] are giving you, it's a problem.—Rank-and-file staffer[1]

Who you trust to tell you what is going on is what is relevant.—Leadership staffer[2]

How much influence legislative leaders can leverage from the informational asymmetries in Congress is shaped, to a degree, by how much their rank and file trust them. When leaders enjoy ample trust among their followers, the tactics described in this book can yield tremendous influence. However, when distrust is prevalent or when a subset of followers is skeptical of them, their influence may be limited. This chapter explores the limits of information-based leadership.

Although information is a strong source of power, it is a double-edged sword. As this chapter reveals, legislative leaders' aggressive use of information tactics may have the side effect of eroding trust, especially among moderate members and others outside their party's orthodoxy. These members know that their leaders' policy priorities sometimes conflict with the preferences of their constituents. Consequently they grow skeptical about what their leaders tell them and ultimately may be less influenced by it than other members of their caucus.

This chapter draws on the interviews conducted with lawmakers and their staffs to investigate the effect trust has on leadership power in the House, particularly regarding the use of informational tactics. Uncovered is a legislative body where few are satisfied with the way business is conducted, yet majority members have little appetite to push for changes to procedures that, at the very least, guarantee their party will win the day. Furthermore, the interviews demonstrate that moderate lawmakers and other unorthodox partisans put less faith than others in the information their leaders provide. In the second half of the chapter I examine these findings by looking at some of the notable struggles the new Republican leadership had at the beginning of the 112th Congress. In sum, this chapter demonstrates that while leaders can be hampered by a lack of trust among their rank and file, their ability to lead largely persists.

Trust and Leader-Follower Relationships

Beyond leadership selection, scholars of Congress have paid little attention to the nature and consequences of the relationship between legislative leaders and rank-and-file lawmakers. Other than recognizing the importance of contextual factors, such as the level of agreement within a party caucus, they have drawn few systematic conclusions about when leaders' standing among their followers will be stronger or weaker (see, for example, Cooper and Brady 1981; Aldrich and Rohde 2000). This is remarkable given the emphasis placed on the nature of the relationship between leaders and followers in the study of organizations. Among other variables, one key factor in this relationship is *trust*. Trust can powerfully shape these relationships and ultimately a group's ability to act efficiently and effectively, affecting followers' willingness to fall in behind leaders and allow them the freedom to act (see Burke et al. 2007).

Of course, trust among leaders and followers follows from numerous antecedents, including the traits of the leader (e.g., benevolence, integrity, and ability) (Mayer, Davis, and Schoorman 1995), the length of their relationship (Lewicki and Bunker 1995), and the congruence among the values held by leaders and followers (Govier 1997; Jung and Avolio 2000; Sitkin and Roth 1993). Another factor affecting the trust followers have in their leaders is the quality of information sharing and communication. Leaders who are perceived as more forthright in providing information, or who provide better explanations for their actions, have been shown to engender more trust (see Roberts and O'Reilly 1974; O'Reilly 1977; O'Reilly and Roberts 1977; Folger and Konovsky 1989; Konovsky and Cropanzano 1991). Dirks and Ferrin (2002), in a meta-analysis, found that followers' confidence in their leaders correlates with their belief in the information they provide. Perhaps most important here, a number of studies have found that open communication between leaders and followers enhances trust among all involved (Butler 1991; Farris, Senner, and Butterfield 1973; Hart et al. 1986).

In Congress, leaders' efforts to leverage their informational advantages into power and influence are likely to damage their relationship with many among their rank and file. The tactics they use—especially in restricting information and providing skewed information—are essentially the opposite of open communication. Consequently, the aggressive use of informational tactics is likely to foment distrust. These tactics persist because leaders and followers approach the legislative process with different priorities and because the party benefits collectively from their use, but the benefits come at a cost.

The rank-and-file lawmakers and staff interviewed varied dramatically in their reactions to their leaders' use of informational tactics and to their characterization of their trust in their leaders. Although some grew agitated in discussing their leaders' actions, others were less concerned or even indifferent. The most prevalent division appeared to be between orthodox, mainstream members of each party and moderate lawmakers representing swing districts that were often out of step with their party's policy proposals. For mainstream partisans, the way leaders use information is not so troublesome. Many of these lawmakers saw the priorities of the party and those of their constituents as fairly well aligned.[3] These lawmakers can put more trust in what their leaders tell them because what is good for the party's electoral fortunes is often good for their individual fortunes as well.

By contrast, lawmakers out of step with the party's orthodoxy, especially moderate lawmakers representing moderate or cross-pressured districts, often find that the party's priorities do not match theirs or their districts'. For them, the way leaders restrict and use information is troublesome. These lawmakers know they need to learn and consider the details of any bill before they decide to support or oppose it, because they have learned from experience that what their party wants is not always in their best interest. They become tremendously frustrated when they cannot find the information they need independently.

A closer look at the statements made by the rank-and-file lawmakers and staff interviewed demonstrates this dynamic. Each was asked to describe how informational tactics influenced their views of the legislative process and of their legislative leaders. Since the interviews were only semistructured, the initial responses often led to a different array of follow-ups. Nonetheless, that the initial questioning on this subject was the same for each interviewee allows me to compare their reactions. Specifically, each of them could be categorized as to whether they expressed frustration at the use of informational tactics generally and whether they trusted the information they got from their party and committee leaders.

In evaluating and categorizing interviewees' responses, I had to look at more than just words. Often their body language and tone of voice were just as telling. Since these questions were asked near the end of the interviews, I had typically been able to deduce something about their personalities by the time we broached the subject of trust. Since some interviewees were excitable about whatever was discussed, an excited response to this line of questioning did not necessarily mean they were agitated. Conversely, when an interviewee had been calm throughout the interview but displayed great agitation on this subject, it signaled something very important. In fact, it was not uncommon for the interviewees to really come alive during this line of questioning.[4]

To ensure that the conclusions drawn here are solely about followers, I limited this analysis to lawmakers and staffers who could be understood as purely rank and file. In other words, I compared only the statements of lawmakers who had never held a leadership post and of staffers who had never worked in a leadership or committee office.[5] This left fifteen lawmakers and staffers. To distinguish between mainstream members of the party and relative moderates, I used the DW-NOMINATE scores of each interviewee, or the scores of staffers' bosses. For retired members of Congress I used the average first-dimension DW-NOMINATE score for their whole careers, because I asked these former members to reflect on their entire time in office. For sitting members, I used the score for the Congress during which the interview took place. For staffers I used their bosses' scores at the time of the interview.[6] I then compared each of these scores with the range of scores from their party during the same period. Lawmakers and the staffs of lawmakers in the most moderate 20 percent of their party at the time of the interview (or in the case of former members, those who averaged out to being in the most moderate 20 percent during the span of their careers) were designated as moderates, while the rest of the interviewees were understood as mainstream.[7]

Table 7.1 summarizes the categorization of the interviewees and the views they expressed. Among the fifteen individuals, I categorized ten as mainstream and coded the other five as moderates. Generally, main-

TABLE 7.1. **Ideology and the responses of rank-and-file members and staffers**

Ideological group	Frustrated?	Trust in party information	Trust in committee information
Mainstream	yes	no	yes
Mainstream	yes	no	yes
Mainstream	yes	yes	yes
Mainstream	no	no	yes
Mainstream	no	yes	yes
Mainstream	no	yes	yes
Mainstream	no	no	yes
Mainstream	no	yes	yes
Mainstream	no	yes	yes
Mainstream	no	yes	yes
Moderate	yes	no	yes
Moderate	yes	no	yes
Moderate	yes	no	yes
Moderate	yes	no	no
Moderate	no	no	yes

Source: Interviews with rank-and-file lawmakers and staff. See appendix A.

stream lawmakers and staff were more positive and expressed less frustration about informational tactics, though the feeling was far from unanimous. Of the ten mainstream individuals interviewed, just three expressed frustration; by contrast, four of the five moderates did. Mainstream members and staff felt that though their legislative leaders' actions might not have been ideal, they could still do their jobs well enough and were informed enough to make decisions. Some of these people were very positive about their ability to get the information needed: "We had great information on the bills and the pros and cons actually with those who were for it and against it."[8]

One former member who had sat on a committee dealing with rather technical issues provided a typical positive response about whether he felt the hurried consideration of some bills left him and his staff enough time: "Yes, there was usually enough time. No surprises on the committees I was on. The chairman let you know what was in it."[9]

Two staffers for mainstream lawmakers said that while the information they got may not have been comprehensive, they usually were able to get enough information to do their job. According to one: "What the leadership would give you was mostly vote recommendations and talking points. Not a whole lot of substance. Sometimes there isn't enough time to get all the information you want, but you do the best you can."[10]

Another staffer even explained how her boss's rather orthodox district allowed her to trust the information they were getting from the leadership: "Our district is not that atypical, so in most circumstances the information [the party leaders] have on the national level is going to be helpful in understanding how things will work in our district."[11]

Others said that while they would have liked more time to review legislation, they understood why the leaders managed the process as they did:

> RANK-AND-FILE MEMBER: I was there during one of the busiest Congresses of all. Of course I would have liked more time to look at legislation, but the leadership did the best they could. . . . Certainly we were criticized for speed with the health care bill, but a lot of that was misinformation. Generally things were not done so quickly that I was uninformed.[12]
>
> RANK-AND-FILE STAFFER: If something is being compressed it's being done for a reason. Things are always done quickly for a reason. Obviously it's always better to go through regular order; that should always be the goal. But sometimes it's just not possible.[13]

Of course the mainstream individuals interviewed were not uniformly positive. One staffer for a mainstream lawmaker still expressed frustration about the inability of their office to get their voices heard and achieve their legislative goals:

> RANK-AND-FILE STAFFER: I will say that it can be stressful in that there are times when we want to offer amendments or there is limited time, as I mentioned earlier, to entirely analyze something and to offer a change to it, a fix to what we would want. Normally, at least, our leadership will work with you if there is something that is really important to your district or to the congressman and try to come up with a solution, but that's not always the case. That can be frustrating.[14]

Another former member who could generally be considered part of the mainstream in his party expressed concern that the speed of legislative process could let the majority leadership abuse the system and give lawmakers little time to consider the implications:

> RANK-AND-FILE MEMBER: Clearly, at the beginning of last year when the stimulus legislation was brought to the floor there was a great deal of de-

tail in there that I don't think rank-and-file members had an opportunity to review. I view that as problematic. . . . In fact, I think that is a large abuse, and it creates a situation where you are voting on things that literally you haven't had time to review![15]

By comparison, the moderate lawmakers and staff interviewed were more routinely negative about the use of informational tactics and expressed far more frustration. In some instances these moderates understood why their leaders did what they did, but they were still displeased with the process:

> RANK-AND-FILE MEMBER: I wish the party leadership was more honest with us, because no legislation is perfect. But I also know they have incentives to not provide full information to the members about what is going on. That's just how things work here.[16]
>
> RANK-AND-FILE MEMBER: I was skeptical of information provided by the party leadership. Leaders would put out information to try to get the response they wanted from their members. The information was always perfectly valid, but it was also one-sided. You can play with language like that.[17]

One staffer in particular became quite animated in discussing the way one of his boss's committees would withhold information. This staffer, quoted on the same subject in chapter 4, when asked about trust sarcastically reiterated his disgust with receiving information from other offices before he received it from his party's committee staff: "Not infrequently I will get copies of the bills from outside stakeholders or from minority offices before I get them from the majority committee staff. Minority committee staff have a very different approach to the legislative process. I hope I'm not sounding too bitter about it."[18] Later this staffer became very blunt concerning the way many rank-and-file offices feel about their leaders: "At the end of the day, personal office staffers often feel that committee staff is not trying to help us in any way, and in fact they are actually working against us because they want to compress the timetable such that we cannot review and change the legislation so that the legislation can be exactly what they want. And that's exactly what happens."[19]

Some of these moderates made explicit reference to their relative positions in their parties or the nature of their districts in describing their reaction to the information they received:

RANK-AND-FILE MEMBER: I was more skeptical of the information that came from the party leadership because my district required me to be.[20]

Even one fairly mainstream lawmaker said the information coming from the party leadership was not particularly helpful in these instances:

RANK-AND-FILE MEMBER: [Leadership information] was useless for some-body from a swing district. I couldn't image it actually being useful to any-one like me. Perhaps people who were like-minded could use it politically, but it wasn't good information. I would have preferred they made better ar-guments for their side. I needed information that attacked the other side's argument in a cogent and effective way, but that's not what they gave you.[21]

Generally, as shown in table 7.1, lawmakers and staffers regardless of their ideological orientation were somewhat skeptical of the informa-tion coming from their party leaders. All together, only six of the inter-viewees said they trusted what their leaders told them. Most understood that this information was biased and that it largely amounted to parti-san political arguments in favor of the leadership's position. Neverthe-less, mainstream lawmakers and staff still often saw the information as useful, especially as a way to explain their votes on major legislation to their constituents:

RANK-AND-FILE MEMBER: The information they gave us was useful primar-ily as back-up information. But it was especially useful when they gave you information specific to your district.[22]
RANK-AND-FILE STAFFER: As far as paper, the whip's office puts more out now than they ever had, I think, which is really good. Instead of just saying what the schedule will be, they'll really describe the bill.[23]

Moderate lawmakers, by contrast, typically cannot make the same use of information from the party leadership. Unlike many of their mainstream colleagues, they cannot rely on a sizable party base within their constituency for reelection, and partisan talking points will not be as helpful as they try to explain their actions.

Interestingly, while most of the rank-and-file lawmakers and staffers interviewed were wary of party leadership information or understood it to be superficial, all but one expressed some trust in the information provided by committees and committee staffers. These included several lawmakers who expressed deep skepticism about their party leadership:

RANK-AND-FILE MEMBER: All of the information was shared. That's how we operated on the [omitted] Committee.[24]

RANK-AND-FILE STAFFER: Sometimes the committee will provide you with unsolicited information if they know it is important to your boss. Most of the time, however, you have to ask. But if you develop the right relationships with the committee staff you can get good information.[25]

Often lawmakers and staff would say, unprompted, that they relied on committee information. Early in the interviews, when I asked them how they became informed about legislation or what sources they primarily turned to, committees and committee staff were almost always among the first sources mentioned:

RANK-AND-FILE MEMBER: You go to the appropriate committee chairman first.[26]

RANK-AND-FILE MEMBER: Committee staff are a useful source of information, as is CRS.[27]

JC: How did you go about becoming informed about the bill?

RANK-AND-FILE MEMBER: My staff would go to the committee to find out.[28]

By contrast, the party leadership was never spontaneously mentioned as an initial source of information.

Some of the leadership staffers interviewed acknowledged that the way they managed information might not be ideal for some rank-and-file lawmakers, and that they knew not everyone was happy about it. As one staffer put it, keeping members in the dark was regrettable, but ultimately unavoidable:

LEADERSHIP STAFFER: The nature of the negotiations with the president and the Senate forced us to have to often leave our members, and even committee chairmen, in the dark about what was going on. . . . It happens quite a bit that poor communication causes these problems. But really it's unavoidable.[29]

One former leadership staffer summarized the dilemma quite well:

LEADERSHIP STAFFER: The complaints that are raised [by the rank and file] against it are very legitimate. But of course the leadership always has their legitimate reasons for doing so. It's just a matter of how much trust you put in the leadership to be doing the right thing. I think members on both sides now have to have that kind of delegation and trust in their leadership to do the right thing and protect the majority or get it back in the next election.[30]

Ultimately, it appears that some lawmakers, especially those from relatively partisan districts or those who fall within the mainstream of their party's orthodoxy on most issues, are more willing to trust their leaders and the information they provide than are those who are outside the party's orthodoxy or who represent swing districts. This suggests that leaders may have to try harder to get some lawmakers to stand with the party on votes, or that in some instances it may simply be more difficult to persuade recalcitrant lawmakers to get in line. The following discussion of the challenges faced by Speaker Boehner and the Republican leadership during the 112th Congress speaks to this point.

Limits to Leadership and the New Republican Majority

The lessons of this chapter are instructive in part because they suggest where the limits to the information-based powers of legislative leaders may lie. Leaders' abilities to restrict and control information are always beneficial in hampering the opposition of the minority—at least as long as they manage the information effectively.[31] If they are to influence their own rank and file, however, their lawmakers need to trust them enough to give credence to what they are saying. Recall that chapter 3 noted that trustworthiness was a key factor in what information lawmakers seek out and consider. But as noted above, using informational tactics too forcefully may erode lawmakers' trust in their leaders, and those with less trust express less willingness to take what their leaders tell them at face value. At times this limitation may temper leaders' inclinations to use the tactics at their disposal as aggressively as they could. For our understanding of congressional leadership, this limitation also suggests that when a leader or group of leaders seems less credible to the rank and file, they may be less effective in using their informational advantages.

The experience of the Republican leadership after the 2010 elections provides an opportunity to further investigate these claims. The 2010 midterm elections were a stunning victory for congressional Republicans. Just two years after a twenty-one-seat electoral loss, Republicans gained sixty-three seats and established a commanding forty-nine-seat majority to start the 112th Congress. This new Republican majority included eighty-four freshmen—more than one-third of the conference. This was not the first time a new majority had a substantial number of new members. At the 1994 midterms, seventy-four freshmen Republicans were elected (about 32 percent of the conference) as the GOP took control of the House for the first time in forty years. However, there are key differences between the storied freshman class of the Republican Revolution and those of the 2010 elections. The freshman class of the 104th Congress entered with remarkable loyalty to Speaker Newt Gingrich. Since the late 1980s, Gingrich had worked to personally recruit and support Republican congressional candidates, and during the election almost half of the new Republicans in 1995 had been closely advised and supported by Gingrich's GOPAC training organization.[32] In fact, Gingrich's strongest bases of support during the 104th Congress were freshmen and sophomore Republicans, many of whom he had personally recruited and supported during their initial runs for Congress.[33]

The Republican class elected in 2010 held no similar loyalty to Speaker John Boehner or the senior Republican leadership. Unlike the Republican Revolution, which was a top-down movement led by Gingrich and other congressional Republicans, the Tea Party movement that energized the Republican electoral victory in 2010 is better understood as bottom-up. The early Tea Party rallies were coordinated by umbrella groups, such as Tea Party Patriots and Tea Party Nation, and were funded and supported by libertarian groups such as FreedomWorks, which were organized and operated by conservative elites and former lawmakers, not by sitting representatives in Congress or anyone in a Republican leadership organization. The movement had a decidedly anti-establishment flavor as well, and many Tea Party affiliates saw as one of its goals purging the Republican Party of those deemed not conservative enough (see Gervais and Morris 2012, 246). While the Tea Party is best understood as a "new incarnation of long-standing strands in U.S. conservatism," its organization and operation was decidedly divorced from the Republican Party and from elected Republican elites (Williamson, Skocpol, and Coggin 2011, 26).

Many of the eighty-four new Republican lawmakers had benefited from or were strongly supported by Tea Party–affiliated groups. Karpowitz et al. (2011), for example, note that endorsements from these groups significantly affected Republican congressional primaries throughout 2010 and that voters supporting Tea Party candidates felt less strongly attached to the Republican Party than other Republican voters. Many of these new lawmakers did not owe much to the Republican leadership; in fact, they may have felt determined to establish their independence from "establishment" figures. This created a dynamic where many of the new conservative members of the House Republican Conference were skeptical of their leaders from the start and less willing to give significant credence to information and cues they provided.

After their election, this freshman class and other conservative lawmakers influenced by the Tea Party coalesced in a way that may have undermined the ability of Speaker Boehner and the Republican leadership to leverage their informational advantages. While the media made much of Representative Michele Bachmann's (R-MN) Tea Party Caucus, the real manifestation of the skepticism the Tea Party and other conservatives felt about their leadership has been the Republican Study Committee (RSC). The RSC was founded in the 1970s by conservative activist and Heritage Foundation founder Paul Weyrich and Representative Phil Crane (R-IL) to create an organization for conservative Republicans on Capitol Hill. Working in unison with the Heritage Foundation, the RSC develops conservative policy options and alternatives and helps coordinate action and information sharing among its members.

Priding itself on placing ideological purity over partisan loyalty, the RSC has always been skeptical of the Republican leadership. In fact the organization was founded in part because of conservative dissatisfaction with President Richard Nixon and Minority Leader Gerald Ford (R-MI).[34] Modeling it after the Democratic Study Group, formed by liberal Democrats to counterbalance senior conservatives in their party, the founders of the RSC recognized the need for staff and other resources to counterbalance their own leaders: "Members soon realized that pressuring leadership required real resources—staff members to churn out studies, charts, and memos, and to organize the logistics of a new, independent caucus. To accomplish this, Crane and his staff designed a system to hire apparatchiks for their new organization by putting them on multiple payrolls. That way, say, five lawmakers might split the cost of one operative."[35]

The RSC still pools resources to hire staff. *Politico* notes that during the 112th Congress RSC members paid dues that varied with their seniority and position. Freshmen members had to pay $2,500 to join, other rank-and-file members owed $5,000, and senior members and steering committee members paid $10,000.[36] In addition, the RSC benefits from its connection with the Heritage Foundation, with its multimillion-dollar annual budget and large staff.

For years the threat of the RSC was minimal for the Republican leadership. Membership in the caucus was small—never more than a dozen lawmakers—and while the Republicans were in the minority throughout the 1970s and 1980s the Democratic Party was a much bigger threat to conservative ideals. Nevertheless, Gingrich recognized its potential when he took the Speakership in 1995 and abolished the RSC along with all other legislative study organizations. Ironically, this led to a rebirth and revitalization of the RSC as new conservatives in the party were motivated to maintain the caucus within the rules. Nonetheless, the group remained small, never having more than forty members in the 1990s.[37]

Since the 2010 elections, however, the RSC has become a major force in the Republican conference. Throughout the 2000s the group grew in prominence among conservative Republicans. Fueled by Tea Party influence over conservative members of the party in general, but especially among the incoming freshmen class, the RSC's membership ballooned to 164 at the start of the 112th Congress—over two-thirds of the party's total membership. The RSC came to represent a large subset of Republicans who felt at least some skepticism toward their formal leaders and the messages, information, and cues coming from the party. With more members the RSC took in more dues for more staff and more resources, making it even more viable as a competing source of information.[38] Combined with the Tea Party movement, the growth and revitalization of the RSC created a second power center and a secondary source of information and perspectives within the new Republican majority.

For the current Republican leaders this means that as much as two-thirds of their party's members at any time may look to the RSC for information to balance what their formal leadership is telling them. And there are many reasons to believe the message coming from the RSC often conflicts with the party's. One of the staffers interviewed for this study was closely associated with the RSC. He described its mission and efforts:

CAUCUS STAFFER: We pull our leadership to the right or our party to the right, in general. Right now we have the bonus of being in the majority, so we try to force conservative solutions into law. And I say force, because with these things it's always a process. There's no conservative anything that's going to just naturally become law, especially since we have a Democratic president and a Democratic Senate. But frankly, even when Republicans had control of all three there was nothing conservative that was just naturally occurring.[39]

During the interview I focused on trying to ascertain the nature of the relationship between the RSC and the Republican leadership. At one juncture I asked the staffer if he could recall an instance when the RSC and the leadership worked closely together on a policy proposal:

CAUCUS STAFFER: Let's see. The fact that I have to pause to think about it should probably tell you something. Yeah, it's not that often. It's not that we never agree with them, but it's usually they're doing their thing and we'll do our thing, and if we talk and happen to agree, great. But it's pretty rare that we work together on some big initiative, which is kind of a shame if you think about it.[40]

Generally, the staffer described a situation where, even though some members of the Republican leadership team, like Majority Leader Eric Cantor (R-VA), were members of the RSC, it was a somewhat adversarial relationship in which the leadership and the RSC each pursued its own legislative goals. He noted that when the leadership did attempt to work with the RSC, it was generally out of fear that members of the caucus would oppose its position on the floor:

CAUCUS STAFFER: They'll work with us if they fear us—if they fear us bringing something down. They don't work with us because they love the RSC's ideology or energy. It's a different motivation. . . . They want our votes or don't want our no votes, or are afraid we'll blow something up.[41]

In many ways the RSC works to manage information the way legislative leaders do. It holds regular meetings with members and staff to discuss issues, find out what the caucus is interested in, and dispense cues and talking points. It also is aggressive in distributing information and materials to help members view policy options through a conservative lens. However, the RSC seems more receptive and interactive with the whole of its membership than many leaders. It can act this way because, unlike the party leadership, it has complete control over its membership. Whereas anyone elected to Congress as a Republican gets to be part of the Republican conference, RSC members "have to pay dues, and we have a steering committee that approves members. So, we kind manage membership in the group."[42] As the staffer described it, the RSC has reached a place where it makes sure key members and groups within the caucus are on board before it rolls out a proposal or an official position. In the 112th Congress, especially, this meant making sure the more than sixty members of the freshman class who joined the RSC were on board with whatever it did:

> CAUCUS STAFFER: Anything we do we try to make sure there are freshman involved. They just carry a certain weight these days. They are a very large class. They were sent here from the Tea Party, you know, they are supposedly tied in to the grass roots more than members who have been there for sixteen years. And [our chairman] knows that, so anything that we do we try to push freshmen out to the front. We did this welfare reform bill. First, it was a Jim Jordan bill. Then it was a Jim Jordan–Scott Garrett bill. Then they were like, we need a freshman. Now it's a Jim Jordan–Scott Garrett–Tim Scott of South Carolina. It often works that way. If we don't do that we at least do a press conference with a freshman. Even for our budget, [the chairman] said to me today, "Let's make sure it's our freshmen pitching this. Not, Jim Jordan says this is the RSC budget, but the freshmen say this is the RSC budget."[43]

As a result, there is much more unity among RSC members, and potentially a lot more trust, than among all Republicans. As noted earlier, open communication, sharing, and unity of opinion breed the kind of trust than can make leadership effective. With the RSC, this approach can make what its leadership and staff communicate that much more influential during policymaking.

The fingerprints of the RSC can be seen on some of the Republican leadership's most notable struggles since the party took power in 2011. One example is the fiscal year 2011 spending standoff that took place during the first four months of the 112th Congress. Throughout the 2010 elections, Republicans, including Boehner and his leadership team, pledged to cut federal spending by $100 billion. However, on taking control of the House in January the leadership backtracked, suggesting the actual cuts would necessarily be much smaller.[44] Realizing that finding $100 billion in cuts would be difficult with almost half of the fiscal year already over, the leaders began to temper expectations. The RSC, however, was committed to the $100 billion target and sent a letter, with ninety cosigners, urging the leadership to work to uphold the pledge.

Initially the leadership floated a bill that would cut spending by $35 billion for the rest of the fiscal year, but this proposal faced a stiff backlash within the party. During a closed-door meeting, freshmen and conservative members clashed with more senior Republicans over the nature of the cuts.[45] The Republican leadership ultimately acceded to crafting a bill that made deeper cuts.[46] In mid-February the leadership unveiled H.R. 1, which would cut roughly $60 billion in spending over the rest of the fiscal year. The leaders worked to sell the bill as a $100 billion cut, since its $1.028 trillion total spending level was roughly $100 billion below the budget request President Obama had made a year earlier. As Majority Leader Cantor put it, "What we heard here was a commitment to the $100 billion reduction number, and that's what we said we're going to do and we're going to do it."[47] However, the president's request had never been enacted, and some Republicans remained unhappy. In fact, ahead of H.R. 1's consideration, Representative Jim Jordan (R-OH), chairman of the RSC, unveiled H.R. 408, the Spending Reduction Act of 2011, which would cut $80 billion over the rest of the fiscal year and $2.5 trillion over ten years. The contents of this proposal would counter options the Republican leadership floated over the subsequent months.

Wary of defections if they tried to ram the bill through the chamber, the leaders placed H.R. 1 on the floor, open for debate and amendment, requiring only that members have their amendments printed in the *Congressional Record* a day before consideration. By allowing the rebellious and boisterous members to debate and vote on even more aggressive spending cuts, the leadership hoped they would support and pass a spending bill that could be used to negotiate with Senate Democrats before a March 4 deadline to keep the government operating. As Boehner put it, the House would work its will.[48] The result was a marathon four-day session in which more than four hundred amendments were offered, including dozens aiming to further reduce federal spending. Many of them passed, sometimes over the leaders' objections. Perhaps the most conspicuous of these was an amendment eliminating funding for the F-35 Jet Engine Program, an amendment Boehner strongly opposed.[49] Ultimately the bill passed the House on February 19 by a nearly perfect party-line vote, 235–189. Just three Republicans opposed its final passage. The RSC ultimately indicated its support for the bill through a press release before the vote. Jordan noted that while they would have liked to see deeper cuts, they viewed H.R. 1 as only the beginning.[50]

The passage of H.R. 1 has to be seen as a win for the RSC and something of a failure for the Republican leadership. The RSC pulled the leadership and the party to the right, securing almost double the spending cuts initially proposed. As the caucus staffer quoted above put it, "The C.R. was the best example of what can be done. The RSC went and got more spending cuts in place in the bill and forced it to happen. There wasn't any other entity that could have done it that way. That was great."

The leadership thus had been unable to get its message across and persuade the party to stand with the original proposal. Conceding to the RSC and the boisterous freshman class meant new headaches for the party leadership. They would still need to negotiate with Senate Democrats and the White House to craft a bill that could pass both chambers and obtain the president's signature. While the $35 billion package the leadership initially floated might have served as a reasonable starting point for such negotiations, the new $61 billion bill was well beyond anything Senate Democrats would consider, and the White House warned that it would be vetoed if it came to the president's desk. In addition, many of the amendments adopted on the floor had policy implications that Democrats would never accept, including defunding Planned Parenthood and the Affordable Care Act and altering the Environmental Protection Agency's climate-change policies. The leadership now needed to find a way to secure a spending package that its conservative wing could accept but that would pass the Senate and find support from the president. This task was to prove challenging.

As the March 4 deadline approached, Boehner said he could not accept even a temporary extension that did not include at least some new spending cuts: "I am not going to move any kind of short-term C.R. at current levels. When we say we're going to cut spending, read my lips: We're going to cut spending."[51] On February 25, the Republican leadership floated a proposal to end the impasse. The bill (H.J.Res. 44) would be a two-week extension with $4 billion in cuts to earmarks, education, and transportation programs that President Obama had previously indicated he would eliminate.[52] This proposal struck the right balance for the leadership. Cutting $4 billion in a two-week extension was enough to obtain the support of conservatives in their caucus, while targeting unobjectionable cuts made it hard for Democrats to say no. The bill passed with bipartisan support. However, it did not solve the problem for the leadership but only bought more time.

Over the next two weeks House Republicans and Senate Democrats held tight to their positions. Senate Democrats passed a bill, supported by the White House, that would cut $6.5 billion, while Republicans continued to insist on deeper cuts that came closer to the $61 billion total in H.R. 1.[53] On March 11, with the support of the leadership, House Appropriations Chair Harold Rogers (R-KY) proposed a three-week extension (H.J.Res. 48) cutting $6 billion and allowing negotiators more time to reach a resolution. Like the previous extension, it eliminated more earmarks and federal programs that the White House had already slated for elimination and again avoided making deep cuts or attaching controversial policy riders, so that again it would be hard for Democrats to object.[54] However, the new plan drew criticism from the RSC. Republican leaders worked to assuage the discontent and convince its conservative flank that the fight over fiscal year 2011 spending was just the first act and that the upcoming fiscal year 2012 budget would be the party's real opportunity to make substantial cuts to federal spending.[55] Despite these efforts, Jordan indicated the RSC leadership would oppose the bill, stating that it could support only a plan that cut spending for the rest of the fiscal year and made deep cuts or eliminated funding to Planned Parenthood, the Affordable Care Act, and the Environmental Protection Agency.[56] On the final vote on H.J.Res. 48 numerous RSC members swung against its passage. Although it prevailed 271–158, fifty-four Republicans opposed it, and it needed the support of the Democrats to pass.

With three more weeks to negotiate, the Republican leadership once again faced the challenge of finding a resolution that could hold the support of enough RSC members to pass but would also be acceptable to Senate Democrats and the White House. Now, having seen the RSC's power to sap the votes of conservatives, the leadership had to be more careful to ensure that its right flank would hold. Although the three-week extension obtained enough Republican support to pass, another attempt that made anything less than substantial cuts might result in a larger defection among RSC-aligned Republicans and possibly an embarrassing failure for the leadership.

Not long after the passage of the extension, it appeared that Senate Democrats might accept a spending bill that made between $30 billion and $40 billion in cuts, similar to what Boehner had initially proposed in January. However, Democrats remained fundamentally opposed to the policy riders included in H.R. 1. With the RSC insisting on those riders, the standoff could not be resolved.[57] As it persisted over the subsequent weeks, House Republicans passed a series of largely symbolic measures making big cuts to some programs and providing funding to others, and the battle lines generally remained unchanged. Conservatives continued to insist on deep cuts and policy riders, and Democrats continued to insist they would support neither. Some conservatives even criticized the $30 billion in cuts floated by Democrats as too small, with or without the policy riders. Meanwhile Republican leaders continued to try to convince their caucus that the upcoming 2012 budget resolution was the "real fight."[58]

With just hours remaining before a government shutdown was set to begin on April 9, Democratic and Republican leaders announced they had reached a deal. The agreement would fund the government for the rest of the fiscal year, making $39 billion in cuts along the way but, reflecting public pressure to avoid a shutdown, the bill excluded the policy riders.[59] Boehner and the Republican leadership worked to sell the agreement as a win. In a closed-door meeting, Boehner told his party that the cuts were the steepest he could possible wring from Democrats and that they represented the "largest real dollar spending cut in American history."[60] Boehner's sales pitch initially appeared to have some impact with many Republicans, including some conservatives and RSC members who said they were satisfied with the deal. Representative Todd Rokita (R-IN), for example, stated, "Instead of politicians talking about how much they wanted to increase spending, the entire debate of the last two months was about how much spending to reduce and where. . . . This is progress."[61] Representative Alan Nunnelee (R-MS) also noted his support for the deal: "Now that an agreement has been made, we can advance our fight from saving billions of dollars to saving trillions of dollars. . . . While we would have liked more, I think that the deal reached was the most anyone could have expected under the circumstances."[62] Some even parroted the leadership's talking point that this was just the beginning in the fight over spending. Freshman Kristi Noem (R-SD), for example, offering her tentative support for the deal, predicted, "There will be more opportunities to address our spending issues and to come to an agreement on how better to be more, much more responsible with our taxpayer dollars."[63]

Others remained skeptical. The statements of several RSC members noted that they might have a hard time supporting a deal that fell short of their $100 billion pledge. Representative Louie Gohmert (R-TX), for example, noted, "I have to wait to hear what it is, but $39 billion is not what we pledged to do."[64] As details about the plan emerged, opposition among the conservative ranks appeared to grow. Before the vote, Jim Jordan and former RSC chair Mike Pence (R-IN) registered their opposition.[65] Other conservatives, RSC members, and freshmen followed suit. For example, Representative Jason Chaffetz (R-UT) said he would likely oppose the plan: "We have to make a bigger dent faster."[66] Freshman Bill Huizenga (R-MI) likewise expressed his disappointment in the plan: "It doesn't go far enough or fast enough for me, based on what we've seen so far."[67]

Ultimately the deal (H.R. 1473) passed the House 260–167, but with 59 Republicans voting no. With just 179 Republicans voting in support, the leadership again needed dozens of Democratic votes for the plan to pass. Once again, RSC opposition had damaged the Republican leadership's ability to maintain support within the conference. The influence of the RSC on this vote and the other fiscal year 2011 spending proposals and continuing resolutions in the House can be further assessed and summarized with logistic regression analyses predicting the votes of lawmakers on each roll call (see table 7.2). Included in each analysis is a variable for each lawmaker's party, first- and second-dimension DW-NOMINATE score,[68] and whether each was a member of the RSC.[69] The RSC membership variable indicates which lawmakers would likely be listening to and influenced by the positions and messages of the RSC leadership. The results suggest that support and opposition from the RSC leaders played a meaningful role in the roll-call outcomes. Recall that on the first two votes, the passage of H.R. 1 and the two-week extension passed on March 1 (H.J.Res. 44), the RSC was supportive. In each of these analyses the RSC membership variable is not statistically significant—it did not meaningfully influence the votes. Republican leaders were able to hold the party together. However, the opposition noted by Jim Jordan on the three-week extension (H.J.Res. 48) and the final deal (H.R. 1473) appears consequential. On those votes, RSC membership predicts a decreased likelihood of support. Specifically on the final vote, while the model predicts non-RSC Republicans had, on average, a

TABLE 7.2. **Predicting yea votes on major fy 2011 spending bills, February to April 2011**

	H.R. 1 (February 19)	H.J. Res. 44 (March 1)	H.J. Res. 48 (March 15)	H.R. 1473 (April 14)
Republican	–	−4.919*** (1.574)	2.650*** (0.933)	3.235*** (0.939)
DW-NOMINATE first dimension	10.620*** (1.738)	9.037*** (1.639)	−0.022 (0.795)	−0.603 (0.793)
DW-NOMINATE second dimension	−0.250 (1.335)	1.426*** (0.504)	1.898*** (0.341)	2.289*** (0.354)
RSC member	−0.288 (1.145)	−1.189 (0.929)	−1.568*** (0.467)	−1.558*** (0.455)
Constant	−1.647** (0.762)	3.897*** (0.693)	−0.279 (0.353)	−0.621* (0.354)
N	424	426	429	426
ePCP	0.983	0.832	0.629	0.631

Note: Coefficients estimated using logistic regression; significance tests are two-tailed. The "Republican" variable is excluded in the analysis of H.R. 1 because it dropped out during the calculations.
*$p < .10$
**$p < .05$
***$p < .01$

92 percent likelihood of supporting the final deal, RSC Republicans had just a 72 percent likelihood of voting with their leadership.

These effects underscore the influence the RSC and Tea Party Republicans would have on the Republican leadership's ability to lead throughout the 112th Congress. It also underscores that when legislative leaders cannot control and manage information among their followers, when they are unable to shape the debate surrounding a bill, when they are unable to get their followers to buy into leadership messages and cues, then their ability to corral their caucus and lead the chamber is weakened. During the 112th Congress the RSC used its clout and resources to function as a second source of information and cues for conservative and Tea Party–backed lawmakers hesitant to follow Boehner and the party leadership. During the fiscal year 2011 budget fight they were able to affect decisions made by the leadership—keeping them from bringing their original spending plan to the floor, influencing their decisions to bring H.R. 1 to the floor under an open rule, and pushing Boehner to take a hard line during negotiations with the White House and the Senate Democratic leadership. This pattern would reemerge on other major policy battles throughout the 112th Congress, including the debt ceiling standoff later that year. In short, with informational advantages reduced, legislative leaders' efficiency is also reduced.

However, this case study also shows the persistence of certain informational advantages that only formal legislative leaders have, and it shows how these advantages allow leaders to continue using informational tactics to lead even when their informational hegemony is imperiled. No matter what other informational power centers exist, leaders still have information about activities such as behind-the-scenes negotiations that other actors cannot know. Additionally, only legislative leaders can control the procedural mechanisms, such as self-execution or reducing layover times, that allow them to restrict the rank and file's access to bill language. Only the leadership can still control what information is available about major legislative proposals and when.

Despite the challenge of the RSC, Boehner and his leadership team wielded these powers effectively. Recall that when the final spending deal was announced, the leadership's message was that $39 billion in cuts was the most that could be extracted from Senate Democrats. The RSC, not being part of these negotiations, could not as legitimately claim otherwise. Furthermore, the Republican leadership controlled the release of the final deal's language and gave its members very little time to review it before the vote. Under these conditions Republican rank-and-file had to decide whether to take what the leadership had negotiated for them or get nothing at all.

Furthermore, while the spending fight and negotiations unfolded in a manner the leadership might not have preferred, the final deal looked at lot more like the $35 billion plan Boehner had initially proposed in January than the $100 billion plan the RSC had demanded. And though 59 Republicans opposed the final deal, 179 supported it, including numerous RSC members and Tea Party–backed freshmen. Apparently the leadership's message resonated with enough Republicans to keep most of them on board. In fact, before the vote several of the 84 freshmen noted that they saw the deal as a win and echoed that message. Representative Mo Brooks (R-AL) stated, "It shows that we're serious and we're determined in the fight to cut spending to amounts that we can afford. . . . This was one battle in the war, and we won the first battle — and it resumes tomorrow."[70] Others even noted that they were beginning to trust the Speaker. Freshman Representative James Lankford (R-OK) called the deal a win and noted, "[Boehner's] really building trust with a lot of the freshmen."[71]

In sum, the struggles Boehner and his leadership team had during the 112th Congress stemmed in part from the skepticism many rank-and-file

Republicans had about their leaders, as manifested in the RSC. However, it is also apparent that the informational advantages the Republican leadership enjoyed still allowed it to lead, keeping on the party line many conservatives and Tea Partiers who may have found reasons to side with the RSC and passing a bill that looked a lot like the one the leadership initially proposed. This highlights not only the role of trust in legislative leadership, but also the resilience of information-based power.

Conclusion

As this chapter shows, legislative leaders cannot simply run roughshod over the House members, and their influence is somewhat limited by the trust their followers place in them and in the information they provide. This underscores why, as detailed in chapter 4, leaders make very strategic decisions about when to restrict access to information, focusing on the most important bills and on legislation where their informational dominance is threatened. While legislative leaders likely are always gathering information from and providing messages to their members, they cannot use every weapon in their arsenal on every bill lest they engender dissatisfaction and ultimately distrust among their rank and file.

Nonetheless, this should not be seen as an extremely stringent limitation on leaders' abilities to leverage their informational advantages. Even in a case like the 112th Congress, where the House Republican leadership faced a caucus that was significantly skeptical about them, Boehner and his leadership team still had substantial influence over the final legislation passed regarding fiscal year 2011 spending, the debt ceiling, and other major policy battles. Even given skepticism and opposition among their members, legislative leaders still enjoy far more resources than their rank and file, including information, and control over the procedural levers of the chamber.

The findings of this chapter suggest something else as well. They suggest that the way legislative leaders manage the House, leveraging their informational advantages into influence, is making both parties less comfortable for political moderates and anyone else outside the party's orthodoxy. For members of Congress whose policy opinions typically align with the leadership or who are elected from solidly partisan districts, there is often little reason to be skeptical of the messages coming from party leaders or committee chairs. If it is in the party's interest,

it is probably in their interest as well. But for members who are elected
from swing districts, or from districts that tend to support the presidential candidate from the other party, following the leadership can be haz-
ardous. As one former rank-and-file member put it during an interview,
"You've got absolute Democrats who once the leadership makes a decision they decide they will vote with the party. And it's the same with the
Republicans. I was never one of those. If I at any time had voted with
the Democratic Party more than 60 percent of the time I would have lost
early in my career."[72]

These lawmakers have the most to lose from the informational imbalance described in this book. They are also the ones who are going
to cause the most headaches for the leadership. They will be the ones in
the majority trying to slow the process, maximize the deliberations, and
in the eyes of legislative leaders, endanger the passage of the legislation.
Political moderates and other nontraditional partisans consequently are
going to find themselves out of favor with their leaders and out of step
with their party. They will frequently be frustrated, unable to get the information they think they need to make safe decisions or to effect the
changes they want in legislation considered in committee or on the floor.

This is of course just one implication of the style and extent of leadership influence described here. The next chapter delves more comprehensively into the conclusions we can draw from this study and how its findings affect how we understand the United States Congress.

CHAPTER EIGHT

Representation in the Dark

A place where every interest and shade of opinion in the country can have its cause even passionately pleaded . . . is in itself, if it answered to no other purpose, one of the most important political institutions that can exist anywhere, and one of the foremost benefits of free government.—John Stuart Mill 1975 (1861), 227

Yet, for government to function, the obstructions of the constitutional mechanism must be overcome, and it is the party that casts a web, at times weak, at times strong, over the dispersed organs of government and gives them a semblance of unity.—V. O. Key 1952, 693

Congress is responsible for representing the interests of the public as laws are drafted, debated, enacted, and executed. Yet the preceding chapters show that the abilities of different lawmakers to represent the interests of their particular constituents at any time, and on any bill, are highly unequal. Hall (1996) demonstrated that lawmakers' patterns of participation are driven by their interests as they put forth more effort on issues of particular importance to them or their constituents and remain less involved on others. This book speaks to inequities in a different way. On many bills, lawmakers simply do not have the necessary information to participate in most of the legislative process, and their input is limited to casting votes. In other words, beyond an intensity bias in Congress, there is an *information* bias. Those who have the resources to obtain information can participate meaningfully and extensively. All the rest are left to represent their constituents in the dark.

The preceding chapters explore the various ways legislative leaders in the House of Representatives are empowered by their informational advantages. Leveraging their substantial staff resources, both party leaders and committee leaders can gather intelligence about the preferences and opinions of their rank and file, the minority, and outside interests and can use this information to strategically draft legislation and craft messages, talking points, and cues to shape the preferences of their rank and file and keep them in line on votes as well as counter the opposition tactics of the minority. On bills of special importance, or when their informational hegemony is threatened, leaders can use a number of tactics to restrict access to information about the legislation being considered so as to keep the chamber in the dark, make their rank and file rely more on leadership cues, and further undercut the minority. This method of leadership power and influence is demonstrated through evidence culled from elite interviews, participant observation, quantitative data analyses, and case studies. Combined, the evidence shows how legislative leaders in the House can take the lead and exercise substantial control over House policymaking.

This book concludes by considering the ways leaders' informational powers shape the House and our understanding of it. Among other things, the findings presented here underscore the importance of inequities in the course of policymaking, the pervasive power of party leaders and committee chairs, and the crucial role information plays in congressional politics. However, the greatest implication is that legislating in the dark affects the fundamental character of the House of Representatives. The leader-centric nature of the chamber, with its asymmetrical access to information, allows leaders to get their heterogeneous party members to act as responsible, programmatic parties and support and pass partisan platforms. But it comes at a cost to the deliberative character of the chamber. Deliberation is minimized and most lawmakers are excluded from most of the legislative process, unable to represent the interests of their unique constituencies as policymaking proceeds and laws are made.

Inequities in the House of Representatives

As noted in the introduction, few studies of Congress fully engage with how institutionalized inequities among lawmakers affect policymaking in the House of Representatives. In particular, inequities in the information different lawmakers hold have not been appreciated. While most studies do not a priori deny that informational asymmetries affect congressional politics, most concentrate on aspects of policymaking that equalize lawmakers, primarily by stressing lawmaker preferences and roll-call voting. However, while lawmakers may be equals in the number of votes they can cast, when we consider the broader legislative process, to paraphrase George Orwell, some are more equal than others.

Without adequate information or the resources to obtain it, rank-and-file lawmakers are hindered as they try to engage in the legislative process. Without an invitation from a committee chair or the majority leadership, helping to draft most major legislation is simply not possible. Insofar as leaders keep what they are doing quiet, rank-and-file lawmakers will know only what they are told, which is often very little. Lawmakers can try to counteract this on one or two issue areas by developing expertise and committing their time and resources to being persistent with the leadership, asking the right questions, earning a place at the table, and over the long run developing a reputation as a force on those issues. But as Hall (1996) finds, the rank-and-file lawmakers who ultimately can become involved on any bill are very few. Furthermore, on all issues and bills besides the ones they have specialized on, they will simply be unable to become very involved.

Rank-and-file lawmakers are hindered in the subsequent stages of the legislative process as well. Without information about what is being drafted, and often without access to legislative language until very late in the game, it is hard for them to make changes to legislation during committee markups or floor consideration. Without the time to analyze a bill, members often have almost no chance of offering well-crafted amendments. Even when they do, leaders can deflect at least some amendments by appealing to their own superior information. For example, when an amendment is offered that a committee chair opposes, he or she can claim that such language was ruled out during negotiations with the administration or the Senate and that inserting it into the bill might unravel the carefully crafted compromise and jeopardize its ultimate passage into law. Legislative leaders can credibly make these claims, which can sway the votes of majority lawmakers.

Despite having formal equality at the voting stage, at least in having the same number of votes, rank-and-file lawmakers are hindered by their informational inequalities at this stage as well. Lawmakers want to make the best decision on each of the roll-call votes they cast. They know their votes are the aspect of their legislative records that is most easily assessed and that voting out of line with their constituents on the wrong bill could end their political careers. But finding the information they need to cast the best vote is difficult, and lawmakers often must get information and cues from their leaders. Thus the preferences that rank-and-file lawmakers hold and develop on particular bills are shaped by what their leaders tell them. Since most legislation is multifaceted and multidimensional, many lawmakers on both sides of the aisle could find reasons to support or oppose most important bills. But if the information they use to make these calculations is biased, they typically will decide to stand with their leaders, whether or not that is the best decision or the one they would have made under different conditions.

These consequences of informational asymmetries, conversely, empower those in the know. Insofar as legislative leaders are the ones endowed with the valuable information, these dynamics will always bolster their power and influence. Combined with their procedural powers, their informational advantages allow leaders to manage what is drafted into legislation, control what other actors know about that legislative language and when they know it, minimize the ability of rank-and-file lawmakers or the minority to alter that legislation, and then line up their rank and file to support final votes. This view of legislating places party leaders and committee chairs at the center and relegates rank-and-file lawmakers to the sidelines.

This perspective on congressional policymaking affects how we might understand and evaluate existing scholarly conceptions of congressional action. It poses a distinct challenge to preference-based models, especially those that use spatial and formal modeling approaches assuming perfect or near perfect information among all lawmakers (see, for example, Krehbiel 1998). This study shows that such an assumption is tenuous and questionable and that congressional policymaking is deeply affected by who has what information and how they use it. What is more, the findings in this book speak to how we understand the lawmaker preferences that form the foundation of these and other theories. With their ability to manipulate what information their rank and file consider when forming preferences about legislation, leaders can sometimes shape the very preferences that are supposed to drive congressional action. Consider the case of the REAL ID Act (presented in chapter 6). The Republican leadership worked to get their rank and file to see the bill as a national security issue in line with the recommendations of the 9/11 Commission and consistent with IRTPA, rather than as a harsh anti-immigration bill or a bill full of provisions that were deemed too extreme to pass just months earlier. In doing so they shaped some lawmakers' preferences on that bill before its consideration and before the vote. Thus, preference-based theories presenting lawmakers' preferences as exogenously defined or finding it unnecessary to model legislative leaders as part of policymaking misunderstand the influence of leaders and probably overstate the importance of rank-and-file preferences in congressional politics.

In short, informational inequalities are an important aspect of power dynamics and policymaking in the House of Representatives, and scholars should take them into account when studying or theorizing about the forces driving congressional actions. This is particularly true for our understanding of the power and influence of party leaders and committee chairs.

Leadership Power and Influence

Perhaps the clearest implication of this book is that information is an important source of leadership power and influence in the House of Representatives. This deduction allows for a more pervasive and significant understanding of their power than that reached by most scholarship on Congress. Establishing a scholarly basis for understanding such influence is necessary, in part, because journalists', practitioners', and close observers' accounts on the subject differ greatly from the findings of most academic studies.

As pointed out in chapter 1, while studies of Congress typically recognize leaders as important, the focus is often on the limits to their power, such as contextual constraints, or on means of influence that are inherently limited. Journalistic accounts, in contrast, present congressional action as leader-centric, focusing on the moves and negotiations of party leaders and committee chairs and how these actions make or break legislative efforts in Congress. Similarly, remembrances of past leaders often extoll their influence. We call Lyndon Johnson "master of the Senate," Joseph Cannon and Thomas Reed "czars," and Henry Clay "the great compromiser." Practitioners and close observers of Congress also recognize legislative leaders as very powerful. Lee Hamilton, a former representative from Indiana, describes leadership power in Congress this way:

> Leaders are the ones in a position to determine which issues will come forward for consideration, and which will be set aside; what oversight will be

done and what ignored; what will get the media spotlight and what will remain in the shadows; which programs will be included in appropriations bills
and which won't. They have enormous power, in other words, over both the
substance and the style of Congress. (Hamilton 2008)

The preeminent scholarly conceptions of leaders and their power cannot easily explain a view of them as expansively powerful and integral
to policymaking in Congress. However, an information-based perspective can.

Consider explanations of leadership influence that focus on their ability to distribute or withhold legislative and electoral resources as carrots
and sticks to compel their rank and file to act a certain way. As noted in
chapter 1, leaders rarely hand down punishments. To use this source of
power regularly, they would have to be making threats repeatedly while
rarely following through. But hollow threats are unlikely to bother the
rank and file. Perhaps more important, wielding resources for leverage is
risky. If leaders punish their members too aggressively, for example, by
refusing to help them with their campaigns, these lawmakers' individual
electoral chances might be damaged, which in turn will damage the collective fortunes of the party. Thus, relying on punishments to keep lawmakers in line can have negative consequences for the party as a whole.
This means leaders are likely to be very constrained in employing these
tactics.

Informational powers, if well directed, carry less risk. While leaders
are concealing from their rank and file aspects of legislation that may be
unappealing or may be unpopular in their districts, they are obscuring
this information from the opposition and the public as well. In general,
leaders' messaging tactics are aimed at framing a bill and presenting it
in a positive light—at controlling the policy debate. If they can do that
well, they not only will persuade their rank and file to stand with them
but will provide ways for them to justify their votes and undercut arguments from the opposition. Because informational powers carry less risk
to the party and may carry broader benefits, leaders can use them frequently and aggressively to lead the chamber. This mechanism thus better explains why journalists and practitioners see leadership power as so
widespread.

Information-based power also explains significant leadership more
easily than contextual theories. While contextual theories can present leaders as active and deeply involved in every step of the legislative

process, the decisions about what is to be done and how far leaders can go remain, theoretically at least, with the rank and file in each party, so leaders are significantly constrained by their preferences. The steps taken to advance a bill reflect agreement and consent among the party's members, not the independent force of a leader acting as a master or a czar, or exercising "enormous power." Under the informational perspective forwarded here, leaders can sometimes shape the very preferences that are supposed to limit them, giving them more leeway than most contextual theories suggest.

In many ways the findings in this book are compatible with principal-agent approaches to the study of leader-follower dynamics in Congress. Principal-agent theories, like Kiewiet and McCubbins's (1991), note that "hidden information" is a potential risk in delegating authority and resources to party leaders and committee chairs. Within this framework leaders are expected to make independent decisions, including those that the broader membership may not have made collectively. As Cox and McCubbins (2005) put it, parties delegate authority to senior partners to ensure that the party can overcome the problems inherent in collective action. However, studies employing principal-agent approaches typically theorize or find that agency loss and hidden information are minimized by institutional design or by the terms of the delegation—for example, through majority vote checks on leaders' decisions. This study differs in recognizing that the effects of hidden information actually are magnified by institutional design. In allocating resources and information so disproportionately to those holding leadership posts, congressional parties weaken their ability to check their leaders' actions. With limited time to consider the legislative packages crafted by their legislative leaders, rank-and-file lawmakers must depend on information *from* their leaders in order to evaluate the bill and make a voting decision. This gives leaders much more leeway to take the reins of the chamber than is expected in most principal-agent theories.

Of course, leadership influence is not without its limits. As chapter 7 emphasizes, for these informational powers to be effective, members must have some trust in what their leaders tell them, and using informational tactics aggressively over time is likely to erode that trust. This is especially true for those outside the party's orthodoxy, who have the most to lose from being influenced to follow their leaders. However, despite these limitations leaders' informational powers provide a basis for understanding significant and pervasive leadership influence in

Congress in a way that is consonant with the accounts of journalists and practitioners and in a way that existing theories cannot.

Party Strength versus Representative Deliberation

These findings about informational inequalities and leadership power speak to a larger tension in congressional policymaking. While these informational powers serve as an underpinning of party power and discipline in the House and help leaders induce their followers to pass programmatic party platforms, they sacrifice deliberation and undermine individual lawmakers' abilities to represent the interests of their districts and constituents as policymaking unfolds. Uncovered here is that party strength and representative deliberations appear to conflict with each other in the House of Representatives.

As citizens and scholars we profess a desire for both. On one hand, we want Congress to act with dispatch to address the nation's problems and provide solutions. Gridlock and inaction are seen as symptoms of Congress's ills, since the public believes extended political conflict and debate are largely unnecessary and a sign that lawmakers are corrupt or out of touch (see Hibbing and Theiss-Morse 2002). The doctrine of responsible parties that has often served as a normative guide for studies in American politics similarly underscores the value placed on active congressional parties, suggesting that political parties acting with unity to pursue clear policy goals generally improve the public's ability to hold government accountable and thus better the health of our political system (see American Political Science Association, Committee on Parties 1950; Ranney 1962). On the other hand, we want Congress to be a deliberative assembly where participation is broad and different voices, concerns, and interests are heard and reflected as decisions are made and laws enacted. For many political theorists, deliberation is at the heart of democratic legitimacy (see, for example, Mill 1975 [1861]; Gutmann and Thompson 2004). While scholars disagree on how much deliberation is necessary, there is general agreement on its essential characteristics: "public spiritedness, equal respect, accommodation, and equal participation" (Thompson 2008, 504). We hope to find these essential characteristics in the congressional policymaking process.

This book strongly suggests that the informational powers afforded to leaders strongly benefit party strength at the expense of the quality of deliberations. Compared with legislatures in other parts of the world, especially those in parliamentary systems, the United States Congress is not a place we expect to find strong parties. As Mayhew once put it, "the specified resources and incentive arrangements conducive to party unity among [members of the British Parliament] are absent in the congressional environment" (1974, 25). Even though congressional parties are far more unified today than in the past, they remain diverse, since each lawmaker represents a unique geographic district and leaders cannot control who is nominated to run for office. Coordinated party action requires institutional structures and incentives that solve collective action dilemmas and encourage cooperation. The asymmetrical distribution of information and the ability of legislative leaders to influence what information their lawmakers have when making decisions are such structures. Because lawmakers already have numerous incentives to support their parties and their leaders (see Lee 2009) and typically default to standing with them unless they have compelling reasons not to (Ripley 1967, 139–59; Matthews and Stimson 1975; Kingdon 1989), being able to influence what their rank and file are looking at, considering, and thinking about as they make decisions helps leaders reinforce partisan behavior. The institutionalized unequal distribution of information in the House helps leaders do their job and hold their party's members together in committee and on the floor. It helps them get their rather heterogeneous rank and file to act like responsible parties.

However, what is gained in terms of party strength is lost in deliberative character. In leveraging their informational advantages, legislative leaders do not just reinforce partisan behavior; they limit lawmakers' abilities to participate meaningfully and independently in policymaking. In a deliberative assembly, we want the policies produced and the courses of action taken to result from meaningful discussion and debate among lawmakers representing diverse interests, at the very least among those in the majority party. However, on many occasions the opinions, stances, and statements rank-and-file lawmakers bring to committee hearings and markups and to floor consideration and debate are based on information from their leaders. Rather than displaying the pluralistic policy views of a diverse membership representing distinct geographic constituencies, debates in Congress largely reflect messages that legislative leaders have constructed to frame the issues. This can hardly be called deliberation. It gets worse when leaders actively restrict the information available on legislation. When decisions are made and bills are drafted behind closed doors by party leaders and committee chairs and presented to the rest of the chamber just hours before the vote, the participation of most lawmakers is minimal. Essentially, their involvement is reduced to accepting or rejecting what has already been done. For most members most of the time, it makes the most sense to follow their leaders on these decisions. This may be efficient, but it is not representation, nor is it deliberation.

The loss of deliberation is particularly disconcerting when the perspectives and opinions silenced are not random. In other words, if viewpoints outside the party's orthodoxy are disproportionately muzzled, and if the participation of lawmakers who fall in the moderate or extremist wings of each party is particularly limited, then the representative nature of the chamber is fundamentally at risk. Party loyalists and leaders do not have a monopoly on good policy ideas. For all the gains in terms of responsible party government, something much more intrinsic may be lost if legislative leaders can routinely silence the unique voices of the chamber.

Assessing Lawmaking "in the Dark"

How should we evaluate this style of leadership and lawmaking? Undoubtedly it tilts the balance between action and deliberation overwhelmingly, and possibly inappropriately, toward action. But while many readers may rush to judgment, decrying the lack of input and influence on any bill from most members of Congress, I want to close by urging caution. We should be mindful of what contemporary congressional policymaking might look like were legislative leaders to have less influence or were the House structured to elevate equality, deliberation, and debate. There is little doubt that citizens, scholars, and observers alike would complain that this hypothetical House could not take any action. Popular dissatisfaction with the slow-moving, obstructionist Senate, and with the frequent gridlock caused by the broader system of checks and balances, substantiates this point. Without powerful party leaders *or* committee chairs, there would be no one to herd the cats and direct the chamber toward some resolution. The House would be all talk and no action. While John Stuart Mill (1975 [1861], 227) might have been satisfied with such a legislature, "where every interest and shade of opinion in the country can have its cause even passionately pleaded," but where no other action was ever taken, it is unlikely that many others would agree.

Unfortunately, deliberation and action are unavoidably in conflict. Congress cannot closely consider policy proposals and maximize deliberation and input among its members without significantly slowing the legislative process and inviting stalemate. As Barbara Sinclair puts it, "If we expect a Congress that gives all interests a full and fair hearing on each issue and then, in every case, expeditiously passes legislation that both satisfies a majority, preferably a large one, and effectively addresses the problem in question, we are doomed to be disappointed" (Sinclair 2012, 274). Unquestionably, a balance between deliberation and action is ideal, and scholars and practitioners alike should strive to better understand how the House of Representatives, or any other legislature, can allow for meaningful participation and deliberation without tactlessly harming the ability of a majority to pursue legislative ends.

But how is such a balance achieved? Complete coverage is beyond the scope of this study, but some suggestions are worth brief mention. Simply giving lawmakers more time to consider proposals is probably not enough. As many of those interviewed noted, legislation is often complex, and it takes specialized knowledge and context to fully understand and assess it. Lawmakers need access to expert information that does not come from political actors or offices with explicit agendas. Restoring and bolstering congressional support offices that can supply this would be a good first step, including revoking the ban on the Office of Technology Assessment and other legislative service organizations (see Kelly 2012, 2013). LSOs were once a major source of policy and technical information accessible to all members of the chamber. These organizations, banned by Speaker Gingrich in 1995, employed policy experts, produced reports on policy proposals, and answered lawmakers' inquiries. Dissolving them gave legislative leaders and interest groups even more power as sources of knowledge and policy information.

Restoring these entities and protecting their independence, as well as bolstering the resources available to the Congressional Research Service (CRS) and the Congressional Budget Office, could help lawmakers obtain more policy knowledge without having to turn to their leaders. This development need not be entirely internal to Congress. The hundreds of research universities in the United States are a tremendous source of information and knowledge on a variety of technical and complex topics and policy issues. Public-private partnerships between these entities and offices such as CRS to develop and share expert knowledge with Congress could help lawmakers gain some additional information independently.

These suggestions are not a panacea. Although they would at least guarantee that additional perspectives are available, leaders would still have access to unique knowledge, such as the content of draft legislation in progress and the nature of negotiations with the other chamber or the White House. More important, doing too much to dilute leaders' advantages could lead to undesirable unintended consequences such as more gridlock. However, insofar as legislative leaders in the House of Representatives are inappropriately powerful, changes are needed to pull the legislative process out of the darkness.

Appendix A: Notes on the Qualitative Methods

This appendix provides additional information about the participant observation and elite interview methods I used for this book. I hope that parts of it can serve as a guide to other scholars engaging in similar research on Capitol Hill.

Participant Observation

As I noted in chapter 1, my participant observation research, along with the elite interviews, forms the backbone of this study. Particularly, the insights I garnered through two experiences participating in and observing congressional politics let me uncover the insights presented here about the important role that information and information asymmetries play in policymaking in the House. Each of these experiences is detailed below, as are my efforts to obtain and maintain access during these experiences. I also assess the trustworthiness of the knowledge I acquired from these experiences.

Details of my Participant Observation

I engaged in two distinct periods of participant observation on Capitol Hill. The first was as a fellow with the majority staff of the House Appropriations Committee's Subcommittee on Financial Services and

General Government, from May through August 2007. I was an entry-level staffer on the subcommittee. As such, I was not involved in drafting the subcommittee's annual spending bill, but primarily conducted background research on spending requests from members of Congress and the executive branch agencies under our jurisdiction.[1] I also helped organize meetings, markups, and briefings for the subcommittee and aided the committee's leadership during floor consideration of its bill.

My second experience was as an American Political Science Association (APSA) congressional fellow in the Office of Representative Daniel Lipinski (D-IL), from January through August 2012. I was roughly the equivalent of a legislative assistant (an LA), assisting the lawmaker in legislating on a particular subset of issues. LAs answer directly to the member, but also to the chief of staff and legislative director, who help coordinate action among the various LAs, legislative correspondents, administrative assistants, interns, and other employees. My portfolio—the set of policy issues I was responsible for—included science and technology, education, telecommunications, cybersecurity, budget, and veterans affairs. I also helped out at various points on transportation policy and defense policy and was responsible for managing two member caucuses that my congressman cochaired: the STEM Education Caucus and the Zoo and Aquarium Caucus. Some of the specific tasks I engaged in included researching active legislation and amendments on these issues and recommending support or opposition, drafting original legislation and amendments, drafting questions and statements for committee hearings, liaising with constituent, stakeholder, and government groups on these issues, writing speeches, and seeking out public relations opportunities.

These experiences were in-depth and immersive, and they allowed me not only to observe legislative staffers and members of Congress as they did their work, but also to participate myself and develop a sensibility, or understanding, for what it is like to be an actor on Capitol Hill. My methods of immersion in this world are detailed below, but it is worth noting some details about working on Capitol Hill. The hours are intense—these are not nine-to-five jobs. While committee offices often have slightly more regular hours (except when their legislation is under consideration), the schedules for members' offices are often long, harried, and unpredictable, dictated by the scheduling decisions of the majority party leaders and committee chairs. When the House was in session, the day would start by 9:00 a.m. and continue until an unspecified time in the evening, depending on what was happening on the floor or elsewhere around the Capitol. At the earliest, office hours would end between 6:00 and 7:00, but often the workday stretched beyond that. On occasion we would work past midnight. The day itself was often packed with committee hearings, briefings, the occasional markup, meetings with constituent and stakeholder groups, e-mail and phone communications, meetings and briefings with the member, reading, research, and other tasks. In the evening it might be necessary to attend a reception or two to speak with other important individuals or groups or be briefed by a think tank over dinner. At home, smart phone in hand, separation from the job was never absolute, since I needed to be ready to promptly answer important e-mails, or even return to the office. In short, working on Capitol Hill requires full immersion if the researcher is to make sense of its world.

Initial Access

For interpretive methods, like participant observation research, access is ongoing. As Schwartz-Shea and Yanow put it, "'Access' is not simply a matter of knocking on the door, literally or figuratively, in order to get in. . . . Participant observer sociologists and others doing interview-based studies also came to understand 'access' in a less literal sense, linked to the more interpersonal notions of establishing rapport with their interlocutors" (2012, 58–59).

In other words, getting your foot in the door is one thing, but gaining access to private conversations, important happenings, culturally specific insights, and other often sensitive information requires something more. This section describes how I got my foot in the door; the next section describes that "something more."

For participant observation in Congress, a researcher is not in a position to "select" the place to be immersed; you have to convince a congressional office that you are worth the risk of making you part of the staff. More than anything, offices want to know that you will not cause problems, become an embarrassment, or waste limited office space. They also want to know that you will contribute to their mission. For each experience I had to provide assurances that I would be a constructive, enthusiastic, and trustworthy member of the team and that I would produce good work.

For my first foray, which resulted in my time with the Appropriations

Committee, I planned to investigate committee politics, so I sought a position on the majority staff of nearly every committee on Capitol Hill. Having no experience in Congress beyond a college internship, I could not claim any expertise, and it was difficult to demonstrate that I would be a productive member of a staff. I presented myself in four ways: First, I made it clear that I would work without pay. Second, I stressed my time as a member of the College Democrats of New York to present myself as a committed Democrat who wanted to help achieve Democratic party aims. Third, I emphasized my level of education (then as a PhD student) to portray myself as intelligent, adaptable, and having strong research skills. Fourth, I emphasized my willingness to do any work the committee needed and to do it with a smile. The subcommittee ultimately offered me a position. As a new subcommittee, they were short on staff (just four full-time staffers) and needed assistance. Free labor from a graduate student was hard to pass up. The initial agreement was that I would help research funding requests made to the subcommittee in return for being allowed to observe and engage in the committee's work and ask whatever questions I wanted.

Gaining initial access was easier the second time around. Having acquired some experience on Capitol Hill, I could more easily demonstrate my value. My status as an APSA congressional fellow also provided legitimacy, especially with offices that had previously employed APSA fellows. This time I applied broadly, not caring about the type of office, whether committee, leadership, or rank and file. My appeal emphasized my knowledge of Capitol Hill culture and work, which would allow me to begin working effectively on day one, with less of a learning curve than most fellows. In each cover letter I also appealed to the office's sense of mission, describing my interest in the lawmaker, my enthusiasm for the work the office was doing, and my desire to help those efforts by doing whatever work was needed, no matter how boring or banal. This type of personal appeal is essential, because member offices want staffers who believe in their member of Congress.

These efforts paid off in each case, granting me initial access within Capitol Hill offices and opportunities to participate directly in policymaking. However, to truly engage in sensemaking during these experiences, I had to take steps to fully immerse myself and to maintain "access" by establishing trust and rapport with those working alongside me.

Continued Access and Immersion

Once in the door, a researcher seeking immersion for participant observation research has to develop a presentation of self. Interpretive researchers cannot separate themselves from the environment they are studying. They are inherently part of it. Consequently, their identities, attitudes, and actions can significantly affect how other participants react to them, and ultimately how enmeshed they can become and how much knowledge they can accrue (Feldman, Bell, and Berger 2003; Shehata 2014). My approach was to blend into the world of Capitol Hill as much as possible, minimizing the ways I could be seen as different from other congressional staffers or making those I was trying to understand uncomfortable so that they altered their behavior in some way.

Among those I worked with directly within each of the offices where I was employed, this was a challenge. They knew I was an outsider, knew I was a researcher, and knew I was ultimately there to study and understand what they did. To the degree that they felt "watched" they might act differently. My approach to mute this effect was threefold. First, I talked as little as possible about my life as an academic and researcher. I did not bring up my identity as a political scientist with my coworkers, and I avoided conversations about this as much as possible. I never carried a notebook or wrote down anything anyone said in their presence. The goal was to lessen their seeing me as anything other than a colleague. Second, I strove to gain their trust as a coworker by working very hard, arriving early, staying late, offering to help, and doing as much as I could to show that I cared and that I took the job as seriously as they did. I personally invested in the mission of each office and became part of the team. Basically, I acted the way anyone in a new job would act to gain the trust of coworkers and their boss.

Third, I worked to develop rapport on a personal level. I got to know my coworkers, asked about their kids, and met them for happy hours after work and for barbecues on the weekend. In short, I socialized as anyone would in a close-knit office environment. During my first week in one office, I even subjected myself to the junior staff's initiation ritual: doing shots of cheap whiskey and climbing onto the roof of a House office building to bask in the warm glow of the Capitol Dome, just out of sight of the Capitol police.

Blending in was simpler with those outside the offices I worked in.

These people did not know I was a researcher, and they did not need to know. The business cards I carried were the same as any other staffer's. When people asked who I was or introduced themselves, I replied, "Jim Curry, Congressman Lipinski's office," or "Jim Curry, House Appropriations." Only a few people outside my offices even knew I was a fellow, but this meant very little in terms of their perception of my identity. Washington is full of fellows who are there to contribute to policymaking rather than study or understand it.[2] The APSA Congressional Fellowship Program is the exception in this sense, and it is less well known than many of the policy-focused fellowships. Consequently, those who saw me as a fellow did not consider me unusual.

These efforts worked. In both of my experiences, as I gained trust, developed rapport, and immersed myself as a congressional staffer, I was given more important work and trusted with more information, which exposed me to more interesting and insightful tasks and experiences. I was able to participate as fully as the others and develop the "ethnographic sensibility" of a congressional staffer (Schatz 2009). Outside these offices I could interact with members of Congress and staffers as one of them, taking part in their conversations about everything important to them, from policy, to process, to gossip.

To be sure, these experiences were natural and enjoyable, and the connections I developed both professionally and socially were and are real. These things cannot be faked. In immersing myself as I describe, it is inevitable that the distinction between research relationship and friendship blurs, as many field researchers attest (see, e.g., Beech et al. 2009). Indeed, I left Capitol Hill with new friendships. For some this may raise concerns about "contamination" of the research site or the worry that my efforts to fit in caused me to "go native" and lose some necessary emotional or cognitive distance or "objectivity." However, for interpretive research such distance and objectivity are neither realistic nor desirable (see Schwartz-Shea and Yanow 2012). Without full immersion and developing these connections, including emotional connections, my sensemaking of the world of congressional actors would be incomplete. Ignoring the emotional side of legislating in Congress would have distorted my understanding of the motives that drive the behavior of these actors. Furthermore, those with such concerns imply that scholars and researchers cannot recognize their biases as they accrue, analyze, and reflect on their research experiences. This is off the mark. As Schwartz-Shea and Yanow put it, "To presume that humans cannot be aware of their 'biases' is to reject human consciousness—the possibility of self-awareness and reflexivity—and human capacity for learning" (2012, 98). Ultimately, all types of research—positive or interpretive—include some bias or limitation, but many of the insights in this book were made possible only by this immersed participant observation research.

Field Notes

I did not take regular or extensive field notes during my research for several reasons. As noted above, I did not want to make those I worked with uncomfortable or wary of my presence. My demanding "job" requirements often left little time during the day for reflection or for note taking, and by the end of many workdays it was often very late, and I was sufficiently tired that I was not in the right frame of mind to collect my thoughts. Finally, I found that when I tried too hard to commit the things I saw or experienced to memory I would forget more and remember less, and that if I tried to record things as they were happening I would miss important details or misinterpret things, not properly taking the full context into account. Thus I would infrequently—perhaps once a week or so, at the end of a day that did not end so late—organize my thoughts and write down some impressions of what I experienced, observed, or learned. However, it is worth repeating that the greatest benefit of this participant observation was not what I observed, but what I gained in terms of "ethnographic sensibility," of understanding the logic of the actors in the world I was studying.

Assessing My Participant Observation

There are several criteria for assessing interpretive research and the trustworthiness of its findings (see Schwartz-Shea and Yanow 2012, 91–114; Schwartz-Shea 2014). The information above implicitly addresses some of these, but a few means of assessment merit particular attention. One such criterion is "reflexivity," or consideration of how my own sensemaking, identity, and particular circumstances may have affected the knowledge I assessed and the conclusions I ultimately drew. My particular identity was probably an advantage in this regard. As a young white, middle-class male (I was twenty-three and twenty-seven to twenty-eight during my periods of participant observation), I fit the profile of most congressional staffers (see Congressional Management Foundation 2003). Consequently, I could blend in both physically and culturally. Along with my efforts to fit in through my actions, my similarity to most congressional actors who interacted with me meant they were likely to behave "normally" around me. Having two distinct experiences helped as well. Spending one period of participant observation as a committee leadership staffer and the other in a rank-and-file member's office allowed me to see the role of information in congressional policymaking from both sides and to avoid developing a bias toward one perspective or the other. The elite interviews I conducted, mostly between the two periods of participant observation, likely broadened my perspective as well, exposing me to the opinions and perceptions of actors in various roles in Congress as well as to some who were no longer in office.

In a couple of ways, though, my experiences surely limited my exposure to some aspects of Hill politics. For one, Appropriations is rather unique among committees, including a dedication to process that is a bit more bipartisan than most. My experience working in that committee may have understated the partisan conflict found in most committees. My time in Representative Lipinski's office may have limited my perception as well. A moderate Democrat, Lipinski and his staff work most often with other moderates and are more committed than most congressional offices to advancing legislation in a bipartisan manner. Primarily, this meant that my interactions with lawmakers and staffers on the ideological extremes of both parties were less frequent and usually antagonistic. However, I was aware of these factors before beginning each period of participant observation and was careful to take them into account when recording my thoughts, analyzing my experiences, and writing this book.

My experiences may have limited the knowledge I acquired in another way. Generally, I cannot rule out that some of the knowledge and impressions I accrued might have been slightly altered had my roles in each office been different. For example, as a legislative assistant, my view of the policymaking process and congressional politics may have differed in some ways from the view of a chief of staff or an elected representative. Again, however, these concerns are mitigated by the multiple methods I adopted. In conducting interviews I was able to expose myself to the views of those holding other positions, and by conducting quantitative analyses I could evaluate my research questions in another light.

In addition to reflexivity, interpretive researchers can check their sensemaking by taking steps to think broadly, suspend judgment, or generally keep an open mind about the patterns of knowledge they perceive. This is obviously difficult, but it is something I worked to achieve. Again, having two distinct periods of participant observation in very different offices helped in this regard. Furthermore, my note-taking method (described above), though driven primarily by other concerns, was likely helpful. By not taking notes in the moment, but only after longer periods of evaluation and reflection, I was able to avoid snap judgments about what I experienced and put things into a broader perspective. I did not record anything about my experiences during my first month in each office, but focused on becoming acclimated and achieving some sense of my environment before attempting to record anything concrete. Finally, my multiple methods were helpful once again: with interview evidence and quantitative analyses pointing toward similar conclusions, I can have more confidence in the knowledge I gained through participant observation.

All together, the steps I took reduced favoritism toward any single set of actors as much as possible, so that the knowledge I gathered through participant observation allowed me to gain a well-rounded view of congressional politics. With the addition of interview evidence and quantitative analyses, the findings in this book should inspire confidence.

Elite Interviews

I conducted elite interviews with members of Congress and staff, past and present, between January 2010 and December 2013, with all but two occurring between the two periods of participant observation. Because it is important to provide as much information as possible to increase readers' confidence in interview evidence (Bleich and Pekkanen 2013), in this section I describe the interviewees, how I obtained the interviews, the interview procedure, and my method of transcribing and ascribing meaning to the interviews.

The Interviewees

Each interview was conducted with the promise of anonymity in part to make it more likely that those I asked would agree to an interview, but also to encourage the interviewees to speak candidly without fearing retribution or harm to their careers. Although the identities of these

TABLE A.I. **The interviewees**

By party

Democrat	20
Republican	12

By role

Party leadership	9
Committee leadership	7
Rank and file	15
Caucus	1

Member or staff

Member	9
Staff	23

In or out of office

In office	20
Out of office	12
Total	**32**

thirty-two individuals must be protected, I can provide some description. Table A.1 summarizes information about those interviewed. Interviewees are categorized by their party, whether they were currently serving in Congress or had served previously, whether they were members or staffers, and their role. The first three categorizations are straightforward, but the fourth requires some explanation. For sitting members of Congress and staffs, their role was defined by the position they held at the time of the interview. Those designated as party leaders include anyone in the Speaker's office, in the offices of the majority or minority leader, in the offices of the majority or minority whip, or on the staff of the Rules Committee. Committee leaders include full committee chairs and ranking members, but not subcommittee chairs or ranking members, for the reasons I noted in chapter 1. Committee staffs are any staffers who worked solely in a committee office. All other sitting members and staffers are categorized as rank and file. Former members and staffers are harder to categorize, since some, at different times in their careers, might have been both rank and file and leaders. I based the categorization on the focus of the interview. If the interview concentrated on their time as a committee chair, for example, or a party leadership staffer, they would be categorized as such. If it focused on their time as rank and file, they would be coded that way.

Taken together, the sample is diverse. It leans Democratic, with

63 percent of the interviewees being Democrats, but it includes a good number from both sides of the aisle. It also includes a variety among the roles: 47 percent are rank and file, 28 percent are party leaders, and 22 percent are committee leaders or staff. One interviewee was designated as a "caucus" staffer since he formally worked for a caucus. Nine members of Congress are in the sample, and the rest of the interviewees are staffers. Finally, 63 percent of the interviewees were working in Congress at the time of the interview; the rest were out of Congress.

Obtaining Interviews

As described in chapter 1, I obtained the interviews primarily by using a snowball selection technique, but I cold-contacted offices as well. Notably, individuals referred to me through the snowball method were much more likely to agree to an interview. All together, 71 percent of the interviews were obtained after a referral, reflecting what Ross Baker (2011) terms the importance of "credentials." Every potential interviewee was contacted by e-mail using a customized form letter like the one printed below:

[Name of potential interviewee],

[Name of reference] and I recently had a conversation and [he/she] suggested I get in contact with you. I am a political science professor at the University of Utah and I am currently conducting research about the role communication and information play in the legislative process in the House.

Given your experience, I would appreciate the opportunity to briefly discuss the topic with you in an interview. Any information we discuss would only be used anonymously and for my academic research, and all records from the interview would be securely stored and accessible only by me. I understand that you have an exceedingly busy schedule and promise to not take up too much of your time.

I would greatly appreciate it if you would be willing to speak with me. I can be flexible on times and dates to match your schedule. I hope to hear from you soon. If you have any questions about the interview or interview process I will be happy to answer them.

Best,
Jim Curry

From one e-mail to the next, the only changes were the name of the reference and the position I held at the time. If I was contacting the person without a reference, I left out the first sentence. Some people required additional reassurance, and some asked about the purpose of the study, what the interview would be used for, when and how it might be published, and if anyone else would have access to the records. I gave them more details about the questions I would ask, the security of files, and the way they would be described in any publications, and I assured them that the statements made would be used only in my academic research.

Interview Process

The interviews were in-depth and semistructured, and I asked primarily open-ended questions. I had the dual goals of keeping the interviews open enough so that I might discover things I had not anticipated, while keeping them structured enough to be comparable, addressing similar themes and topics. Meeting these dual goals meant asking all the interviewees a similar set of initial questions, with follow-up questions that allowed the interviews to go in different directions. The interviews typically lasted twenty to forty minutes. I conducted all but seven in person and the rest over the phone.

Every interview began the same way. I gave interviewees some basic background on the project and the interviews, then assured them that the interviews were anonymous and that anything discussed would be used only in my academic research and that they would be identified only in the most basic way: as a current or former member of Congress or staffer who was rank and file, a committee leader, or part of the party's leadership. I then asked each one if I could record the interview. All but one of the in-person interviewees allowed me to use the tape recorder. None of the phone interviews were recorded. From there the interviews differed slightly based on whether the person was rank and file, a committee leader or staffer, or a party leadership staffer.

With rank-and-file members and staffers I asked how they obtained information about legislation, whom they turned to and trusted for that information, the difficulties of obtaining information, and how different processes and procedures altered these things. Interviews with committee and party leaders and staffers focused on how they gathered, distributed, used, and restricted information. With committee leaders and staffers, for example, I would ask how they communicated the contents of bill drafts to committee members, what considerations determined how they communicated that information, and other questions about their communication with member offices. I asked party leaders similar questions aimed at how they collected intelligence about their members, what they communicated to their membership about legislation, how they communicated it, and how they employed their procedural prerogatives.

More often than not, the interviews became more interesting with the follow-up questions. A challenge in doing interviews on Capitol Hill is knowing not only what to ask, but how to ask it (Beckmann and Hall 2013). Here my experience as a participant observer was helpful. Through my time with the Appropriations subcommittee I had become familiar with "Hill speak"—the jargon actors on Capitol Hill use to describe and discuss their work. I had also become familiar with how members of Congress and staffers *think* about what they do. This knowledge helped me formulate my questions and develop rapport with the interviewees, and it should give readers confidence that my questions tapped relevant information.

Even so, different interviewees required different approaches. While some gave very detailed and complete answers to the initial questions, others came alive only after a few follow-up queries or in discussing specific bills or issues. Generally the interviews were most rewarding and insightful when they became more conversational and less formal. The study benefited from these variations among the interviews, allowing me to gain information and insights that I had not anticipated and aiding the theoretical and empirical development of the project.

Transcription and Interpretation

The way I transcribed and subsequently organized, understood, and used the interview evidence here follows the interpretive tradition. In assessing the meaning of what the interviewees were trying to convey, I had to go beyond the spoken words. Additional features—including tone of voice, posture, and even silences—spoke volumes. Furthermore, I considered what each interviewee conveyed in a broader context. Statements, discussions, and narratives were considered and reconsidered, evaluated and reevaluated in light of the other interviews and the inferences that emerged more generally from the study. In addition, when analyzing the interview transcripts I also relied on my participant observation experiences to put the words into context and uncover meaning. Joe Soss describes this manner of evaluation well:

> The open-ended format of my conversations with clients, and the large bodies of text they produced, made it possible to explore how individual comments fit together as parts of a more meaningful whole. Indeed, the parts and the whole, as I gradually came to understand them, could be used as a kind of commentary on one another. Small, seemingly isolated statements hinted at broader conceptions; their patterns of convergence and discord offered a way to develop, assess, and revise an emerging account of latent understanding. At the same time, as my inferences about broader conceptions took shape, they offered a contextual standpoint for making sense of each individual comment and for linking seemingly unconnected remarks. (2014, 162–63)

The goal was to develop as complete an understanding as possible of what each interviewee was trying to convey, how it fit within or against the broader framework of my theory and evidence, and to uncover the narrative that all the interviews combined formed about information and power in Congress.

My method of transcription reflected these goals. Since most of the interviews were recorded, I could use my notepad to jot down other features of the interviewee and the interview. For example, I could characterize posture, tone, or level of agitation at different points in the interview—things that would not be clear on the recording. With the seven phone interviews I could not jot down visual impressions, but I could note when the interviewees became excited, or when there were noticeable changes in how they spoke. With every interview I tried hard to complete the transcription within twenty-four hours, while the conversation was fresh in my mind, so I could note these additional elements. The anger, frustration, and sarcasm that several of the interviewees conveyed in both verbal and nonverbal ways were ultimately very important for construing meaning. These notes on tone, posture, and other features are reflected in how the interviews are presented in this book. At times, I use italics to show interviewees' clear emphasis. Words and sentences followed by exclamation points show where interviewees yelled or got excited. At other times I describe their tone or mood in the text immediately before or after the quotation.

These interviews provide the insights of influential lawmakers and staffers with years of congressional experience on the topic of this book. Combined with the evidence I culled from participant observation and statistical data analyses, the information I present in this book is multifaceted and provides a compelling basis for my conclusions.

Appendix B: Notes on the Quantitative Methods

Dataset of Important Legislation, 1999–2010

Table B.1 provides an overview of the bills in the dataset of important legislation.

Issue Coding Details

The Policy Agendas Project codebook I used is the version updated in April 2013. The primary issue coding of eight bills was altered from that provided in the Congressional Bills Project's (CBP) data because I

TABLE B.1. **Information on the dataset of important legislation**

Legislation by type	
Bill	479
Resolution	7
Joint resolution	20
Concurrent resolution	12
Total	518

Legislation by Congress	
106th	123
107th	85
108th	64
109th	69
110th	88
111th	89
Average per Congress	86

strongly disagree with the code given there. I made the changes for a variety of reasons, detailed in table B.2.

Matching the Issue Coding with the Center for Responsive Politics' Industries

To develop the *interest group interest* measure, I matched each of the Center for Responsive Politics' industry sectors with one or two of the Policy Agendas Project's nineteen major issue areas. The results of the matching are presented in table B.3.

TABLE B.2. **Changes from the Congressional Bills Project's issue coding**

Bill	Congress	CBP Coding	New Coding	Reason
H.R. 4520	108th	Productivity and Competitiveness of US Business, US Balance of Payments (code 1806)	Taxation, Tax Policy, and Tax Reform (code 107)	The bill as introduced deals with taxation beyond promoting the international competitiveness of US businesses
H.R. 3	109th	Police, Fire, and Weapons Control (code 1209)	Transportation— General (code 1000)	The bill reauthorizes the Department of Transportation
H.R. 6	110th	Civil Defense and Homeland Security (code 1615)	Energy—General (code 800)	Substance of the bill deals directly with energy production
H.R. 2669	110th	National Budget and Debt (code 105)	Higher Education (code 601)	The bill deals with college costs and student loans
H.R. 2701	111th	Government Efficiency and Bureaucratic Oversight (code 2002)	Military Intelligence, CIA, Espionage (code 1603)	The bill is an Intelligence reauthorization
H.R. 2892	111th	Government Operations—General (code 2000)	Civil Defense and Homeland Security (code 1615)	The bill reauthorizes the Department of Homeland Security
H.R. 4314	111th	Government Operations—Other (code 2099)	National Budget and Debt (code 105)	The bill increases the federal debt ceiling
H.R. 4872	111th	Taxation, Tax Policy, and Tax Reform (code 107)	Comprehensive Health Care Reform (code 301)	The is the reconciliation bill that accompanied the Affordable Care Act

TABLE B.3. **Matching the Policy Agendas Project's issue coding to the Center for Responsive Politics' issue industries**

Center for Responsive Politics Industry Sector	Policy Agendas Project	
	Issue topic 1	Issue topic 2
Agricultural Services and Products	Agriculture	
Crop Production and Basic Processing	Agriculture	
Dairy	Agriculture	
Food Processing and Sales	Agriculture	
Forestry and Forest Products	Agriculture	Public Lands and Water Management
Livestock	Agriculture	
Poultry and Eggs	Agriculture	
Tobacco	Agriculture	
Miscellaneous Agriculture	Agriculture	
Building Materials and Equipment	Banking, Finance, and Domestic Commerce	Foreign Trade
Construction Services	Banking, Finance, and Domestic Commerce	Foreign Trade
General Contractors	Banking, Finance, and Domestic Commerce	Foreign Trade
Special Trade Contractors	Banking, Finance, and Domestic Commerce	Foreign Trade
Accountants	Banking, Finance, and Domestic Commerce	
Commercial Banks	Banking, Finance, and Domestic Commerce	Foreign Trade
Credit Unions	Banking, Finance, and Domestic Commerce	
Finance / Credit Companies	Banking, Finance, and Domestic Commerce	Foreign Trade
Insurance	Banking, Finance, and Domestic Commerce	
Real Estate	Banking, Finance, and Domestic Commerce	
Savings and Loans	Banking, Finance, and Domestic Commerce	
Securities and Investment	Banking, Finance, and Domestic Commerce	Foreign Trade
Miscellaneous Finance	Banking, Finance, and Domestic Commerce	
Beer, Wine and Liquor	Banking, Finance, and Domestic Commerce	Foreign Trade
Business Associations	Banking, Finance, and Domestic Commerce	Foreign Trade
Business Services	Banking, Finance, and Domestic Commerce	Foreign Trade
Casinos/Gambling	Banking, Finance, and Domestic Commerce	Foreign Trade

(*continued*)

Center for Responsive Politics Industry Sector	Policy Agendas Project	
	Issue topic 1	Issue topic 2
Food and Beverage	Banking, Finance, and Domestic Commerce	Foreign Trade
Lodging/Tourism	Banking, Finance, and Domestic Commerce	Foreign Trade
Miscellaneous Manufacturing and Distributing	Banking, Finance, and Domestic Commerce	Foreign Trade
Miscellaneous Services	Banking, Finance, and Domestic Commerce	Foreign Trade
Recreation / Live Entertainment	Banking, Finance, and Domestic Commerce	Foreign Trade
Retail Sales	Banking, Finance, and Domestic Commerce	Foreign Trade
Steel Production	Banking, Finance, and Domestic Commerce	Foreign Trade
Textiles	Banking, Finance, and Domestic Commerce	Foreign Trade
Miscellaneous Business	Banking, Finance, and Domestic Commerce	Foreign Trade
Abortion Policy/Pro-Choice	Civil Rights, Minority Issues, and Civil Liberties	
Abortion Policy/Pro-Life	Civil Rights, Minority Issues, and Civil Liberties	
Gun Rights	Civil Rights, Minority Issues, and Civil Liberties	
Women's Issues	Civil Rights, Minority Issues, and Civil Liberties	
Clergy and Religious Organizations	Civil Rights, Minority Issues, and Civil Liberties	
Home Builders	Community Development and Housing Issues	
Defense Aerospace	Defense	
Defense Electronics	Defense	
Miscellaneous Defense	Defense	
Education	Education	
Electric Utilities	Energy	
Fisheries and Wildlife	Energy	Public Lands and Water Management
Mining	Energy	Public Lands and Water Management
Oil and Gas	Energy	
Environmental Services/ Equipment	Energy	Environment
Waste Management	Energy	
Miscellaneous Energy	Energy	
Environment	Environment	
Civil Servants/Public Officials	Government Operations	
Health Professionals	Health	
Health Services/HMOs	Health	
Hospitals and Nursing Homes	Health	

Pharmaceuticals / Health Products	Health	
Miscellaneous Health	Health	
Foreign and Defense Policy	International Affairs and Foreign Aid	Defense
Pro-Israel	International Affairs and Foreign Aid	
Building Trade Unions	Labor, Employment, and Immigration	
Industrial Unions	Labor, Employment, and Immigration	
Miscellaneous Unions	Labor, Employment, and Immigration	
Public Sector Unions	Labor, Employment, and Immigration	
Teachers' Union	Labor, Employment, and Immigration	Education
Postal Union	Labor, Employment, and Immigration	Government Operations
Transportation Unions	Labor, Employment, and Immigration	Transportation
Gun Control	Law, Crime, and Family Issues	
Computers/Internet	Science, Space, Technology, and Communications	
Printing and Publishing	Science, Space, Technology and Communications	
Telecom Services and Equipment	Science, Space, Technology, and Communications	
Telephone Utilities	Science, Space, Technology, and Communications	
TV/Movies/Music	Science, Space, Technology, and Communications	
Electronics Manufacturing and Services	Science, Space, Technology, and Communications	
Miscellaneous Communications/Electronics	Science, Space, Technology, and Communications	
Human Rights	Social Welfare	
Air Transport	Transportation	
Automotive	Transportation	
Railroads	Transportation	
Sea Transport	Transportation	
Trucking	Transportation	International Affairs and Foreign Aid
Miscellaneous Transport	Transportation	
Lawyers/Law Firms	None	
Lobbyists	None	
Democratic/Liberal	None	
Republican/Conservative	None	
Miscellaneous Issues	None	
Nonprofit Institutions	None	
Other	None	

Bill Complexity Index

Table B.4 provides the full categorization of the Policy Agendas Project's major issue areas by issue complexity.

Majority Leadership Priority Issues

Table B.5 notes the issues identified as *majority leadership priority* issues by assessing the primary issue addressed by each of the bills inserted into the first ten bills slots (H.R. 1 . . . 10) in each Congress (and the eleventh slot in the 111th Congress).

TABLE B.4. **Complexity and the Policy Agendas Project's major policy topics, 106th to 111th Congresses**

Major policy topic	Percentage of bills	Level of complexity	Percentage by complexity
Macroeconomics	8.9	High	27.7
Agriculture	3.5		
Environment	0.8		
Energy	4.1		
Banking, Finance, and Domestic Commerce	8.1		
Space, Science, Technology and Communications	2.3		
Health	6.0	Moderate	65.4
Labor, Employment, and Immigration	4.1		
Education	2.9		
Transportation	2.4		
Social Welfare	2.1		
Community Development and Housing Issues	1.9		
Defense	10.6		
Foreign Trade	2.9		
International Affairs and Foreign Aid	5.2		
Government Operations	21.9		
Public Lands and Water Management	4.5		
Civil Rights, Minority Issues, and Civil Liberties	3.1	Low	7.0
Law, Crime, and Family Issues	3.9		

Note: Major issue topics are those of the Policy Agendas Project.

TABLE B.5. **Majority leadership priority issues, by Congress**

Congress	Issues
106th Congress	Elderly issues and elderly assistance programs (including Social Security Administration) Elementary and secondary education Taxation, tax policy, and tax reform Defense—general Manpower, military personnel and dependents, military courts Banking, finance, and domestic commerce—general
107th Congress	Education of underprivileged students Health—general Taxation, tax policy, and tax reform Energy—general Employee benefits
108th Congress	Prescription drug coverage and costs National budget and debt Poverty and assistance for low-income families Comprehensive health care reform Energy conservation Taxation, tax policy, and tax reform Military intelligence, CIA, espionage
109th Congress	Transportation—general Employment training and workforce development Comprehensive health care reform Alternative and renewable energy Taxation, tax policy, and tax reform Voting rights and issues
110th Congress	Civil defense and homeland security Fair labor standards Health—research and development Prescription drug coverage and costs Higher education Energy—general
111th Congress	Government operations—general Health—infants and children Civil rights, minority issues, and civil liberties—general

Tests of the Proportional Hazards Assumption

The proportional hazards assumption can be evaluated using several tests: the link test, Harrell's ρ, and plots of Schoenfeld residuals. The results of each test confirm that the assumption holds. An insignificant link test suggests that the null hypotheses that the assumption holds cannot be rejected.

Link Test

$$y^2 = 0.053 \ (0.358); p = 0.628$$

Harrell's ρ tests for each variable and the full model (global test) likewise cannot reject the null hypothesis that the assumption holds.

TABLE B.6. **Harrell's ρ**

Variable	ρ	χ^2	p
Majority leadership priority bill	−0.056	1.510	0.219
Presidential priority bill	−0.027	0.350	0.556
Presidential priority bill × Divided government	−0.014	0.080	0.775
Interest group interest	0.008	0.030	0.868
Public salience	0.074	0.720	0.397
Committee chair relative ideology	−0.041	0.460	0.498
Polarization of key lawmakers	0.028	2.000	0.157
Appropriations bill	0.003	0.000	0.972
Number of committees	−0.050	0.000	0.954
Considered under suspension of the rules	−0.002	1.210	0.272
September 11 bill	0.010	0.050	0.823
Days left in a Congress	0.009	0.040	0.848
Global test		8.79	0.947

Additional Analyses from Chapter 5

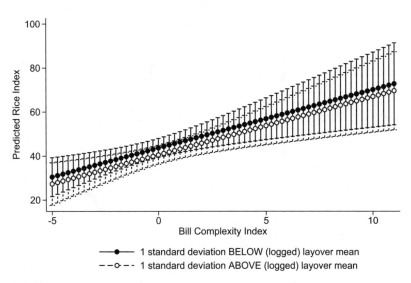

FIGURE B.I. Interactional effect of layover and bill complexity in predicting the Rice index.

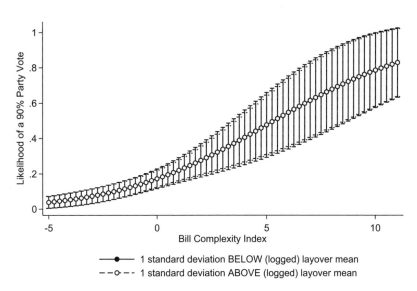

FIGURE B.2. Interactional effect of layover and bill complexity on the likelihood of a 90 percent party vote.

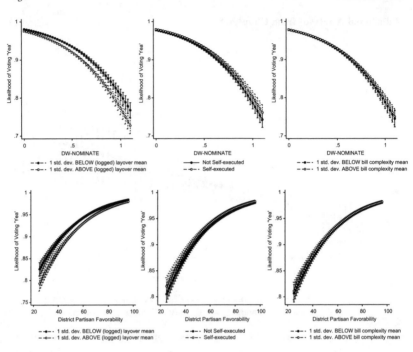

FIGURE B.3. Effect of information-restricting tactics varying with majority lawmaker ideology and district partisanship on the likelihood of voting Yea.

Notes

Chapter One

1. From remarks at a National Press Club luncheon in July 2009: Paul Blumenthal, "Rep. Conyers: Don't Read the Bill," *SunlightFoundation.org*, July 27, 2009; retrieved June 10, 2013.

2. Quoted in Representative John Boehner (R-OH), "Conference Report on H.R. 1, American Recovery and Reinvestment Act of 2009," *Congressional Record* 155, pt. 30, February 13, 2009, H1566.

3. Carver (1992) reports that two hundred words a minute is the average reading speed among college students aiming to understand enough to pass a multiple-choice test on the material being read. Cognitive understanding beyond this level may require one to read as slowly as 138 words a minute.

4. Some excellent studies of congressional leaders and leadership have been published in recent decades. These most notably include Strahan's (2007) study of conditional leadership in the House, Green's (2010) study of leadership among House Speakers, Peters's (1997) study of the House Speakership, and Peters and Rosenthal's (2010) study of Speaker Nancy Pelosi (D-CA). This book builds on the foundation of these studies.

5. Most studies highlighting inequities, or differences in influence, among members of Congress focus not on institutional inequalities but on inequalities based on race and gender (e.g., Hawkesworth 2003), socioeconomic class (Carnes 2013), members' willingness to follow institutional norms (e.g., Matthews 1960; Fenno 1962), and their policy expertise (e.g., Fenno 1973). Inequalities in terms of the information and resources different lawmakers possess have not been adequately studied.

6. Kiewiet and McCubbins do have a chapter on the delegation of authority to party leaders, but their analyses establish only that parties select ideological "middlemen" for those positions.

7. In fact, the 2001 Nobel Prize in Economics was awarded to George Aker-

lof, Michael Spence, and Joseph E. Stiglitz for their research on information asymmetries and market dynamics.

8. This form of leading by following is often illustrated with the story of a French revolutionary who, sitting in a café, exclaims, "There goes the mob. I am their leader. I must follow them!" (as conveyed in Burns 2010, 265).

9. On the discipline-wide trend toward quantitative study and formalistic approaches, as well as reactions to it, see Monroe 2005.

10. See Jeffrey Goldberg, "Adventures of a Republican Revolutionary," *New York Times Magazine*, November 3, 1996, 42.

11. The Appropriations Committee may be the exception to this rule. Traditionally, Appropriations subcommittee chairs, often referred to as "cardinals," exercise substantial influence over their jurisdictions.

12. Interviewee 10 attested to this dynamic. The interviews and interview process I used are described below and in appendix A.

13. Interview 25.

14. Interpretive approaches to the study of politics have a long lineage (see Schwartz-Shea and Yanow 2012), even if they are rarely used in the study of Congress. Some notable exceptions include the work of Richard Fenno (e.g., 1990), Ross Baker (e.g., 2011), and Patrick Sellers (2010). Additionally, the American Political Science Association's Congressional Fellowship Program has for decades afforded scholars the opportunity to learn about government by participating in Congress.

15. The Policy Agendas Project data and issue coding were originally collected by Frank R. Baumgartner and Bryan D. Jones, with the support of National Science Foundation grant numbers SBR 9320922 and 0111611, and were distributed through the Department of Government at the University of Texas at Austin. Neither NSF nor the original collectors of the data bear any responsibility for the analyses reported here.

16. There are a few exceptions. Specifically, the primary issue topic is changed from the Congressional Bills Project's coding on eight bills. These are detailed in appendix B.

17. Budget resolutions, by definition, address all nineteen major issue areas. No nonbudget bill addressed more than fifteen.

Chapter Two

1. Interview 27.

2. See Ryan Grim and Sabrina Siddiqui, "Call Time for Congress Shows How Fundraising Dominates Bleak Work Life," *Huffingtonpost.com*, January 8, 2013; accessed at http://www.huffingtonpost.com/2013/01/08/call-time-congressional -fundraising_n_2427291.html.

3. Both these dollar totals are on top of the $1.5 million committee chairs and majority party leaders received to run their personal offices.

4. Lee (2013) notes that in the late 2000s, 20 to 30 percent of these leadership staffers focused on partisan communication strategies. While this is a substantial number, it also means that 70 to 80 percent concentrated specifically on legislative issues. Furthermore, although communications are aimed primarily toward the media and the public, these messages may be related to the ones leaders disseminate to their rank and file to influence their decisions as well (see chapter 3 on leaders' messaging efforts).

5. The most famous example of leader removal is Speaker Joseph Cannon's overthrow in 1910. However, Cannon's behavior has to be viewed as the most extreme case of power abuse in congressional history. That he was stripped of his powers only after egregious abuses should be seen not as an example of a sufficient check, but rather as a demonstration of just how far a leader has to go to spur a caucus to revolt.

6. See Longley and Oleszek 1989, 294–306, for a more detailed discussion of this case study.

7. These goals reflect those identified by Strahan 2007 and Green 2010. Strahan identifies good public policy, historical reputation, and remaining as a leader as major leadership goals. Each of these is included within my three categories. Green identifies a broader set of goals that also includes reelection to Congress, representation of the institution, and support of the president. Leaders' relationship with the president is subsumed in my goal of passing partisan policy priorities, but I do not explicitly consider reelection to Congress or representation of the institution as goals. I bypass these because they are relatively minor compared with the other three. Green himself points out that leadership in fulfillment of these goals is far less common than for the others. The three given here are not the only goals a legislative leader could hold, but they represent the major motivators of leaders' actions.

8. Majority Leader Eric Cantor's (R-VA) 2014 primary defeat at the hands of a political amateur speaks volumes about this point.

9. To some degree, developing a historical reputation could also drive leaders in the House to position themselves to seek even higher office—the Senate or the even the presidency. Doing so, however, may spur self-interested behavior that is contrary to party goals. A leader who has an eye toward a statewide or national election may support or oppose legislation in a way that hurts the party caucus. Richard Gephardt's (D-MO) support for the 2002 Iraq War Resolution, against the majority of his own caucus, is a prime example. In this instance Gephardt put his own presidential ambitions ahead of the good of the party, forfeiting the Iraq War as a political issue for the Democrats in the 2004 elections.

10. It is prudent to note that Waters faced an ethics investigation in 2010 for allegedly helping a bank to which her husband had financial ties obtain federal

relief funds. Nonetheless, in 2012 Waters was cleared of wrongdoing by the Ethics Committee. Furthermore, it would be a stretch to attribute her evolution on financial issues to her husband's business dealings, which had been ongoing for years before her public shift.

11. See Ben Protess, "The Mellowing of Maxine Waters," *New York Times*, May 11, 2013.

12. Quoted in ibid.

13. It is worth briefly considering how the Republican Party's self-imposed six-year term limits on committee leadership posts might affect the difference in perspective between leaders and rank-and-file lawmakers. Between 1995, when the Republicans first imposed these limits, and 2012, forty-two chairpersons reached the six-year limit. Of these, twenty-seven (64 percent) chose to retire or run for higher office, were immediately appointed to another chairmanship or joined the party leadership, or were granted a waiver to remain chairs of their committees. Of the remaining fifteen lawmakers, within two years six either had been given another chairmanship or had left the chamber. This leaves just eight lawmakers over the course of eighteen years who had been committee leaders and went back to being rank-and-file lawmakers for any extended time. Even then, as of 2014, four of those eight have lost their chairmanships within the past two years, so it is hard to say how long they will remain as rank and file or stay within the chamber. In short, there are not many former leaders masquerading as rank and filers in the House, so the divisions between leaders and rank-and-file lawmakers remain pretty firm.

Chapter Three

1. Interview 17.
2. Interview 3.
3. Interview 3.
4. Interview 2.
5. Interview 4.
6. Interview 15.
7. Interview 20.
8. Interview 20.
9. Interview 20.

10. One interesting difference that emerged between staffers and members in leadership posts is that staffers, on the whole, tended to be more hard-line about these opinions. Many of them had held positions in Congress only with committees or with a leadership organization. As such, they were particularly insensitive to the views of their rank and file. Those members holding leadership posts, on the other hand, had all spent parts of their careers as rank-and-file legislators.

Nonetheless, both staffers and members expressed this general orientation toward the legislative process when talking about their roles as leaders.

11. For an overview of much of this literature, see Ansolabehere and Jones 2011.

12. Interview 17.

13. This section of the chapter relies heavily on my participant observation, drawing on my own experiences seeking information for my boss as well as from informal conversations with other legislative staffers about how they did their jobs. This discussion will not perfectly describe how every member office gathers information—there is certainly a great deal of variation. But the general description of what information is sought and how should ring true to anyone who has spent time on Capitol Hill.

14. Interview 31.

15. Interview 32.

16. Interview 17.

17. Interview 13.

18. Interview 6.

19. Interview 21.

20. Interview 19.

21. Interview 21.

22. For more information, see Lee Drutman, "Turnover in the House: Who Keeps—and Who Loses—the Most Staff," *Sunlightfoundation.org*, February 6, 2012.

23. On confirmation bias and motivated reasoning, see Nickerson 1988; Lord, Ross, and Lepper 1979; Tabor and Lodge 2006; and Westen et al. 2006. On motivated reasoning among members of Congress, see Anderson and Harbridge 2014.

24. For more on this point, see chapter 7.

25. Interview 4.

26. The "chairman's mark" is Capitol Hill vernacular for the draft of a bill that is to be considered by the committee after alterations are made by the chair. It is described in more detail in chapter 4.

27. Interview 4.

28. Interview 8.

29. Interview 4.

30. Interview 4.

31. Interview 4.

32. Interview 21.

33. Interview 4.

34. This example is discussed in more detail in chapter 6.

35. Interview 8.

36. Interview 4.

37. Interview 24.

38. Interview 8.

39. Interview 4.

40. Interview 8.

41. Interview 8.

42. Interview 7.

43. Interview 24.

44. Interview 10.

45. Interview 3.

46. Interview 10.

47. Interviews 3 and 10.

48. Interview 9.

49. Interview 3.

50. Interview 3.

51. Interview 3.

52. Interview 3.

53. Interview 3.

54. Interview 9.

55. Interview 25.

56. Interview 3.

57. Interview 3.

58. This topic is discussed in more detail in chapter 4.

59. Interview 19.

60. The details presented here come from documents I obtained during my time as a participant observer on Capitol Hill.

61. Eight Democrats, compared with just three Republicans, missed the markup.

62. Interview 17.

63. Although the minority is typically allowed to invite one witness to each hearing, the committee's majority staff usually retains the right to veto the minority's selection.

64. Interview 7.

65. Interview 19.

66. Interview 19.

67. Interview 17.

68. Interview 24.

69. Interview 6.

70. Interview 10.

71. Interview 10.

72. Interview 10.

73. Interview 2.

74. Interview 10.

75. Interview 27.
76. Interview 10.
77. Interview 14.
78. Interview 24.
79. Interview 24.
80. Interview 17.
81. Interview 21.
82. Interview 6.
83. Interview 11.

Chapter Four

1. The important bills dataset is described in chapter 1 and in appendix B.

2. There is every reason to believe that the use of information-restricting tactics in committee is likely just as effective as it is for party leaders, if not more. While many bills considered on the floor have previously been subject to work in committee, and thus have been publicly evaluated and discussed at some level, during committee work often no one has yet read or analyzed the bill in question. Consequently, committee leaders can keep their members in the dark in ways party leaders may envy.

3. Interview 4.

4. Interview 8.

5. Interview 19.

6. Interview 4.

7. The 109th and 110th Congresses were chosen for this table to control for the possibility that party control influences committee rules. The 109th Congress rules represent requirements under recent Republican control, and the 110th Congress rules represent requirements under recent Democratic control. There are seemingly no systematic differences between Democratic and Republican control. For most committees the rules are consistent. Where there are differences, they do not appear to become more or less restrictive between the two Congresses.

8. It is interesting to consider why these rules vary so much from committee to committee, but the answer is not immediately clear. It is possible that committees that have historically been more centralized and hierarchical have adopted and held on to rules that allow chairs more leeway to restrict information. However, it is possible that committees with more collaborative and nonhierarchical histories have less well-defined rules. This is a question worthy of further study, but not within this text. Most important here is how often these rules are ignored.

9. Interview 2.

10. Interview 4.

11. Interview 8.

12. Interview 6.

13. Interview 24.

14. Interview 19.

15. Interview 17.

16. Interview 24.

17. Interview 19.

18. Interview 19.

19. Interview 24.

20. Interview 5.

21. Interview 15.

22. Many committee-produced bills are not even formally introduced in the chamber until after the markup, meaning there isn't even an "as introduced" version of the bill that lawmakers or the public can access until after committee consideration is finished.

23. Language is taken from H.Res. 809 from the 110th Congress. Clauses 9 and 10 of rule XXI pertain to earmarking procedures.

24. Interview 1.

25. The values in figure 4.1 include layover times for all bills in the dataset that moved past the committee stage, including those that were never brought up for consideration on the floor. With these bills, layover time is considered to have expired at the end of the Congress. As such, the values presented here understate how frequently bills are considered after very brief layovers.

26. Interview 6.

27. Interview 14.

28. Interview 31.

29. Interview 10.

30. Interview 10.

31. In the Congresses studied here the proportion of the first ten bill slots used by the leadership varied. In other words, the majority leadership did not insert a bill into every one of the slots in every Congress. For example, in the 106th Congress, all ten slots were used, whereas during the 111th Congress just H.R. 1 and H.R. 2 were filled.

32. During the 2006 congressional elections, the Democrats' coordinated campaign focused on six pieces of priority legislation that they promised to pass if they took control of Congress. This agenda, formally called "A New Direction For America" consisted of a "phased redeployment" of American troops from Iraq; implementation of the 9/11 Commission's national security recommendations; a labor bill to raise the minimum wage and punish companies that exported jobs overseas; an education bill to make college more affordable for students by increasing access to loans and expanding grant programs; energy

legislation to invest in renewable energy and end tax breaks for oil companies; health care legislation aimed at lowering costs of medication and ending the ban on stem cell research; and a promise to stop any plan to privatize or endanger Social Security.

33. See appendix B for more information on the issues identified as priority using this method.

34. Some readers may find this measure too blunt, since this coding scheme counts all bills considered that year on each subject. However, it is worth emphasizing again that because the dataset analyzed here comprises just "important" legislation, this means relatively few bills are included each year. Specifically, the dataset includes roughly forty-three bills a year, so few bills address each topic each year. For example, just two bills primarily addressed the national budget and debt (code 105) in 2009. More important, because all these bills are major or important bills, it is likely the president would be concerned with all that address his priority issues. As a result this measure is unlikely to be assigning a priority to bills a president does not care about and is less blunt than it may appear.

35. It is worth noting that these two measures are relatively uncorrelated ($r = 0.18$).

36. An alternative measure, using the total number of lobbyists hired each year by each industry, was employed instead of this spending measure in replications of each test. The results were neither statistically nor substantively different.

37. Because annual budget resolutions attract the attention of nearly all industries and are subject to intense lobbying efforts, each receives an interest group interest coding of 99 percent. General tax bills (bills that deal with general tax rates rather than taxes targeting specific people or industries) are difficult to code for interest group interest. These bills are coded as having the median value of interest group interest. Alternative coding of these bills does not affect the results statistically or substantively.

38. The following is an example of the language in a self-executing rule (taken from H.Res. 615 in the 110th Congress): "The amendment printed in part A of the report of the Committee on Rules accompanying this resolution shall be considered as adopted in the House and in the Committee of the Whole. The bill, as amended, shall be considered as the original bill for the purpose of further amendment under the five-minute rule and shall be considered as read. All points of order against provisions in the bill, as amended, are waived."

39. Interview 1.

40. The time series in figure 4.4 begins with the 101st Congress because the use of self-executing provisions was fairly rare before this Congress and not recorded by the Rules Committee. See Donald R. Wolfensberger, "House Executes Deliberation with Special Rules," *Roll Call*, June 16, 2009.

41. Interview 1.

42. Interview 1.

43. Interview 10.

44. Interview 13.

45. Interview 17.

46. Interview 22.

47. Interview 14.

48. Interview 24.

49. Interview 21.

50. Interview 22.

51. Interview 10.

52. Interview 6.

53. Size and scope are taken from Krutz's (2001, 46) definition of bill complexity.

54. Readability metrics are becoming common in the study of political phenomena (see Bligh, Kohles, and Meindl 2004; Coleman and Phung 2010; Owens, Wedeking, and Wohlfarth 2013; Law and Zaring 2010). The Flesch Reading Ease metric is especially appropriate for this study, since it is designed to assess the readability of, among other things, legal documents like legislation.

55. The index itself is additive, since the presence of complexity in more than one factor should not be multiplicative. From the perspective of a member of Congress, it seems complex subject matter in a bill would add to the complexity of a long bill, rather than those two factors' multiplying each other's effect. For more details on this measure, see Curry 2013.

56. Another method scholars have used to assess the salience of different issues is to consider responses to survey questions asking what individuals believe to be the nation's "most important problem" (see Burden and Sanberg 2003). However, that measure is not well suited for this analysis because it may bias responses toward issues respondents view negatively. People may think an issue is very important, but if they approve of government action and performance on the issue, they may not see it is as a "problem" (Wlezien 2005). Consequently it may not capture the true salience of each issue with the public.

57. NOMINATE is a scaling technique developed initially by Poole and Rosenthal (1997) that locates the voting patterns of lawmakers in an n-dimensional space. It is commonly used as a measure of the ideologies of members of Congress, though that interpretation carries certain flaws (see Lee 2009, 41–44). For more on DW-NOMINATE, see Carroll et al. 2009.

58. For robustness, the analyses were also run calculating the absolute difference between the majority leadership and chairs. The primary results were not substantively or statistically different.

59. This measure is not included in analyses of self-execution because bills considered under suspension of the rules do not come to the floor under a special rule and as such cannot be self-executed. In other words, the variable's inclusion in the tests perfectly predicts failure.

60. Because the inclusion of this variable is specifically meant to predict short layover times, it is not included in the analyses of self-execution or bill complexity.

61. There are various duration models, but the CPH model is ideal for this test because it is nonparametric. Parametric models are typically used to predict specific duration times of individual cases by assuming some general distribution in the data, such as a Weibull or log-normal distribution. However, the assumption of an unknown distribution can lead to false inferences (Box-Steffensmeier and Jones 2004). For the purposes of this test, I am most interested in understanding the effect of covariates on layover times, rather than predicting the length of layover of specific bills. The CPH model does not assume any distribution, reducing the likelihood that the predicted effects of the variables are biased. CPH models, however, require that a proportional hazards assumption be met. This assumption is simply that the effects of variables do not vary over time. In other words, the effect of covariates does not increase or decrease as the duration of time studied continues. There are several tests of this assumption. Two prominent tests are the link test and Harrell's ρ test. The results of these tests for each variable, and for the model as a whole, do not reject the null hypothesis that the proportion hazards assumption holds. The results of these diagnostics can be found in appendix B.

62. Note that, unlike other more commonly used regression models, CPH models do not report a constant term.

63. An example of front-loading is the effort by the new majority Democrats to pass their Six for '06 agenda during the first hundred hours of the 110th Congress. Bills addressing their six campaign tenets were drafted behind the scenes before the 110th Congress formally began and passed rapidly in its opening days.

64. Predicted probabilities derived from logistic regression analyses in this book are calculated using the method suggested by Hanmer and Kalkan 2013.

65. The results of the truncated model are not presented but can be obtained from the author. The truncated model's predictions for all other independent variables are neither statistically nor substantively different from those presented table 4.3.

66. This analysis is available from the author.

67. Interview 1.

Chapter Five

1. Interview 17.

2. Quoted in Edwin Mora and Adam Brickley, "Congressmen Say They Didn't Have Chance to Read Full 1,200-Page Climate Change Bill Before Vote," *cnsnews.com*, June 27, 2009. Accessed at http://www.cnsnews.com/news/article/

congressmen-say-they-didnt-have-chance-read-full-1200-page-climate-change
-bill-vote.

3. Quoted in Rachel Weiner, "Boehner Calls Climate Bill 'a Pile of Shit,'" *Huffingtonpost.com*, June 29, 2009. Accessed at http://www.huffingtonpost .com/2009/06/28/boehner-calls-climate-bil_n_221995.html.

4. Of course it is likely that both causal arguments are partially true. On one hand leaders, since they use these tactics on issues they consider important to the party and on issues that attract substantial interest group influence, they are often applying them to rather contentious legislation, meaning partisanship is already somewhat heightened. However, using these tactics is likely to heighten partisanship even further, for all the reasons theorized about in the previous chapters.

5. As discussed in chapter 3, with floor consideration, bill text will typically have to have been made public in some way, and if any committee work has been done earlier, there is likely more information floating around than before. In committee, members sometimes do not see the final bill language until they take a seat on the dais for the markup. In an even more restricted environment, the information committee leaders provide should be even more influential, and committee chairs' abilities to line up votes should be even more impressive.

6. See chapter 4 under "Bill Complexity."

7. Each analysis was also conducted replacing the Congress-specific dummies with a measure of the difference between the first-dimension DW-NOMINATE party medians in each Congress. The results are not substantively or statistically different from those reported here.

8. See figure B.1 in appendix B.

9. These predicted probabilities are derived from the analysis presented in table 5.2, column 4.

10. See figure B.2 in appendix B.

11. Some readers may question the assumption that the majority leadership will be in favor of passing every bill that comes to the floor. Across the universe of all bills considered in the House, there are undoubtedly cases in which the majority leadership is in opposition. But among "important bills" these cases should be rare or nonexistent. Nearly every bill in the dataset analyzed here passed with strong majority support, suggesting that the majority leadership either supported its passage or at least was ambivalent. Analysis of the roll-call results indicates that on roughly 96 percent of the 453 bills analyzed here, both the majority leader and majority whip voted yea, indicating clear unified majority leadership support (the Speaker of the House casts roll-call votes only intermittently). Cox and McCubbins (2005) provide further discussion of how infrequently the majority leadership opposes bills considered on the floor.

12. An additional set of analyses, not shown here, assesses how restricting information affects majority lawmakers' voting decisions differently across ideologies and districts. I conducted these tests because the previous chapters suggest

that moderate lawmakers from swing districts may be more skeptical of information given them by leaders. The results are inconsistent. Across the tests, the effect of restricting information is not noticeably greater across variations at more extreme or moderate ideologies, or among more or less partisan districts. There are some small divergences among the tests of layover time, but they are not substantively significant. These results are found in figure B.3 in appendix B.

Chapter Six

1. Specifically, the bill scores 21.3 on the *interest group interest* variable introduced in chapter 4. This puts it in the seventy-third percentile of the variable.

2. See John M. Broder, "Geography Is Dividing Democrats over Energy," *New York Times*, January 27, 2009, A1.

3. See Felicity Barringer, "Climate Legislation Sends Chill through Areas Fueled by Coal," *New York Times*, April 9, 2009, A17.

4. See John M. Broder, "House Bill for a Carbon Tax to Cut Emissions Faces a Steep Climb," *New York Times*, March 7, 2009, A13.

5. See Coral Davenport, "A Temperature Take on the Climate Bill," *CQ Weekly*, July 6, 2009, 1568–70.

6. Ibid.

7. Quoted in Office of Congressman Jim Matheson, "Matheson: Climate Change Draft Bill Disappoints," Press Release, Washington, DC, March 31, 2009.

8. See US House, Committee on Energy and Commerce, *The American Clean Energy and Security Act* (Washington, DC: Government Printing Office, 2009), Hearing.

9. Ibid.

10. Ibid.

11. See US House, Committee on Energy and Commerce, *The American Clean Energy and Security Act* (Washington, DC: Government Printing Office, 2009), Markup, Day 1.

12. This further underscores why the layover time measure employed in chapters 4 and 5 is noisy. Using that measure, this bill had a nearly three-day layover. However, most members had far less time than that to digest the legislation.

13. Quoted from US House, Committee on Energy and Commerce, *American Clean Energy and Security Act*, Markup, Day 3.

14. Ibid., Markup, Day 2.

15. Ibid., Markup, Day 3.

16. Ibid., Markup, Day 2.

17. Ibid., Markup, Day 2.

18. Ibid., Markup, Day 3.

19. Ibid.

20. Ibid.

21. Ibid.

22. Ibid.

23. Ibid., Markup, Day 4.

24. Ibid.

25. Ibid.

26. Ibid., Markup, Day 3.

27. Ibid., Markup, Day 4.

28. Ibid.

29. Specifically, two votes resulted in five Democrats' defecting from the chairmen's position. These were both amendments offered by Representative Stearns regarding nuclear power.

30. Representative Gene Green (D-TX) cast one vote opposed to the chairmen.

31. One could argue that these eight votes were the key to the bill's moving through committee safely and successfully. With four Democrats likely to vote against the bill (and who ultimately did), these eight votes were crucial to maintaining a majority on each vote. On many votes, including final passage out of committee, eight votes represented the margin of victory for the Democrats.

32. Bush even emphasized his support for a guest worker program during his 2005 State of the Union address just a week before the REAL ID Act would be considered on the floor of the House.

33. Quoted in Jennifer A. Dlouhy, "Immigration Fight Looms," *CQ Weekly*, January 31, 2005, 246.

34. The opposition of these groups was noted on the floor by Representative Alcee Hastings (D-FL), "Providing for Consideration of H.R. 418, REAL ID Act of 2005," *Congressional Record* 151, pt. 13, February 9, 2005, H449–50.

35. These were noted by, among others, Representative Barney Frank (D-MA) during both days of debate.

36. See Patrick O'Connor, "Sensenbrenner and Davis Bills Square Off," *The Hill*, February 1, 2005.

37. Quoted in Representative Pete Session (R-TX), "Providing for Consideration of H.R. 418, REAL ID Act of 2005," *Congressional Record* 151, pt. 13, February 9, 2005, H442–43.

38. Quoted in Representative Roy Blunt (R-MO), "Providing for Consideration of H.R. 418, REAL ID Act of 2005," *Congressional Record* 151, pt. 13, February 9, 2005, H444.

39. Quoted in Representative David Drier (R-CA), "Providing for Consideration of H.R. 418, REAL ID Act of 2005," *Congressional Record* 151, pt. 13, February 9, 2005, H451.

40. Quoted in Representative Jane Harman (D-CA), "Providing for Consid-

eration of H.R. 418, REAL ID Act of 2005," *Congressional Record* 151, pt. 13, February 9, 2005, H444–45.

41. Quoted in Representative Tom Davis (R-VA), "REAL ID Act of 2005," *Congressional Record* 151, pt. 13, February 9, 2005, H461.

42. Ibid.

43. Quoted in Jennifer A. Dlouhy, "Immigration Fight Looms," *CQ Weekly*, January 31, 2005, 246.

44. Quoted in Jennifer A. Dlouhy, "Lawmakers Spar over Asylum," *CQ Weekly*, February 14, 2005, 402.

45. The opposition of such groups was repeatedly mentioned by Democratic representatives during floor debate.

46. Quoted in Representative Jim McGovern (D-MA), "Providing for Consideration of H.R. 418, REAL ID Act of 2005," *Congressional Record* 151, pt. 13, February 9, 2005, H444.

47. Quoted in Representative Linda Sanchez (D-CA), "REAL ID Act of 2005," *Congressional Record* 151, pt. 13, February 9, 2005, H456.

48. Quoted in Representative Jerrold Nadler (D-NY), "REAL ID Act of 2005," *Congressional Record* 151, pt. 13, February 9, 2005, H456.

49. Quoted in Representative Alcee Hastings (D-FL), "Providing for Further Consideration of H.R. 418, REAL ID Act of 2005," *Congressional Record* 151, pt. 14, February 10, 2005, H528.

50. Representative Hastings mentioned this rule bending on the floor during debate on the rule on February 10.

51. Quoted in Representative James Sensenbrenner (R-WI), "Providing for Further Consideration of H.R. 418, REAL ID Act of 2005," *Congressional Record* 151, pt. 14, February 10, 2005, H532.

52. Quoted in Representative Jerrold Nadler (D-NY), "Notice of Intention to Offer Modification to Nadler Amendment to REAL ID Act," *Congressional Record* 151, pt. 14, February 10, 2005, H536.

53. Quoted in Representative James Sensenbrenner (R-WI), "REAL ID Act of 2005," *Congressional Record* 151, pt. 14, February 10, 2005, H549.

Chapter Seven

1. Interview 22.

2. Interview 20.

3. For few lawmakers are these priorities likely to align perfectly, but this alignment is far greater for some than for others.

4. See appendix A for more details on my method of transcribing and interpreting the interview evidence.

5. The coding of lawmakers and staffers as rank and file, party leadership, or committee leadership is discussed in more detail in appendix A.

6. Two of the interviews took place during the 113th Congress. Since this Congress was not yet completed when I finished the manuscript of this book, I used these lawmakers' first-dimension DW-NOMINATE scores from the Congress before our discussion. One interviewee worked for a freshman member in the 113th Congress, which made it impossible to rely on DW-NOMINATE. I instead relied on my impressions of the member and her voting record to date for the categorization.

7. Deciding on the cut-points for "moderates" is unavoidably arbitrary (see Fleisher and Bond 2004). A 20 percent cut-point, however, largely conformed to my view of the lawmakers at the time of the interview. Regardless, blunt categorization like this is necessary for this analysis. The precise DW-NOMINATE scores of the lawmakers and staffers could not be used without the risk of making the anonymous interviewees identifiable. While it is likely that lawmakers from the extremist wing of their party may also have less trust in their leadership, none of the lawmakers or staffers I interviewed came from the most extreme 20 percent, making it impossible to test for this.

8. Interview 28.

9. Interview 22.

10. Interview 21.

11. Interview 31.

12. Interview 23.

13. Interview 32.

14. Interview 24.

15. Interview 6.

16. Interview 17.

17. Interview 14.

18. Interview 19.

19. Interview 19.

20. Interview 14.

21. Interview 22.

22. Interview 23.

23. Interview 28.

24. Interview 13.

25. Interview 21.

26. Interview 6.

27. Interview 22.

28. Interview 13.

29. Interview 27.

30. Interview 1.

31. The battle between Waxman and Dingell described at the start of chap-

ter 4 is an example of the failure of a legislative leader (Dingell) to effectively manage information.

32. See Gloria Borger, "The Majority of One," *U.S. News and World Report*, January 16, 1995.

33. See Jackie Koszczuk, "Unpopular, yet Still Powerful, Gingrich Faces Critical Pass," *CQ Weekly*, September 14, 1996, 2573.

34. See Tim Alberta, "The Cabal That Quietly Took Over the House," *National Journal*, May 23, 2013.

35. Quoted in ibid.

36. See Marin Cogan and Jake Sherman, "Republican Study Committee is GOP's 'Circular Firing Squad,'" *Politico*, October 10, 2011.

37. See Alberta, "Cabal That Quietly Took Over the House."

38. Using the dues amounts reported by *Politico*, the total budget of the RSC in 2011 was likely between $500,000 and $1 million.

39. Interview 25.

40. Interview 25.

41. Interview 25.

42. Interview 25.

43. Interview 25.

44. See Jackie Calmes, "Republicans Lower Goal for Cuts to Budget," *New York Times*, January 4, 2011.

45. See Carl Hulse, "House Republicans Battle Turmoil in Their Ranks," *New York Times*, February 9, 2011.

46. See Carl Hulse, "Republican Leaders Yield to a Push for More Budget Cuts," *New York Times*, February 10, 2011.

47. Quoted in Deirdre Walsh and Dana Bash, "Republican Says Government Shutdown Possible, as House GOP Work to Bridge Divisions," *CNN Political Ticker*, February 10, 2011.

48. See Hulse, "House Republicans Battle Turmoil."

49. See Sharyl Attkisson, "House GOP Bucks Boehner, Kills Funding for Extra F-35 Engine," *cbsnews.com*, February 6, 2011.

50. See Republican Study Committee, "RSC Chairman Jordan on House Passage of Bill to Reduce Spending," press release, February 19, 2011.

51. Quoted in Brian Friel and Sam Goldfarb, "Lawmakers, President Brace for Government Shutdown," *CQ Weekly*, February 21, 2011, 404.

52. See Carl Hulse, "Republicans Propose Budget Stopgap, Reducing Risk of a Federal Shutdown," *New York Times*, February 25, 2011.

53. See Kerry Young and Brian Friel, "With CR Cleared, Haggling Begins," *CQ Weekly*, March 7, 2011, 526.

54. See Kerry Young and Sam Goldfarb, "House GOP Offers Three-Week CR," *CQ Weekly*, March 14, 2011, 582.

55. Ibid.

56. See Republican Study Committee, "RSC Chairman Jordan to Vote against 3-Week Spending Bill," press release, March 14, 2011; Carl Hulse and Jennifer Steinhauer, "Conservatives Balk at Stopgap Spending Measure," *New York Times*, March 14, 2011.

57. See Carl Hulse, "Boehner Tries to Serve Two Masters in Budget Deal," *New York Times*, March 16, 2011.

58. See Kerry Young and Sam Goldfarb, "Stretched for a Spending Deal," *CQ Weekly*, April 4, 2011, 758.

59. See Kerry Young and Sam Goldfarb, "Shutdown Averted at 11th Hour," *CQ Weekly*, April 11, 2011, 806.

60. Quoted in Carl Hulse, "Last-Minute Budget Deal Averts Government Shutdown," *New York Times*, April 8, 2011.

61. Quoted in Carl Hulse, "Republicans and Democrats Alike Claim Successes in Averting a Federal Shutdown," *New York Times*, April 9, 2011.

62. Quoted in Deborah Barfield Berry, "Mississippi Lawmakers Applaud Budget Deal," Gannett News Service, April 9, 2011.

63. Quoted in Ledyard King, "Disappointment Lingers despite Budget Agreement," Gannett News Service, April 9, 2011.

64. Quoted in Theo Emery, "Shutdown Averted After Furious Push, with Deal for $39B in Cuts: GOP Relents on Including Cut of Planned Parenthood Funds; Plan Must Still Be Approved by Rank and File in Congress," *Boston Globe*, April 9, 2011.

65. See Anna Palmer and Kathleen Hunter, "GOP Can't Pass the CR Deal Alone: A House Vote This Week May Not Show the Party Unity Boehner Had Hoped," *Roll Call*, April 12, 2011.

66. Quoted in Carl Hulse, "Budget Details Stir Republican Dissent Ahead of House Vote," *New York Times*, April 13, 2011.

67. Quoted in Marin Cogan, "Freshmen Embrace Deal to Avoid Government Shutdown," *Politico*, April 9, 2011.

68. DW-NOMINATE spatially locates lawmakers' voting behavior on n dimensions. The first dimension typically reflects the primary divide between the parties. The second dimension typically represents *intra*party divisions.

69. Initial analyses also included variables indicating if a member was part of the Republican leadership team or a committee chair, but these variables were dropped from the analyses owing to collinearity. They perfectly predicted support for each bill.

70. Quoted in Cogan, "Freshmen Embrace Deal to Avoid Government Shutdown."

71. Quoted in ibid.

72. Interview 13.

Appendix A

1. The Subcommittee on Financial Services and General Government was created in 2007 to better align House and Senate subcommittee jurisdictions. It was largely formed from parts of what is now the Subcommittee on Transportation, Housing and Urban Development, and Related Agencies. The new subcommittee's jurisdiction included the Treasury Department, the District of Columbia, the Judiciary, the Executive Office of the President, and a host of independent government agencies including, among others, the Federal Communications Commission, the Federal Election Commission, the Federal Trade Commission, the Harry S. Truman Scholarship Foundation, the Morris K. Udall and Stewart L. Udall Foundation, the National Archives and Records Administration, the Securities and Exchange Commission, and the Small Business Administration.

2. No specific count exists of the number of distinct fellowship programs placing people in Congress or the executive branch to contribute to policymaking, but they likely number in the hundreds.

References

Adler, E. Scott, and John S. Lapinski. 1997. "Demand-Side Theory and Congressional Committee Composition: A Constituency Characteristics Approach." *American Journal of Political Science* 41(3): 895–918.

Ai, Chunrong, and Edward C. Norton. 2003. "Interaction Terms in Logit and Probit Models." *Economic Letters* 80(1): 123–29.

Akerlof, George A. 1970. "The Market for 'Lemons': Quality Uncertainty and the Market Mechanism." *Quarterly Journal of Economics* 84(3): 488–500.

Aldrich, John H., and David W. Rohde. 2000. "The Consequences of Party Organization in the House: The Role of the Majority and Minority Parties in Conditional Party Government." In *Polarized Politics: Congress and the President in a Partisan Era*, edited by Jon R. Bond and Richard Fleisher. Washington, DC: CQ Press.

American Political Science Association, Committee on Parties. 1950. "Towards a More Responsible Two-Party System." Supplement, *American Political Science Review* 44(3).

Anderson, Sarah E., and Laurel Harbridge. 2014. "The Policy Consequences of Motivated Information Processing among the Partisan Elite." *American Politics Research* 42(4): 700–728.

Ansolabehere, Stephen, and Philip Edward Jones. 2011. "Dyadic Representation." In *The Oxford Handbook of the American Congress*, edited by Eric Schickler and Frances E. Lee. New York: Oxford University Press.

Arnold, R. Douglas. 1990. *The Logic of Congressional Action*. New Haven, CT: Yale University Press.

Bach, Stanley, and Steven S. Smith. 1988. *Managing Uncertainty in the House of Representatives*. Washington, DC: Brookings Institution.

Baker, Ross K. 2011. "Touching the Bones: Interviewing and Direct Observational Studies of Congress." In *The Oxford Handbook of the American Congress*, edited by Eric Schickler and Frances E. Lee. New York: Oxford University Press.

Balla, Steven J., Eric D. Lawrence, Forrest Maltzman, and Lee Sigelman. 2002. "Partisanship, Blame Avoidance, and the Distribution of Legislative Pork." *American Journal of Political Science* 46(3): 515–25.

Banks, Jeffrey S., and Barry R. Weingast. 1992. "The Political Control of Bureaucracies under Asymmetric Information." *American Journal of Political Science* 36(2): 509–42.

Baron, David P. 2000. "Legislative Organization with Informational Committees." *American Journal of Political Science* 44(3): 485–505.

Baumgartner, Frank R., and Bryan D. Jones. 2009. *Agendas and Instability in American Politics*. Chicago: University of Chicago Press.

Beckmann, Matthew N., and Richard L. Hall. 2013. "Elite Interviewing in Washington, DC." In *Interview Research in Political Science*, edited by Layna Mosley. Ithaca, NY: Cornell University Press.

Beech, Nic, Paul Hibbert, Robert MacIntosh, and Peter McInnes. 2009. "'But I Thought We Were Friends?' Life Cycles and Research Relationships." In *Organizational Ethnography: Studying the Complexities of Everyday Organizational Life*, edited by Sierk Ybema, Dvora Yanow, Harry Wels, and Frans Kamsteeg. London: Sage.

Behringer, Courtney L., C. Lawrence Evans, and Elizabeth R. Materese. 2006. "Parties, Preferences, and the House Whip Process." Presented at the Annual Meeting of the Southern Political Science Association, New Orleans.

Berry, Frances Stokes, and William D. Berry. 1990. "State Lottery Adoptions as Policy Innovations: An Event History Analysis." *American Political Science Review* 84(2): 395–415.

Biernacki, Patrick, and Daniel Waldorf. 1981. "Snowball Sampling: Problems and Techniques of Chain Referral Sampling." *Sociological Methods and Research* 10(2): 141–63.

Binder, Sarah A. 1999. "The Dynamics of Legislative Gridlock, 1947–96." *American Political Science Review* 93(3): 519–33.

Bleich, Erik, and Robert Pekkanen. 2013. "How to Report Interview Data." In *Interview Research in Political Science*, edited by Layna Mosley. Ithaca, NY: Cornell University Press.

Bligh, Michelle C., Jeffrey C. Kohles, and James R. Meindl. 2004. "Charting the Language of Leadership: A Methodological Investigation of President Bush and the Crisis of 9/11." *Journal of Applied Psychology* 89(3): 562–74.

Bond, Jon R., and Richard Fleisher. 1990. *The President in the Legislative Arena*. Chicago: University of Chicago Press.

Box-Steffensmeier, Janet, and Bradford S. Jones. 1997. "Time Is of the Essence: Event History Models in Political Science." *American Journal of Political Science* 41(4): 1414–61.

———. 2004. *Event History Modeling: A Guide for Social Scientists*. New York: Cambridge University Press.

Brady, David W., and Craig Volden. 1998. *Revolving Gridlock: Politics and Policy from Carter to Clinton.* Boulder, CO: Westview.

Brambor, Thomas, William Roberts Clark, and Matt Golder. 2006. "Understanding Interaction Models: Improving Empirical Analyses." *Political Analysis* 14:63–82.

Brown, George Rothwell. 1922. *The Leadership of Congress.* New York: Bobs-Merrill.

Bryce, James. 1893. *The American Commonwealth.* New York: Macmillan.

Burden, Barry C., and Tammy M. Frisby. 2004. "Preferences, Partisanship, and Whip Activity in the U.S. House of Representatives." *Legislative Studies Quarterly* 29(4): 569–90.

Burden, Barry C., and Joseph Neal Rice Sanberg. 2003. "Budget Rhetoric in Presidential Campaigns from 1952 to 2000." *Political Behavior* 25(2): 97–118.

Burke, C. Shawn, Dana E. Sims, Elizabeth H. Lazzara, and Eduardo Salas. 2007. "Trust in Leadership: A Multi-level Review and Integration." *Leadership Quarterly* 18(6): 606–32.

Burns, James MacGregor. 2010. *Leadership.* New York: First Harper Perennial Political Classics.

Butler, John K. 1991. "Toward Understanding and Measuring Conditions of Trust: Evolution of a Conditions of Trust Inventory." *Journal of Management* 17(3): 643–63.

Calvert, Randall L. 1985. "The Value of Biased Information: A Rational Choice Model of Political Advice." *Journal of Politics* 47(2): 530-55.

Canes-Wrone, Brandice, and Scott de Marchi. 2002. "Presidential Approval and Legislative Success." *Journal of Politics* 64 (2): 491–509.

Cann, Damon M. 2008. *Sharing the Wealth: Member Contributions and the Exchange Theory of Party Influence in the U.S. House of Representatives.* Albany, NY: SUNY Press.

Cann, Damon M., and Andrew H. Sidman. 2011. "Exchange Theory, Political Parties, and the Allocation of Federal Distributive Benefits in the House of Representatives." *Journal of Politics* 73(4): 1128–41.

Cantor, David M., and Paul S. Herrnson. 1997. "Party Campaign Activity and Party Unity in the U.S. House of Representatives." *Legislative Studies Quarterly* 22(3): 393–415.

Carnes, Nicholas. 2013. *White-Collar Government: The Hidden Role of Class in Economic Policy Making.* Chicago: University of Chicago Press.

Caro, Robert A. 2002. *Master of the Senate: The Years of Lyndon Johnson.* New York: Alfred A. Knopf.

Carroll, Royce, Jeffrey B. Lewis, James Lo, Keith T. Poole, and Howard Rosenthal. 2009. "Measuring Bias and Uncertainty in DW-NOMINATE Ideal Point Estimates via the Parametric Bootstrap." *Political Analysis* 17(3): 261–75.

Carver, Ronald P. 1992. "Reading Rate: Theory, Research, and Practical Implications." *Journal of Reading* 36(2): 84–95.

Chui, Chang-wei. 1928. *The Speaker of the House of Representatives since 1896.* New York: Columbia University Press.

Clinton, Joshua D. 2012. "Using Roll Call Estimates to Test Models of Politics." *Annual Review of Political Science* 15:79–99.

Clinton, Joshua D., and John Lapinski. 2008. "Laws and Roll Calls in the U.S. Congress, 1891-1994." *Legislative Studies Quarterly* 33(4): 511–41.

Coleman, Brady, and Quy Phung. 2010. "The Language of Supreme Court Briefs: A Large-Scale Quantitative Investigation." *Journal of Appellate Practice and Process* 11(1): 75–103.

Congressional Management Foundation. 2003. "2002 House Staff Employment Study." Washington, DC: US House of Representatives.

Cooper, Joseph. 1970. *The Origins of Standing Committees and the Development of the Modern House.* Houston, TX: Rice University Publications.

———. 1977. "Congress in Organizational Perspective." In *Congress Reconsidered,* edited by Lawrence Dodd and Bruce I. Oppenheimer. Longman.

Cooper, Joseph, and David W. Brady. 1981. "Institutional Context and Leadership Style: The House from Cannon to Rayburn." *American Political Science Review* 75(2): 411–25.

Cooper, Joseph, and Martin Hering. 2003. "Proximity Voting versus Party Effects: A Revised Theory of the Importance of Party in Congressional Decision Making." Presented at the Midwest Political Science Association 61st Annual Meeting, Chicago.

Cox, Gary W., and Eric Magar. 1999. "How Much Is Majority Status in the U.S. Congress Worth?" *American Political Science Review* 93(2): 299–309.

Cox, Gary W., and Mathew D. McCubbins. 2002. "Agenda Power in the U.S. House of Representatives, 1877–1986." In *Party, Process, and Political Change in Congress: New Perspectives on the History of Congress,* edited by David W. Brady and Mathew D. McCubbins. Stanford, CA: Stanford University Press.

———. 2005. *Setting the Agenda: Responsible Party Government in the U.S. House of Representatives.* New York: Cambridge University Press.

Curry, James M. 2013. "Bill Complexity and Representation in the U.S. House of Representatives." Presented at the 71st Annual Meeting of the MPSA, Chicago.

Damore, David F., and Thomas G. Hansford. 1999. "The Allocation of Party Controlled Campaign Resources in the House of Representatives, 1989–1996." *Political Research Quarterly* 52(2): 371–85.

Davidson, Roger H., Susan Webb Hammond, and Raymond Smock. 1998. *Masters of the House: Congressional Leadership over Two Centuries.* Boulder, CO: Westview.

Deering, Christopher J., and Steven S. Smith. 1997. *Committees in Congress.* 3rd ed. Washington, DC: CQ Press.

Deering, Christopher J., and Paul J. Wahlbeck. 2006. "U.S. House Committee Chair Selection: Republicans Play Musical Chairs in the 107th Congress." *American Politics Research* 34(2): 223–42.

Dirks, Kurt T., and Donald L. Ferrin. 2002. "Trust in Leadership: Meta-analytic Findings and Implications for Research and Practice." *Journal of Applied Psychology* 87(4): 611–28.

Edwards, George C., and B. Dan Wood. 1999. "Who Influences Whom? The President, Congress, and the Media." *American Political Science Review* 93(2): 327–44.

Epstein, Lee, and Jeffrey A. Segal. 2000. "Measuring Issue Salience." *American Journal of Political Science* 44(1): 66–83.

Esterberg, Kristin G. 2002. *Qualitative Methods in Social Research.* Boston: McGraw-Hill.

Evans, C. Lawrence, and Claire E. Grandy. 2009. "The Whip Systems of Congress." In *Congress Reconsidered*, 9th ed., edited by Bruce I. Oppenheimer and Lawrence C. Dodd. Washington, DC: CQ Press.

Evans, C. Lawrence, and Walter J. Oleszek. 1999. "The Strategic Context of Congressional Party Leadership." *Congress and the Presidency* 26(1): 1–20.

Farris, George F., Eldon E. Senner, and D. Anthony Butterfield. 1973. "Trust, Culture, and Organizational Behavior." *Industrial Relations: A Journal of Economy and Society* 12(2): 144–57.

Feldman, Martha S., Jeannine Bell, and Michele Tracy Berger, eds. 2003. *Gaining Access: A Practical and Theoretical Guide for Qualitative Researchers.* Walnut Creek, CA: Rowman Altamira.

Fenno, Richard F. 1962. "The House Appropriations Committee as a Political System: The Problem of Integration." *American Political Science Review* 56(2): 310–24.

———. 1973. *Congressmen in Committees.* Boston: Little, Brown.

———. 1978. *Home Style: House Members in Their Districts.* Boston: Little, Brown.

———. 1990. *Watching Politicians: Essays on Participant Observation.* Berkeley, CA: Institute of Governmental Studies.

Finocchiaro, Charles J., and David W. Rohde. 2008. "War for the Floor: Partisan Theory and Agenda Control in the U.S. House of Representatives." *Legislative Studies Quarterly* 33(1): 35–61.

Fleisher, Richard, and John R. Bond. 2004. "The Shrinking Middle in the U.S. Congress." *British Journal of Political Science* 34(3): 429–51.

Flesch, Rudolf. 1948. "A New Readability Yardstick." *Journal of Applied Psychology* 32(2): 221–23.

Folger, Robert, and Mary A. Konovsky. 1989. "Effects of Procedural and Distributive Justice on Reactions to Pay Raise Decisions." *Academy of Management Journal* 32(1): 115–30.

Follett, Mary P. 1896. *The Speaker of the House of Representatives*. New York: Longmans, Green.

Forgette, Richard. 2004. "Party Caucuses and Coordination: Assessing Caucus Activity and Party Effects." *Legislative Studies Quarterly* 29(3): 407–30.

Frisch, Scott A., and Sean Q. Kelly. 2006. *Committee Assignment Politics in the U.S. House of Representatives*. Norman: University of Oklahoma Press.

Froman, Lewis A., and Randall B. Ripley. 1965. "Conditions for Party Leadership: The Case of the House Democrats." *American Political Science Review* 59(1): 52–63.

Fuller, Hubert Bruce. 1909. *The Speakers of the House*. Boston: Little, Brown.

Gamm, Gerald, and Kenneth Shepsle. 1989. "Emergence of Legislative Institutions: Standing Committees in the House and Senate, 1810–1825." *Legislative Studies Quarterly* 14(1): 39–66.

Gervais, Bryan T., and Irwin L. Morris. 2012. "Reading the Tea Leaves: Understanding Tea Party Caucus Membership in the US House of Representatives." *PS: Political Science and Politics* 45(2): 245–50.

Glassman, Matthew. 2012. "Congressional Leadership: A Resource Perspective." In *Party and Procedure in the United States Congress*, edited by Jacob R. Strauss. Lanham, MD: Rowman and Littlefield.

Goldstein, Kenneth. 2002. "Getting in the Door: Sampling and Completing Elite Interviews." *PS: Political Science and Politics* 35:669–72.

Goodwin, George. 1959. "The Seniority System in Congress." *American Political Science Review* 53(2): 412–36.

Govier, Trudy. 1997. *Social Trust and Human Communities*. Montreal: McGill-Queen's University Press.

Green, Matthew N. 2010. *The Speaker of the House: A Study of Leadership*. New Haven, CT: Yale University Press.

Green, Matthew N., and Douglas B. Harris. 2007. "Goal Salience and the 2006 Race for House Majority Leader." *Political Research Quarterly* 60:618–30.

Grimmer, Justin, and Eleanor Neff Powell. 2013. "Congressmen in Exile: The Politics and Consequences of Involuntary Committee Removal." *Journal of Politics* 75 (4): 907–20.

Grimmett, Richard F. 2006. "9/11 Commission Recommendations: Implementation Status." Congressional Research Service, RL33742.

Gutmann, Amy, and Dennis S. Thompson. 2004. *Why Deliberative Democracy?* Princeton, NJ: Princeton University Press.

Hall, Richard L. 1987. "Participation and Purpose in Committee Decision Making." *American Political Science Review* 81(1): 105–27.

———. 1996. *Participation in Congress*. New Haven, CT: Yale University Press.

Hall, Richard L., and Alan V. Deardorff. 2006. "Lobbying as Legislative Subsidy." *American Political Science Review* 100(1): 69–84.

Hamilton, Alexander, James Madison, and John Jay. 1999. *The Federalist Papers*, edited by Clinton Rossiter. New York: Mentor Books.

Hamilton, Lee. 2008. "Congress Needs Proper Leadership." Commentaries, Center on Congress, Indiana University, Bloomington.

Hanmer, Michael J., and Kerem Ozan Kalkan. 2013. "Behind the Curve: Clarifying the Best Approach to Calculating Predicted Probabilities and Marginal Effects from Limited Dependent Variable Models." *American Journal of Political Science* 57(1): 263–77.

Hart, Kerry M., H. Randall Capps, Joseph P. Cangemi, and Larry M. Caillouet. 1986. "Exploring Organizational Trust and Its Multiple Dimensions: A Case Study of General Motors." *Organization Development Journal* 4(2): 31–39.

Hasbrouck, Paul D. 1927. *Party Government in the House of Representatives.* New York: Macmillan.

Hawkesworth, Mary. 2003. "Congressional Enactments of Race–Gender: Toward a Theory of Raced–Gendered Institutions." *American Political Science Review* 97(4): 519–50.

Heberlig, Eric, Marc Hetherington, and Bruce Larson. 2006. "The Price of Leadership: Campaign Money and the Polarization of Congressional Parties." *Journal of Politics* 68(4): 992–1005.

Herrnson, Paul S. 2011. *Congressional Elections: Campaigning at Home and in Washington.* 6th ed. Washington, DC: CQ Press.

Hibbing, John R., and Elizabeth Theiss-Morse. 2002. *Stealth Democracy: Americans' Beliefs about How Government Should Work.* New York: Cambridge University Press.

Hinckley, Barbara. 1971. *The Seniority System in Congress.* New York: Midland Books.

Iyengar, Shanto, Mark D. Peters, and Donald R. Kinder. 1982. "Experimental Demonstrations of the 'Not-So-Minimal' Consequences of Television News Programs." *American Political Science Review* 76(4): 848–58.

Jacobson, Gary C. 2009. *The Politics of Congressional Elections.* 7th ed. New York: Pearson Longman.

Jenkins, Jeffery A., Michael H. Crespin, and Jamie L. Carson. 2005. "Parties as Procedural Coalitions in Congress: An Examination of Differing Career Tracks." *Legislative Studies Quarterly* 30(3): 365–89.

Jenkins, Jeffrey A., and Charles Stewart III. 2013. *Fighting for the Speakership: The House and the Rise of Party Government.* Princeton, NJ: Princeton University Press.

Jones, Charles O. 1964. *Party and Policy-Making: The House Republican Policy Committee.* New Brunswick, NJ: Rutgers University Press.

———. 1968. "Joseph G. Cannon and Howard W. Smith: An Essay on the Limits of Leadership in the House of Representatives." *Journal of Politics* 30(3): 617–46.

Jung, Dong I., and Bruce J. Avolio. 2000. "Opening the Black Box: An Experimental Investigation of the Mediating Effects of Trust and Value Congruence on Transformational and Transactional Leadership." *Journal of Organizational Behavior* 21(8): 949–64.

Karpowitz, Christopher F., J. Quin Monson, Kelly D. Patterson, and Jeremy C. Pope. 2011. "Tea Time in America? The Impact of the Tea Party Movement on the 2010 Midterm Elections." *PS: Political Science and Politics* 44(2): 303–9.

Kelly, Lorelei. 2012. "Congress' Wicked Problem: Seeking Knowledge Inside the Information Tsunami." Washington, DC: New America Foundation.

———. 2013. "How Do They Know? Case Studies of Expert Knowledge Support for Elected Leaders." Washington, DC: New America Foundation.

Key, V. O. 1952. *Politics, Parties, and Pressure Groups.* 3rd ed. New York: Crowell.

Kiewiet, D. Roderick, and Mathew D. McCubbins. 1991. *The Logic of Delegation: Congressional Parties and the Appropriations Process.* Chicago: University of Chicago Press.

King, David C., and Richard J. Zeckhauser. 2003. "Congressional Vote Options." *Legislative Studies Quarterly* 28(3): 387–411.

Kingdon, John W. 1989. *Congressmen's Voting Decisions.* 3rd ed. Ann Arbor: University of Michigan Press.

Konovsky, Mary A., and Russell Cropanzano. 1991. "Perceived Fairness of Employee Drug Testing as a Predictor of Employee Attitudes and Job Performance." *Journal of Applied Psychology* 76(5): 698–707.

Krehbiel, Keith. 1991. *Information and Legislative Organization.* Ann Arbor: University of Michigan Press.

———. 1998. *Pivotal Politics: A Theory of U.S. Policymaking.* Chicago: University of Chicago Press.

Krutz, Glen S. 2001. *Hitching a Ride: Omnibus Legislating in the U.S. Congress.* Columbus: Ohio State University Press.

Law, David S., and David Zaring. 2010. "Law versus Ideology: The Supreme Court and the Use of Legislative History." *William and Mary Law Review* 51(5): 1–62.

Lee, Frances E. 2008. "Dividers, Not Uniters: Presidential Leadership and Senate Partisanship, 1981–2004." *Journal of Politics* 70(4): 914–28.

———. 2009. *Beyond Ideology: Politics, Principles, and Partisanship in the U.S. Senate.* Chicago: University of Chicago Press.

———. 2013. "Legislative Parties in an Era of Alternating Majorities." Presented at "Representation and Governance: A Conference in Honor of David Mayhew," New Haven, CT.

Levitt, Steven D., and James M. Snyder. 1995. "Political Parties and the Distribution of Federal Outlays." *American Journal of Political Science* 39(4): 958–80.

Lewicki, Roy J., and Barbara Benedict Bunker. 1995. "Trust in Relationships: A Model of Trust Development and Decline." In *Conflict, Cooperation, and Justice*, edited by Barbara Benedict Bunker and Jeffrey Z. Rubin. San Francisco: Jossey-Bass.

Longley, Lawrence D., and Walter J. Oleszek. 1989. *Bicameral Politics: Conference Committees in Congress*. New Haven, CT: Yale University Press.

Lord, Charles G., Lee Ross, and Mark R. Lepper. 1979. "Biased Assimilation and Attitude Polarization: The Effects of Prior Theories on Subsequently Considered Evidence." *Journal of Personality and Social Psychology* 37(11): 2098–2109.

Matthews, Donald R. 1960. *U.S. Senators and Their World*. Chapel Hill: University of North Carolina Press.

Matthews, Donald R., and James A. Stimson. 1975. *Yeas and Nays: Normal Decision-Making in the U.S. House of Representatives*. New York: Wiley.

Mayer, Roger C., James H. Davis, and F. David Schoorman. 1995. "An Integrative Model of Organizational Trust." *Academy of Management Review* 20(3): 709–34.

Mayhew, David W. 1974. *Congress: The Electoral Connection*. New Haven, CT: Yale University Press.

———. 1991. *Divided We Govern: Party Control, Lawmaking, and Investigations, 1946–1990*. New Haven, CT: Yale University Press.

McCombs, Maxwell. 2006. "The Agenda-Setting Function of the Press." In *The Press*, edited by Geneva Overholser and Kathleen Hall Jamieson. New York: Oxford University Press.

Mill, John Stuart. 1975 [1861]. "Considerations on Representative Government." In *Three Essays*. Oxford: Oxford University Press.

Miller, Gary J., and Terry M. Moe. 1983. "Bureaucrats, Legislators, and the Size of Government." *American Political Science Review* 77(2): 297–322.

Monroe, Kristen R. 2005. *Perestroika! The Raucous Rebellion in Political Science*. New Haven, CT: Yale University Press.

Mulder, Mauk. 1971. "Power Equalization through Participation?" *Administrative Science Quarterly* 16(1): 31–38.

Nelson, Garrison. 1977. "Partisan Patterns of House Leadership Change, 1789–1977." *American Political Science Review* 71(3): 918–39.

Nickerson, Raymond S. 1988. "Confirmation Bias: A Ubiquitous Phenomenon in Many Guises." *Review of General Psychology* 2(2): 175–220.

Niskanen, William A. 1971. *Bureaucracy and Representative Government.* Chicago: Aldine, Atherton.

Oleszek, Walter J. 2007. *Congressional Procedures and the Policy Process.* 7th ed. Washington, DC: CQ Press.

O'Reilly, Charles A. 1977. "Supervisors and Peers as Information Sources, Group Supportiveness, and Individual Decision-Making Performance." *Journal of Applied Psychology* 62(5): 632–35.

O'Reilly, Charles A., and Karlene H. Roberts. 1977. "Task Group Structure, Communication, and Effectiveness in Three Organizations." *Journal of Applied Psychology* 62(4): 674–81.

Ornstein, Norman J., and Thomas Mann, eds. 2000. *The Permanent Campaign and Its Future.* Washington, DC: American Enterprise Institute.

Ornstein, Norman J., Thomas Mann, and Michael J. Malbin. 2008. *Vital Statistics on Congress.* Washington, DC: Brookings Institution.

Owens, John E. 1997. "The Return of Party Government in the U.S. House of Representatives: Central Leadership—Committee Relations in the 104th Congress." *British Journal of Political Science* 27(2): 247–72.

Owens, Ryan J., Justin Wedeking, and Patrick C. Wohlfarth. 2013. "How the Supreme Court Alters Opinion Language to Evade Congressional Review." *Journal of Law and Courts* 1(1): 35–59.

Page, Benjamin I., and Robert Y. Shapiro. 1992. *The Rational Public: Fifty Years of Trends in Americans' Policy Preferences.* Chicago: University of Chicago Press.

Peabody, Robert L. 1976. *Leadership in Congress: Stability, Succession, and Change.* Boston: Little, Brown.

Peters, Ronald M. 1997. *The American Speakership: The Office in Historical Perspective.* 2nd ed. Baltimore: Johns Hopkins University Press.

Peters, Ronald M., and Cindy Simon Rosenthal. 2010. *Speaker Nancy Pelosi and the New American Politics.* New York: Oxford University Press.

Petersen, R. Eric, Parker H. Reynolds, and Amber Hope Wilhelm. 2010. "House of Representatives and Senate Staff Levels in Member, Committee, Leadership, and Other Offices, 1977–2010." Congressional Research Service, R41366.

Polsby, Nelson W., Miriam Gallaher, and Barry Spencer Rundquist. 1969. "The Growth of the Seniority System in the U.S. House of Representatives." *American Political Science Review* 63(3): 787–807.

Poole, Keith T., and Howard Rosenthal. 1997. *Congress: A Political-Economic History of Roll-Call Voting.* New York: Oxford University Press.

Ragusa, Jordan. 2010. "The Lifecycle of Public Policy: An Event History Analysis of Repeals to Landmark Legislative Enactments, 1951–2006." *American Politics Research* 38(6): 1015–51.

Ranney, Austin. 1962. *The Doctrine of Responsible Party Government: Its Origins and Present State*. Urbana: University of Illinois Press.

Rice, Stuart. 1928. *Quantitative Methods in Politics*. New York: Alfred A. Knopf.

Ripley, Randall B. 1967. *Party Leaders in the House of Representatives*. Washington, DC: Brookings Institution.

Roberts, Karlene H., and Charles A. O'Reilly. 1974. "Measuring Organizational Communication." *Journal of Applied Psychology* 59(3): 321–26.

Rohde, David W. 1991. *Parties and Leaders in the Postreform House*. Chicago: University of Chicago Press.

Rudalevige, Andrew. 2005. *The New Imperial Presidency: Renewing Presidential Power after Watergate*. Ann Arbor: University of Michigan Press.

Rudolph, Thomas J. 1999. "Corporate and Labor PAC Contributions in House Election: Measuring the Effects of Majority Party Status." *Journal of Politics* 61(1): 195–206.

Rybicki, Elizabeth. 2006. "Availability of Legislative Measures in the House of Representatives (the 'Three-Day Rule')." Congressional Research Service, RS22015.

Schattschneider, E. E. 1942. *Party Government*. New York: Farrar and Rinehart.

Schatz, Edward. 2009. *Political Ethnography: What Immersion Contributes to the Study of Power*. Chicago: University of Chicago Press.

Schickler, Eric, and Andrew Rich. 1997. "Controlling the Floor: Parties as Procedural Coalitions in the House." *American Journal of Political Science* 41(4): 1340–75.

Schlesinger, Arthur M. 2004. *The Imperial Presidency*. New York: Houghton Mifflin.

Schwartz-Shea, Peregrine. 2014. "Judging Quality: Evaluative Criteria and Epistemic Communities." In *Interpretation and Method: Empirical Research Methods and the Interpretive Turn*, 2nd ed., edited by Dvora Yanow and Peregrine Schwartz-Shea. Armonk, NY: M. E. Sharpe.

Schwartz-Shea, Peregrine, and Dvora Yanow. 2012. *Interpretive Research Design: Concepts and Processes*. New York: Routledge.

Sellers, Patrick. 2010. *Cycles of Spin: Strategic Communication in the U.S. Congress*. New York: Cambridge University Press.

Shehata, Samer. 2014. "Ethnography, Identity, and the Production of Knowledge." In *Interpretation and Method: Empirical Research Methods and the Interpretive Turn*, 2nd ed., edited by Dvora Yanow and Peregrine Schwartz-Shea. Armonk, NY: M. E. Sharpe.

Shepsle, Kenneth A., and Barry R. Weingast. 1987. "The Institutional Foundations of Committee Power." *American Political Science Review* 81(1): 85–104.

Sinclair, Barbara. 2000. *Unorthodox Lawmaking: New Legislative Processes in the U.S. Congress*, 2nd ed. Washington, DC: CQ Press.

——. 2012. *Unorthodox Lawmaking: New Legislative Processes in the U.S. Congress.* 4th ed. Washington, DC: CQ Press.

Sitkin, Sim B., and Nancy L. Roth. 1993. "Explaining the Limited Effectiveness of Legalistic 'Remedies' for Trust/Distrust." *Organization Science* 4(3): 367–92.

Smith, Steven S., and Bruce A. Ray. 1983. "The Impact of Congressional Reform: House Democratic Committee Assignments." *Congress and the Presidency* 10:219–40.

Snyder, James M. 1992. "Committee Power, Structure-Induced Equilibria, and Roll Call Votes." *American Journal of Political Science* 36(1): 1–30.

Soss, Joe. 2014. "Talking Our Way to Meaningful Explanations: A Practice-Centered View of Interviewing for Interpretive Research." In *Interpretation and Method: Empirical Research Methods and the Interpretive Turn*, 2nd ed., edited by Dvora Yanow and Peregrine Schwartz-Shea. Armonk, NY: M. E. Sharpe.

Spence, Michael. 1973. "Job Market Signaling." *Quarterly Journal of Economics* 87(3): 355–74.

Strahan, Randall. 2003. "Personal Motives, Constitutional Forms, and the Public Good: Madison on Political Leadership." In *James Madison: The Theory and Practice of Republican Government*, edited by Samuel Kernell. Stanford, CA: Stanford University Press.

——. 2007. *Leading Representatives: The Agency of Leaders in the Politics of the U.S. House.* Baltimore: Johns Hopkins University Press.

Sullivan, John L., and Eric M. Uslaner. 1978. "Congressional Behavior and Electoral Marginality." *American Journal of Political Science* 22(3): 536–53.

Tabor, Charles S., and Milton Lodge. 2006. "Motivated Skepticism in the Evaluation of Political Beliefs." *American Journal of Political Science* 50(3): 755–69.

Taylor, Andrew J. 1998. "Domestic Agenda Setting, 1947–1994." *Legislative Studies Quarterly* 23(3): 373–97.

Theriault, Sean M. 2008. *Party Polarization in Congress.* New York: Cambridge University Press.

Thompson, Dennis S. 2008. "Deliberative Democratic Theory and Empirical Political Science." *Annual Review of Political Science* 11:497–520.

Truman, David B. 1959. *The Congressional Party: A Case Study.* New York: Wiley.

Waxman, Henry, with Joshua Green. 2009. *The Waxman Report: How Congress Really Works.* New York: Twelve.

Weaver, R. Kent. 1986. "The Politics of Blame Avoidance." *Journal of Public Policy* 6(4): 371–98.

——. 2000. *Ending Welfare as We Know It.* Washington, DC: Brookings Institution.

Weber, Max. 1991. *From Max Weber: Essays in Sociology*. Edited and translated by H. H. Gerth and C. Wright Mills. Abingdon, UK: Routledge.

Weingast, Barry R. 1989. "Floor Behavior in the U.S. Congress: Committee Power under the Open Rule." *American Political Science Review* 83(3): 795–815.

Westen, Drew, Pavel S. Blagov, Keith Harenski, Clint Kilts, and Stephan Hamann. 2006. "Neural Bases of Motivated Reasoning: An fMRI Study of Emotional Constraints on Partisan Political Judgment in the 2004 U.S. Presidential Election." *Journal of Social and Political Psychology* 1(1): 337–63.

Williamson, Vanessa, Theda Skocpol, and John Coggin. 2011. "The Tea Party and the Remaking of Republican Conservatism." *Perspectives on Politics* 9(1): 25–43.

Wilson, Woodrow. 1885. *Congressional Government*. Cleveland, OH: World.

Wlezien, Christopher. 2005. "On the Salience of Political Issues: The Problem with 'Most Important Problem.'" *Electoral Studies* 24(4): 555–79.

Index

Westen, Drew, 237n23

Weyrich, Paul, 182

whip, 14, 33, 51, 59–63, 71, 73, 75, 108, 178,
244n11; check, 59, 60; meetings, 72

Whitten, Jamie, 89

Wilkerson, John, 18

Williamson, Vanessa, 181

Wilson, Woodrow, 10

Wlezien, Christopher, 242n56

Wohlfarth, Patrick C., 242n54

Wolfensberger, Donald, 241n40

Wood, B. Dan, 38

Wright, Jim, 13, 98

Yanow, Dvora, 15–16, 209, 212–13,
234n14

Young, Kerry, 249nn53–54, 250nn58–59

Zaring, David, 242n54

Zeckhauser, Richard J., 10

Chicago Studies in American Politics

A SERIES EDITED BY BENJAMIN I. PAGE, SUSAN HERBST, LAWRENCE R. JACOBS, AND ADAM J. BERINSKY

Series titles, continued from front matter: